The Making of a Moor Woman: A Father's Guide for Raising His Daughter
Volume I: Books One and Two

By Christopher L. McGee

Book's Dedication:

This Book is dedicated to the loving women of the Gilmore, McGee, and Penelton families, and all of the beautiful women of Dillard University.

AuthorHouse™
1663 Liberty Drive
Bloomington, IN 47403
www.authorhouse.com
Phone: 1-800-839-8640

First published by AuthorHouse 9/27/2010

ISBN: 978-1-4520-7102-2 (e)
ISBN: 978-1-4520-7101-5 (sc)

Library of Congress Control Number: 2010913621

Printed in the United States of America

This book is printed on acid-free paper.

authorHOUSE®

The Making of a Moor Woman: A Father's Guide for Raising His Daughter
Volume I: Book One

Table of Content

The Making of a Moor Woman: A Father's Guide for Raising His Daughter
Volume I: Book Two

Table of Content

The Making of a Moor Woman: A Father's Guide for Raising His Daughter
Volume I: Book One

Chapter Outline

Mid-life Malaise / Mid-life Slump

Measure of Age / Physical Age / Menopause / Post Menopause / Death and Dying

The Making of a Moor Woman: A Father's Guide for Raising His Daughter
Volume I: Book Two

Chapter Outline

Section 4: Late Adulthood 236

Section 5: The Community Cure! 264

The Making of a Moor Woman: A Father's Guide for Raising His Daughter
Volume I: Book One

"She is not made to be the admiration of all, but the happiness of one."

Edmund Burke

Chapter 1: Family Planning

Planning Your Woman's Pregnancy

In our society parenthood is considered a basic part of any intimate relationship. Those couples that are biologically capable are having children. However, there are many couples choosing not to have children. Following are some of the reasons that might encourage a couple to have children:

- Their close friends and family members are having children.
- Their parents want grandchildren.
- They feel that having children will strengthen their relationship.
- They want to share in the miracle of birth and creation.
- They love children and they are looking forward to the joys of parenting.

Influences that might discourage a couple from having babies include:

- They have educational goals they have yet to meet.
- They feel they don't have the money needed to provide for a child.
- They feel their careers will get in the way.
- They doubt their ability to be good parents.

Parenting will be one of the greatest challenges of your life. It will bring new dimension to you, as well as your relationship. Your adjustment to parenting will be very difficult. Most couples believe that having children will bring them closer.

With the birth of your first child your life will change in a number of ways. When a man becomes a father, he must find time and create opportunities to learn his new role. A man's ability to rise to this challenge will make the difference between his becoming more efficient and organized or becoming overwhelmed and frustrated.

If both you and your woman have to work, finding child-care can be a problem. Between the cost of child-care, and your concerns for your child's safety, you will not find an easy solution. It is very important for you and your woman to clearly define what responsibilities you expect from each other.

In an old fashion family children are considered assets. The more children a couple have, the better off the family is likely to be. In such families, the children work with their parents to provide for each other. However, in your modern families raising children is a major expense with few financial rewards.

Direct Child-raising Costs. How much money is needed to raise a baby?
(The 1989 USDA Agricultural Research Service provided the information above)
• Food at home. 20.1%
• Food away from home. 2.7%
• Housing (rent, furnishing, utilities). 33.1%
• Transportation. 14.1%
• Education. 2.3%
• Clothing. 6.5%
• Medical Care. 6.6%
• Miscellaneous. 14.2%
The initial costs of starting a family begin with hospital bills, food, diapers, clothes, and furniture. The biggest expense in raising a child is housing. Buying a house or renting a large apartment would be ideal. Some men find it necessary to purchase their home before making any other major purchases. Hold off on buying a car or getting any type of loan against your credit until you get your place. The indirect costs of raising a child refer to the loss of wages due to only one person working. Indirect costs are about half the amount of the direct costs.

Preparation for Parenthood

Parenting never ends. Once you and your woman become parents, the two of you will always be parents. Employment and political views may be turned on or off, but parenting is a life time commitment.

People pick and choose when they want to date or what job they wish to work, but making a baby is not always voluntary. It is not uncommon for a couple to have an unplanned pregnancy. People often have babies before they are ready.

Many people planning a family make the mistake of thinking that parenting skills come naturally. They often begin building their families without any preparation or training. Like womanhood, parenting requires proper instruction and good directions.

Childbirth classes are offered at many hospitals, as well as community educational programs. Taking classes in family planning and parenting can help ease the transition into becoming mother and father. Even if only one partner attends a parenting preparation course, the adjustment for both is less severe.

The major benefits of childbirth and family planning classes are that they are made for both expectant fathers and mothers. These lessons provide information on emotional and physical reactions to pregnancy, delivery, and postpartum care. This is where you and your woman can share the first stages of parenthood.

The two of you will learn breathing patterns and relaxation exercises so that both parents to be can work together during labor. There are also several books and pamphlets with useful information about pregnancy, the baby's development, and infant care. It is in you and your woman's best interest to learn as much as you can about the wonderful journey of becoming parents.

Pregnancy: Prenatal Development

It is very important for you to know what is going on inside your woman's womb. Understanding your baby's prenatal development can help you and your woman protect your new baby. You need to know what precautions are necessary for your wife and baby.

A woman usually carries the developing baby for nine months. She will not likely feel her baby move inside of her until about the fifth month. It is also at this stage you and your wife will likely hear your baby's heartbeat. From conception through the first five months, your baby will do most of his or her important prenatal development.

First Stage

Once you have "knocked up" your woman, her ovum (egg) connected with your sperm creating a zygote. The zygote cell divides over and over again until it become about 90 cells. At this point, the fertilized egg will move through the fallopian tube and connect with the uterus. Two weeks into your woman's pregnancy the fertilized egg will implant into the uterine wall.

Embryonic Stage

From the second week through the eighth week of development, your unborn child is enclosed in an amniotic sac. The sac contains amniotic fluid that maintains baby's temperature and protects the embryo. The umbilical cord carries nourishment and waste to and from your baby.

The umbilical cord is also protected by amniotic fluid. At the time of birth the umbilical cord is 20 to 22 inches long. During this stage your baby will develop essential body systems and organs. Viruses, radiation, drugs, and/or chemicals can harm your baby.

Fetal Period

The fetal period begins after the second week and continues until birth. At this stage the unborn child is called a fetus. The fetus has a developed head, arms, legs and feet. Between the fourth and fifth months, your woman will begin to feel the baby move. As the baby continues his/her growth, he/she will grow from an ounce to about seven pounds.

Prenatal Care

Prenatal care requires regular visits to the doctor. These check-ups are necessary in maintaining the health of your woman and your baby. Good prenatal care is for the most part just common-sense health care. When your woman thinks she is pregnant, it is very important that she confirms it with her doctor.

Most doctors have a standard fee for all prenatal care and delivery, so there is no percentage in your woman putting her medical visits on hold. Regular visits to her doctor mean learning about possible complications. Any complications that arise can be detected and controlled.

Before your woman gets pregnant, there are some tests that she can take to see if she has antibodies against German measles, or rubella. These viruses affect the rate of cell division in the unborn child. These viruses are associated with severe birth defects, including blindness.

If your woman does not have the necessary antibodies, she can obtain the necessary vaccine. Once she is made pregnant, she can not receive the vaccine. This is something that you should definitely discuss with your woman.

An expectant mother needs a proper diet. Your woman is eating for both her and your unborn baby. The baby receives nourishment from your woman's blood stream and through her placenta. Your woman and your unborn child will need a balanced diet that is high in all nutrients.

Your unborn baby needs large quantities of foods containing iron, calcium and folic acids. Your woman should add 300 extra healthy calories a day. Low protein may result in learning difficulties throughout your child's life.

Practical Tips
When your woman is pregnant, she should meet the following minimum food requirements:
• Milk. One quart, daily of whole, low fat, or skim milk; or equivalent values of other dairy products like yogurt or cheese.
• Meat, Fish, or Poultry. At least eight ounce daily. A variety of nuts or legumes may be substituted.
• Fruits. At least one citrus and one other fruit daily.
• Vegetables. One potato and one green, leafy vegetable daily. One yellow vegetable four times a week and two to four servings of other vegetables daily.
• Butter or Fortified Margarine. One to two tablespoons daily.
• Bread and Cereals. Two to four servings daily. Preferably whole-grain or enriched, including enriched pasta.

Weight Gain During Pregnancy		
	Pound	Kilograms
Fetus	7.5	3.37
Placenta	1	.45
Amniotic fluid	2	.90
Uterus (increase)	2.5	1.12
Breast tissue (increase)	3	1.35
Blood (increase)	4	1.70
Maternal nutrients reserves	4 to 8	1.70 to 3.60
	24 to 28	10.59 to 12.49
(Source: S. R. Williams, Essential Nutrition and Diet Therapy, 3rd ed. (St. Louis: C. V. Mosby, 1982).		

Keeping in shape is an important aspect of a healthy pregnancy. Adequate rest and proper exercise is necessary for your pregnant woman. In the earliest stages of pregnancy, your woman will experience fatigue. Even with a good diet, she needs to maintain a balance between rest and exercise. Your woman will need to continue her normal activities and exercises throughout her pregnancy, but she should avoid strenuous activity.

Doctors have linked prenatal nutrition to the growth of a healthy fetus, a healthy brain and nervous system. It is also believed that malnutrition during pregnancy may result in learning problems throughout your child's life. Having a proper diet also helps reduce the chances of your woman suffering from toxemia. Toxemia is an illness that results from kidney malfunction and a build up fluid in the body.

If your woman develops toxemia, she will have swelling in her legs, hands, and feet. She may also develop high blood pressure. While your woman is pregnant, she should not only watch what she eats, but she should maintain a balance of rest and exercise.

Another important part of prenatal care is your woman's visit to her dentist. There are certain types of oral bacteria, fungi, and viruses that can be passed from the mother to her unborn child. These harmful germs can enter the fetus through the mother's blood stream and cause problems with the baby's development and sometimes death.

Potential Hazards

It is important that you help your woman stay clear of hazards that may hurt your baby. This is especially important during the embryonic period. Your woman should avoid having X-rays taken. Radiation is harmful to your baby. If she has to have dental X-rays, the technician and the dentist should be informed of your woman's condition. The dentist should have all of the necessary protective covering to keep your woman and your baby safe.

When your woman takes any kind of medication, the drugs are transmitted through your woman's blood stream to the fetal circulatory system. Your woman should avoid alcoholic beverages. Excess alcohol can cause low birth weight and mental retardation in infants. (See fetal alcohol syndrome.)

Caffeine is a drug found in coffee, tea and many soft drinks. In lab animals, caffeine caused a large percent of birth defects. Researchers are not clear about the amount of caffeine a human being can ingest, so make sure your woman is careful when combining foods that have caffeine.

Your woman should not take any medication, unless it is prescribed by her medical doctor. People often take aspirin, decongestants, or laxatives when necessary. This can be a very dangerous thing. Even daily, over the counter drugs can have a bad impact on your baby's development?

Nicotine is a drug found in cigarettes and cigars, and it also threatens your unborn baby. Smoking, whether direct or second hand, increases the chances that your baby will grow slowly and have a low-birth-weight. Smoking restricts the flow of blood through the placenta. This limits the flow of oxygen and nutrients to your unborn baby.

Potential Complications

High-Risk Infants

All babies need to complete their full nine months in their mother's uterus. Babies born before their time can survive, but each baby often require specialized medical care. Babies have to weigh 5 1/2 pounds or more. Those born too small or too early are considered high risk. Without their mother providing all of life's functions, they are susceptible to a number of health problems.

There are several different diseases common to early birth. Respiratory Disease Syndrome (RDS) results from immature lungs that cannot take in enough oxygen. Hypoglycemia is a condition of low blood sugar caused from the liver's inability to store glucose. Anemia or low iron in the blood is common in early births. An early born baby may also suffer from low body heat due to a lack of body fat.

Women from all walks of life give birth to low-birth weight babies. However, it is understood that young women under the age of fifteen, mothers that are poorly nourished or have health problems are more likely to have high-risk infants. Babies depend on their mothers for nourishment, but the mother has to have the nutrients to begin with.

Infant w/ Birth Defects

Birth defects are generally considered mistakes in body formation or function during development. Birth defects can be caused by heredity, disease, or unknown factors that can affect the growing infant while in the mother's womb. Not all defects are visible at birth. Many will cause health problems later in life.

Major Birth Defects

Caused by inherited factors

Cystic fibrosis-
Description. A malfunctioning of the pancreas and frequent respiratory infections are symptoms.
Medical Care. Detected by sweat and blood tests; treatment of respiratory and digestive problems.

Down's syndrome (mongolism)-
Description. This birth defect includes mental retardation with some physical defects (chromosomal abnormality).
Medical Care. Detected by amniocentesis; treatment by corrective surgery, special training.

Hemophilia-
Description. Blood clotting malfunction (even minor cuts result in extensive bleeding).
Medical Care. Detected by blood tests; treatment by injection of clotting factor.

Huntington's Chorea-
Description. A mental and physical deterioration leading to death are symptoms.
Medical Care. Appears in middle age; treated by special medication.

Phenyketonuria (PKU)-
Description. Body cannot use food to create essential amino acid; can cause mental retardation.
Medical Care. Detected by blood tests at birth; treatment by diet with missing amino acid.

Sickle-Cell Anemia-
Description. Malformed red blood cells deprived of oxygen; affects persons of African background.
Medical Care. Detected by blood tests; treated by blood transfusions.

Tay-Sachs disease-
Description. Enzyme deficiency resulting in mental retardation is symptomatic of this disease. This is disease commonly affects Jewish persons of Eastern Europe background.
Medical Care. Detected by blood and tear tests; amniocentesis; no treatment.

Caused by environmental factors

Congenital Rubella Syndrome-
Description. Infection of mother by German measles causes heart defect, deafness, brain damage in child.
Medical Care. This disease is prevented by rubella vaccine. Detected by antibody tests; treatment by corrective surgery, physical therapy.

Congenital Syphilis-
Description. A mother infected by syphilis may result in multiple abnormalities in an infected child.
Medical Care. Detected by blood test, examination at birth; treatment by special medication.

Caused by inherited and/or environmental factors

Diabetes Mellitus
Description. Insulin deficiency; excess sugar in blood and weight loss are symptoms of this disease.
Medical Care. Detected by blood and urine tests; treatment by special diet, insulin.

Low Birth-weight/ Pre-maturity

Description. Birth-weight under 5 1/2 pounds (2.5 kilograms) is too low. An immature body structure makes survival difficult.

Medical Care. This problem is prevented by proper prenatal care. Detected by examination at birth; treatment by intensive care.

RH Disease

Description. Antibodies in blood RH Negative mother destroy blood of RH Positive baby; loss of oxygen causes mental retardation, death.

Medical Care. This is prevented by RH vaccine. Detected by blood test; treated by blood transfusion.

Your Daughter's Personality

Personality is a person's unique pattern of thoughts, feelings, and behaviors that persists over time and situations and that distinguishes one person from another.

Personalities are often looked at as a commodity, like the paint job on a new car. People often see personality as admirable traits, like affectionate, kind, or happy. There are many aspects and traits to our personalities. Personality refers to those traits that separate one person to another. Your personality is your psychological signature. It marks the attitude, behavior, motives, tendencies, and emotions with which you respond to everything in your environment.

Psychodynamic Theories

Sigmund Freud

He is the best-known personality theorist. Freud introduced a perspective on human behavior. Freud stressed the unconscious or all the thoughts, ideas, and feelings of which we are not normally aware. Psychoanalysis is Freud's personality theory and his type of therapy.

Freud distinguishes two classes of instinct:
- Death instincts- these are the self-destructive, suicidal tendencies when directed towards the self and aggression and war when directed towards others.
- Life instincts- these are the survival of the individual, basic physiological needs, and our libido (sexual instinct).

Life and death instincts make up the id. The id is a "steam kettle" of unconscious continuous urges. The id works along the **pleasure principle**: a lust for pleasure and a fear of pain. The id is the natural reflex action and the wish fulfillment. Wish fulfillment (primary-process thinking) is the dreams, day dreams, and a brilliant imagination when dealing with negative feelings. The id is in the back of your mind.

Freud believed that the ego controls all thinking and reasoning. It is the connection to the external world. The **reality principle** is the ego rationally satisfying the id. "Secondary-process thinking" is a type of realistic thinking where the ego effectively and safely works to satisfy the id. The superego represents the social moral standards we learn growing up. The id, superego, and ego are supposed to work in harmony. The ego, with the approval of the superego, satisfies the demands of the id in a reasonable, moral manner.

How the Pleasure Principle Works
External Stimulus/ Internal Stimulus
Increasing discomfort in the ID----Un-pleasure in the ID-----Release of discomfort by first available means-----Pleasure in the ID
How the Reality Principle Works
External Stimulus/ Internal Stimulus
Increasing discomfort in the ID......Un-pleasure in the ID......Rational thought of ego......Release of discomfort by safest and best available means......Pleasure in the ID

Carl Jung
      This psychologist was greatly influenced by Sigmund Freud.
Jung believed that libido (energy produced from sexual instinct), is a psychic energy that represents all the life forces. Jung, like Sigmund Freud, emphasizes the unconscious mind in determining human behavior. Jung felt that the unconscious mind was the source of vitality and strength for that part of your personality that mediates between your environmental, conscience, and instinctual needs. When looking at personality development, Jung stressed rational and spiritual qualities.

He believed that there were two levels of the unconscious.
- Personal unconscious- contains our repressed thoughts, forgotten experiences, unrealized ideas that may come to the surface if something triggers a recall.
- Collective unconscious- consists of the memories and behavior patterns of your ancestors. Just as we inherit physical traits, we also inherit "thought forms" or collective memories, of experiences common to prehistoric times.

Jung called thought forms archetypes.
- The persona archetype is that part of our personality that is known to other people.
- Anima is the female side of the male. It enables him to build relationships with women.
- Animus is the male side of the female. It guides women in their interaction with males.

Jung believed that everyone could be divided into two general attitudes.
- Extroverts have a deep connection with the external world. They focus on others and

in events going on around them.

- Introverts are concerned with their own private world. They are unsociable and lack confidence in dealing with people.

Jung also divided people into rational and irrational categories.
- Rational people regulate their behavior by thinking and feeling.
- Irrational people base their decisions through sensation and intuition.

Alfred Adler

This psychologist was greatly influenced by Sigmund Freud. Adler believed that people possess innate positive motives and focus on personal and social perfection. Children with a disability learn to improve their lives in other ways. That is known as compensation. Adler believed that a negative, or inferior self-image would not help an individual develop, but would inspire them to do better. When a person becomes paralyzed by an image of inferiority, they develop what is known as an inferiority complex.

Fictional finalism is a term used to identify goals that people set for themselves as a tool of motivation. The personal goals do not have to be attainable, but it is important that the person act as if these goals are attainable. When people focus on their "fictional finalism," they establish beliefs and a particular set of meanings that become their "style of life". Adler stresses positive, socially constructive goals and a focus on ideas of perfection. He believed that individuals are not controlled by their environment, but can function creatively on it.

Karen Horney

This psychologist was greatly influenced by Sigmund Freud. Horney believes that environmental and social factors are the most important thing in shaping personalities. She believes that the most vital factors are the human relationships with which children grow up. Horney believed that putting to much emphasis on sexual drives created poor images of human relationships.

She recognizes the importance of sexuality in personality development, but she argues that many nonsexual factors are equally important. One of the most important nonsexual influences in a person's life is the hierarchy of human needs. Horney believed that rational or irrational anxieties were a much greater influence to our personality development than sexual desire.

Horney believed that people often trade their self-reliance for one or more types of neurotic trends in order to help us deal with emotional challenges and ensure our safety.
- Submission (compliant type) moving towards people/aggression and anxiety.
- Aggression (aggressive type) moving against people/insecurity and anxiety.
- Detachment (detached type) moving away from people/anxiety withdrawing.

People who grow up in a secure environment learn to handle threats to their security without losing themselves to neurotic life-styles. Horney's belief that culture more than biology, shape our growth throughout the life cycle. She believed that understanding the personalities of men and women came from understanding the cultural forces that shape their lives.

<u>Humanistic Personality Theories</u>

Humanistic personality theory- any personality theory that asserts the basic goodness of people and their innate need to strive towards higher levels of functioning.

William James
James believed in the psychological concept of self. He believed that the sum and total of what people refer to as his or hers is the true "self". Everything that fills the blank in, "This is my __," represents a small part of one's greater self.

James divided the self into 4 parts.
- The material self.
- The social self (persona).
- The spiritual self (reason, or emotional disposition).
- The pure ego (that part of our personality that mediates between reality, conscience, and instinctive needs)/ internal consciousness.

Carl Rogers
Rogers was greatly influenced by William James and is perhaps the most popular of several humanistic psychologists. The humanistic scientists believe that personality development is all about a continuing process of striving to reach one's full potential. Rogers believes that every living thing has an innate capacity and talent to which substance is added throughout life. He believed that we are born with a genetic blueprint, and that it is our life's purpose to fulfill it.

Actualizing tendency- Rogers believed that all living things push towards the fulfillment of our natural potential.

Self-actualizing tendency- Rogers believed that during the course of our lives as humans we develop an image of ourselves (or a self-concept). He believed that we strive to fulfill our self-image.

A fully functioning person- When a person's natural blueprint closely parallels his/her self-concept.

Unconditional positive regard- people are brought up to feel valued by others and loved regardless of their feelings, attitudes, and behaviors. (Rogers, beyond all logic and good sense, believed that this was the key to developing a fully functioning person.)

Conditional positive regard- this means that only certain aspects of an individual are valued and accepted. The acceptance, warmth, and love that a person receives from others depend on his or her behaving in a certain way and living up to certain conditions.

(Please refer to the section on logical fallacies.)

People who lose sight of their natural potential often become rigid, and defensive. They are not likely to find satisfaction in the things they do. In some case, they will grow up not knowing whom they are or what they are supposed to do with their lives.

Constitutional and Trait Theories

Personality theories emphasis a few different things, but have many similarities in several respects. They all recognize the importance of early childhood experiences, and they each set basic rules that attempt to account for all human personalities. Some personality theorists concentrate on the way developed personalities differ from each other.

William Sheldon

The constitutional theorists believe that body types and personality are directly related. He asserts that physique dictates personality. Sheldon recognizes three types of human physiques:
- Endomorphs (round, soft bodies with large abdomens)
- Mesomorphs (sturdy, upright bodies with strong muscles and bones)
- Ectomorphs (thin, small-boned, fragile bodies)

Most people have some characteristics of all three of these somatotypes, with one type dominant.

Sheldon divides temperament into three types:
- Viscerotonia- sociable, fond of food and people, and love comfort
- Somatotonia- love of physical activity, risk, adventure, and vigorous activity
- Cerebrotonia- restraint, self-consciousness, and love of privacy

Sheldon believed that....
- Plump endomorphs are likely high in viscerotonia
- Athletic mesomorphs high in somatotonia
- Skinny ectomorphs high in cerebrotonia

Trait Theory

Most trait theorists disagree with Sheldon's idea of people having only a few main personality types. They believe that people have many dimensions to their personality and that some personality traits exist to different degrees. These traits are not directly identified. They can only be inferred through long term observations. Traits are classified in three groups:
- Cardinal traits (very rare traits that influence every aspect of a person's life) ex. a greedy person who is greedy in everything he or she does.
- Central traits (often detectable behavior that does not influence one's whole life) ex.

An aggressive person who will often not display aggression.

- Secondary trait (are attribute that do not form a vital part of the personality and only exists in certain situations) ex. an aggressive soldier who is submissive in the company of a superior officers.

Raymond Cattrell

He is a psychologist who uses a statistical technique called factor analysis in order to identify a set of basic personality traits. Cattrell recognizes 200 characteristics that cluster into groups. He concluded that 16 to 23 traits account for the complexity of human personality. Cattrell asserts that each person consists of a relatively unique constellation of the basic trait.

Trait Theories ("Big Five" Dimensions of Personality)

Surgency or Extraversion

Talkative, bold, active, boisterous, forceful, assertive, spontaneous, active, demonstrative, energetic, enthusiastic, adventurous, outgoing, outspoken, loud, noisy, ambitious, dominant, sociable.

Agreeableness or Pleasantness

Warm, kind, cooperative, unselfish, flexible, fair, polite, trustful, forgiving, helpful, pleasant, affectionate, gentle, good-hearted, sympathetic, trusting, generous, flexible, considerate, and agreeable

Conscientiousness or Dependability

Organized, dependable, conscientious, responsible, hardworking, efficient, planning, capable, deliberate, painstaking, precise, practical, thorough, thrifty, cautious, serious, economical, reliable

Emotional Stability

Unemotional, un-envious, relaxed, objective, calm, at ease, even-tempered, good-natured, stable, contented, secure, imperturbable, undemanding, steady, placid, peaceful

Culture or Intelligent or Sophistication

Intelligent, perceptive, curious, imaginative, analytical, reflective, artistic, insightful, inventive, wise, witty, refined, creative, sophisticated, knowledgeable, intellectual, resourceful, versatile, original, deep, cultured

Personology Profiles for Birthdays

Western Horoscope

Western zodiac is divided into 12 personality types. It is a system based on the constellations to portray human archetype as mythical, celestial creatures. There are only 4 elements in Western astrology. (Appendix III)

Eastern Horoscope

The Chinese zodiac is the oldest in the world. It is rooted firmly in the shifting patterns of life on earth, the seasons, the weather, and complex Oriental philosophy. The system represents 12 personality types that are identified as animals, and they are the basis of the zodiac. There are 5 elements in the Chinese system. Eastern wisdom is based on Taoism, which perceives the universe as an eternal flow of the Yin and Yang. (Appendix II)

Chapter 2: Pregnancy

"You are training for the Big Fight!"

Massage for Pregnancy

A careful, gentle massage would benefit all pregnant women. Massage will relax your woman and help alleviate many of the minor complaints (backache, insomnia, etc.) common during pregnancy. Pregnant women have frequently said that the only time they sleep well is after a massage. When massaging a pregnant woman, make all movements smooth and gentle. Avoid using deep pressure and percussion techniques. Gently massage the abdomen, and it will soften her tummy while helping your baby sleep.

In several African cultures, massage is used at all stages of pregnancy. Before conception, massage is used to increase fertility in women. In Nigeria, women who have trouble conceiving often visit a specially trained masseuse. It is believed that three weeks of daily massage may help barren women make a baby. The masseuse is usually a trained midwife or nurse. With the use of a proper massage technique, he or she is able to change the position of the baby to make the birth easier.

When giving a massage, you want to spend extra time on the abdomen, legs, and back. Concentrate on high tension areas like the lower back and shoulders. If you are advised not to massage any of those areas, then you should focus on massaging her hands, feet, arms and face.

Plenty of cushions and pillows should be used to comfort your partner. When she is lying on her back place:
- Cushions under her knees to relax her abdomen and reduce the curve in her lower back
- Cushion under her shoulder
- Cushion under her head

The back massage, she can lie on her side:
- Cushion under her head
- Cushion at her chest, wrapped in her arms
- Cushion between her knees when legs are closed
- Place cushion underneath the upper knee when legs are spaced apart

The back massage, she can sit astride a chair:
- Cushion at her chest, wrapped in her arms
- Cushion under her forehead
- Cushion under her chin.

Giving a massage:
1. Kneel beside your woman and stroke clockwise around her abdomen with one hand, keeping the strokes smooth, even and gentle.
2. Continue stroking clockwise around the abdomen, but use both hands, one following the other smoothly in a gentle, flowing stroke.

3. Make a full circle with one hand and a half circle with the other, lifting one hand over your other hand as your hands cross.
4. Stroke gently up the side of the waist, one hand after the other. Lift your hands off as they reach the navel and start again.
5. Stroke up the abdomen very gently and glide down the sides. Gradually stroke more softly, until you are barely touching the skin.
6. Cup your hands over the navel for a few seconds until you feel heat gathering underneath. Then, lift your hands very slowly away.

Leg Massage

Leg massage helps relieve swelling and pain in legs, and varicose veins or cramps. Stroking her legs gently from her ankles to the thighs (glide your hands back and forth). Keep all movements gentle and avoid percussion techniques. Alleviate swelling and aching by raising her legs slightly above her head. If there is great swelling in the legs, apply proper technique for lymph drainage. When massaging varicose veins, one should never directly massage the affected veins.

Arm Massage

Massaging your partner arms can be very soothing. Some women get dizzy if they lie on their backs for an extended period of time.
1. Rest her arms palms down, on the sheet and place your hands across her waist, with the pinkie of one next to the thumb of the other. Stroke firmly up the arm with your hands cupped. Give deep pressure over the muscles and light pressure over the bones.
2. When you reach the top of the arm stroke around the shoulder. In one continuous action, reach around the top of her shoulder and glide your hands down the side of the arm back down to the wrist. This should be done 6 or 7 times.

Stroking with one hand

Support the forearm with one hand and stroke up the arm with the other. You should stroke continuously around the shoulder, and down the side of her body. Then change hands so that both sides of the arm is massaged.

Draining the Forearm

This exercise is meant to improve drainage of waste products from the veins of the forearms.
1. Lift up the forearm while supporting the wrist and leaving the elbow on the towel. Clasp your hands around her wrist, with your thumbs firmly on the inside of the wrist.
2. Slide one hand down to the elbow, pressing firmly with thumbs without the use of fingers. Once you reach the elbow, circulate your hands back to the wrist, and then alternate hands. Repeat exercise 3 to 4 times.

Back Massage

A back massage can help your woman relax, lower her stress levels, easing pain and inducing a blissful state of repose. Slow rhythmic strokes will calm her nerves. Fast, brisk movement will invigorate nerves.

Cover her back with a towel and place your hands on it. Place one hand at the nape of the neck, and the other hand at her waist. While focusing on your hands, take deep breathes. This exercise will help both you and your partner make a connection and relax.

The connection you make with your woman will carry the two of you throughout the therapy. After about 45 seconds put the oil on your hands and pull back the towel. Kneel down to one side of your woman and face her head, and begin the massage by spreading the oil with deep, even strokes.

Stroking

1. Start with your hands on the lower back, your thumbs on either side of the spine and your fingers pointing towards the head. With relaxed hands, you should stroke firmly up the back. You should lean onto your hands, using the weight of your body to apply pressure.
2. Pull back down on the muscle at the base of the neck. Then, stroke out across the shoulders and the top of the arms. Allow your hands to mold to the curves of her shoulders, arms, and back. Sweep your hands round the top of the arms and then down the sides of her body.
3. Stroke your hands lightly down the sides of the body, keeping them relaxed and taking care not to drag the skin. At the waist, pull upward and inward. This gives the lovely feeling of having a tiny waist. Repeat ten times.

Fan Stroking

1. This stroke is similar to the first with small interesting variations. Start at the lower back, press firmly up both sides of the spine.
2. Fan your hands out at the base of the ribs circulating down to the lower backs. Repeat the stroke, fanning your hands out a little higher each time until you reach the base of the neck. Be sure to mold your hands to the contours of her body.

Alternate Stroking

1. Continue stroking the back, but use your hands alternately. While one hand strokes upward, the other strokes downward along the sides. Repeat the stroke, until it is smooth and rhythmic. It should be a wonderful, continuous stroke.

During Childbirth/After Childbirth

Massage will be very valuable during childbirth. It will help with backaches, and is a good way to comfort and demonstrate your support. Help her relax by massaging her back, feet, shoulders, face and neck.

Massage is after childbirth. In some cultures, women spend the first 40 days after childbirth being massaged from head to toe, giving special attention to the abdomen. It eases the pain of carrying and picking up the baby. It eases the strain of caring for the baby, and reduces the overall nervousness and stress. Massage afterbirth will be one of the best experiences of her life.

A Personal Touch for Pregnancy

<u>Body Reflexology for Pregnancy</u>

Reflexology Works to Help the Body Heal Itself

Body reflexology will stimulate many processes throughout the whole body. It will activate the nervous system and balance out the vital energies among the various systems in the body. The diagram below demonstrates a blockage and how it interferes with the flow of energy.

Healthy Energy and Circulation Flow				
Watts	25	25	25	25
100	Heart	Kidney	Brain	Muscles

Energy and Circulation Flow Disturbed By Blocked					
Watts		10	10	10	10
100	Blockage	Heart	Kidney	Brain	Muscles

A tender spot indicates a blockage, which means there is trouble in an area that may be far from the tender point. Pressing a certain nerve ending on the body may result in an odd tingling sensation in quite a different area, showing a connection to a particular reflex button.
- Press the pressure point with your finger for a few seconds.
- If it is sensitive, press it several times.

(This is proof that healing pressure is getting through to the source of the blockage.)

- When you get a tingle in a place least expected, you have discovered a "life-giving current" of health. It covers all parts of the body and gets them under control. It keeps corrosion from forming causing more trouble later.

Be patient. The blockage does not appear over night and will not be cleared quickly. You must give your body time to naturally correct it. Sometimes, reflexology will improve rapidly. In some cases, alleviating pain may require a 20 minute to 2 hour stimulation of a pressure point. Do not give up. It will work.

Reflexology to Dissolve Stress and Tension

Stress and anger makes us age sooner and offsets us physically and emotionally. Reflexology is used to help normalize our systems, improving circulation and restoring balance to the body. This section will help your woman relieve stress and improve her disposition. Reflexology will channel the body's distress and transform it into a positive force. We will build up our energy while losing stress.

- Tap your chest and smile your biggest smile to stimulate the thymus gland and lymphatic system.

The movement of bending your wrist while tapping your chest pumps lymph fluids. Smiling and tapping your chest renews energy to the thymus. The thymus and lymph glands help convert proteins into sugar for energy.

Endocrine Glands and Stress Control

Stress
- Put strain on the body.
- Stress is the number one killer.
- It depletes energy.
- It absorbs nutrients from your system.
- Creates hormonal imbalance.

Stimulating Endocrine Glands to Restore Hormones
1. Learn the locations of these glands
2. Work the reflexes on both feet and both hands to energize the body.
3. Work the big toe and thumb to stimulate the brain and pituitary glands.
4. Focus on the thyroid reflex (controls temperature and calms our feelings)
5. Work the reflex to the pancreas (produces insulin which converts sugar to energy)

Adrenal Glands (produces adrenalin for extra energy)
1. The reflex button on the inside of the hand will be near the center of your palm, and up toward the base of the fingers.
2. This is also the reflex for the solar plexus (add relaxation to the nervous system).

These glands are closely interrelated and work together to give the body balance. The endocrine glands influence our personality and mental health. Working these reflexes will open and discharge vital life force from the endocrine glands.

Wringing of the Hands (a natural method of stress relief)
1. The fingers of one hand stimulate the reflex buttons of the other.
2. One hand rolls around inside the other and knuckles press the reflex to the solar plexus and other reflexes

Another Exercise for Calming Nerves
1. Clasp both hands together with both fingers intertwined.
2. Press all the reflexes between the fingers seven times.
3. Loosen each finger and move them up and over the middle knuckles.
4. Squeeze and release them seven times.
5. Press the tips of your fingers together in a press-and-release movement.
6. Close your eyes and breathe deeply (inhale with the squeeze and exhale relaxing the squeeze).
7. Repeat the exercise as needed.

Deep Breathing for Relaxation
- 1/3 of the oxygen we breathe is absorbed into our brain.
- The oxygen we breathe coordinates our mental action and coordinates all of our movements.
- Mentally focus on breathing. Take deep breathes and think positive thoughts for stress relief.

15 Ways to Alleviate Stress and Tension

1. A foot and hand rub.
2. Elevate feet and hands, while thinking happy thoughts.
3. Wear comfortable shoe and go for a walk.
4. Close your eyes and visualize enjoyable experiences.
5. Take time to enjoy a hobby.
6. Exercise and stretch daily.
7. Participate in group sports.
8. Talk to friends with a good sense of humor. Laughter relieves stress.
9. Deep breathing exercises.
10. Water is relaxing. (sit by a lake, look at the ocean, listen to the rain, or take a swim)
11. Get proper rest
12. Have a massage.
13. Prayer and meditation.
14. Be forgiving and make an effort to love openly.
15. Hand reflexology with deep breathing exercises.

* Consult your physician before using any kind of therapeutic or exercise technique.

The Standing 9 Count

First Trimester: 1st Month

What your woman is experiencing.

Physically
- Morning sickness (nausea, heartburn, vomiting.)
- Food craving -or aversions.
- Headaches.
- Fatigue.
- Breast changes: tenderness, enlargement.

Emotionally
- Thrilled that she is pregnant.
- A heightened closeness to you.
- Apprehension about the nine months ahead.
- Mood swings and sudden, unexplained crying.

Your baby's growth and development
About 2 hours after you and your woman laid together, her egg is fertilized. In a little over 24 hours, there will be a very small bundle of dividing cells. Within 30 days, the embryo will be almost 1/4-inch long and will have arm and leg buds.

End of First Month
- About 1/4 inch (6mm) long.
- Heart, brain, and lungs forming.
- Heart starts beating on about the twenty-fifth day.

What you may be feeling.
- Thrills.
- A sense of relief and pride. (The natural ability to make a baby.)
- Irrational fears. (Questioning your woman's loyalty and your ability to get a woman pregnant.)

Morning Sickness
   50% of all pregnant women experience morning sickness. It can strike your woman at any given time and for most women will last for the first three months. Many women commonly associate their vomiting, nausea, and heartburn to morning sickness. These are things you can do to help your woman cope with her bouts with morning sickness.
- Help her maintain a high-protein, high-carbohydrate diet.
- Encourage her to drink plenty of fluids (milk). Keep a pitcher of water and ice chips by her bed at night, and stay away from caffeine. She should never be dehydrated.
- Be mindful of the sights and smells that make her sick. Keep things like that away

from her.

- Encourage her to eat several small meals throughout the day. She should stay away from greasy foods and eat basic foods like rice and yogurt.
- Make sure she takes her prenatal vitamins.
- Provide her with plenty of snacks at the beginning and the end of each day. Make sure that these foods are low in fat, salt, and calories.
- Make sure she gets plenty of rest. Encourage her to relax and let nature take its course.
- Keep your woman away from hot tubs, steam rooms, baths, and saunas. Raising your pregnant woman's body heat just two degrees could be very dangerous for the fetus. Your body regulates heat by pulling blood away from the internal organs (that includes the uterus) and pushing it towards the skin.

Exercises You and Your Woman Can Do Together.
- Aerobics.
- Speed walking.
- Swimming.
- Light-duty weight lifting.
- Golf.
- Light-duty house chores.
- Light-duty gardening.

* Any kind of sport, exercise, or workout program should be discussed with your doctor. Always make sure you have his or her approval.

Stocking Up On the Good Stuff
These are a few choice items that will make for a good snack any time of the day.
- Unsweetened cereals
- Whole-wheat pasta
- Vegetable and fruit juice
- Whole-grain bread
- Skim or 2% milk
- Nonfat cottage cheese
- Low-fat, naturally sweetened yogurt
- Fresh eggs
- Natural peanut butter
- Natural fruit preserves or fruit cocktails
- Bottled water and frozen ice chips
- Crackers with low sodium
- Fresh vegetables and fruit
- Frozen berries and grapes
- Raisins and other dried fruit.

2nd Month

What your woman is going through.

Physically
- Continuing fatigue
- Continuing morning sickness
- Frequent urination
- Tingly fingers and toes
- Breast tenderness

Emotionally
- Ambivalent about being pregnant and at the same time a continued elation
- Inability to concentrate on her work
- Fear that she is no longer attractive
- Continuing moodiness
- Fear of an early miscarriage

Your baby's growth and development
At this stage your baby will grow from an embryo to a fetus. Although it is too early to tell the sex of your baby, stubby little arms, eyes without eyelids, ears, and a beating heart that sits outside of the body.

End of Second Month
- About 1.5 inches (4 cm) long.
- Muscles and skin developing.
- Developing arms, and hands forming.
- Legs beginning to form, along with knees, ankles, and toes.
- Every vital organ starting to develop.

What you maybe experiencing.
- The physical changes she will experience will make her pregnancy feel very "real" to her. For you the pregnancy will be more abstract. You may even find it difficult to remember from one day to the next.
- You may feel excited about being a new father, but a little scared of all the things that can go wrong with a pregnancy (miscarriage, or birth defect).
- Increased or decreased sexual desire during pregnancy and after the birth of your child.

People that are at High Risk for Birth Defects
- If you or your woman have a family history of birth defects.
- A person is a member of a high-risk ethnic group.
- A woman who is 35 years or older.

Reasons for Prenatal Testing
- Ultrasound (sonogram)
- Alfa-Fetoprotein Testing (AFP)

- Other Blood Tests
- Amniocentesis
- Chorionic Villi Sampling (CVS)
- Pre-cutaneous Umbilical Blood Sampling (PUBS)
- Peace of mind. It reassures the pregnant couple that all is well.
- To learn the sex of the baby.

3rd Month
What your woman is going through.

Physically
- Fatigue, morning sickness, breast tenderness, and other early pregnancy symptoms beginning to disappear
- Continuing moodiness
- Thickening waistline

Emotionally
- Heightened sense of reality about the pregnancy from hearing the baby's heartbeat
- Continuing ambivalence about being pregnant
- Frustration and/or excitement over widening of waistline
- Focusing inward -increased focus on internal growth
- Starting to build a bond with your baby

Your baby's growth and development
The fetus looks like a real person and an ultrasound can reveal your baby's sex. Her teeth, fingernails, and hair are growing. By the end of the month, she can turn her head, curl her toes, and even has slight facial expression.

End of Third Month
- About 3 inches (8 cm) long.
- Weighs about 1 ounce (28g).
- Can open and close mouth and swallow.

What you may be feeling.
- A heightened sense of reality
- Feeling left out of the pregnancy experience
- Feeling left out of your woman's relationship with her doctor
- Physical symptoms: Couvade Syndrome (sympathetic pregnancy)
1. Traditional symptoms of pregnant women- weight gain, nausea, mood swing, food cravings. 2. Symptoms not associated with pregnancy- headaches, toothaches, itching, and cysts. (symptoms appear in 3rd month, decrease for a few months, month or two before birth symptoms increase, and all will "mysteriously" disappear at birth
- Feelings of guilt for pregnant woman's suffering

Second Trimester: 4th Month

What your woman is going through.

Physically
- Nipples darkening
- Increasing appetite as morning sickness weakens
- Clumsiness
- She feels slight movement from the baby

Emotionally
- Great excitement towards the sonogram
- Less fearful of a miscarriage
- Real concerns about motherhood
- Continuing moodiness and still forgetful
- Increasingly dependent -needs your physical and emotional support

Your baby's growth and development
She has only grown 4 or more inches in the early part of the month. Your baby girl's heart beat is 120-160 beats per minute. She reacts to light and darkness, and she can tell when your woman is eating something sweet and/or sour.

End of the Fourth Month
- 8 to 10 inches (20 to 25 cm) long.
- Weighs 6 ounces (170g).
- Movement can be felt.

What you may be feeling.
- Increasing sense of your woman's pregnancy
- Growing concerns about the financial debt of making a baby
- Increasing concerns for the safety of your woman and the baby

Pleasing Your Pregnant Woman

- Rub her back and massage her feet
- Date your pregnant woman and do things that you won't be able to do after the baby is born.
- Give her gifts for no special reasons.
- Help her with the chores around the house.
- Hug your woman, and hug your baby by hugging your woman.
- Run her bath.
- When you cannot be with her arrange for others to visit with her.
- Surprise her with take-out and a little taste of her favorite comfort food.

- Mail her a love letter or two.
- Buy or make gifts for her and get separate gifts for the baby.
- Treat the nine months pregnancy as if it is a life time of growth. Praise it as the biggest deal ever.
- Pay attention to her diet.
- Walk for exercise, study baby CPR, explore baby names, take picture, make video, read together.
- Visit local nursery at nearby hospital.
- If you already have children, you can take them out and give her time alone.
- Communicate openly about fears and concerns about your baby.

5th Month
What your woman is going through.

Physically
- Your woman can distinguish the baby's movement.
- Braxton-Hicks contractions (occasional painless tightening of the uterus)
- Continuing darkening of nipples, the appearance of dark lines on her tummy.

Emotionally
- Baby's constant movement gives less worry about possible miscarriage
- Developing deep bond with baby
- Sensitivity about her changing body
- Increase in sexual desire
- Increasingly dependent on your support
- Feelings of jealousy towards the baby

Your baby's growth and development
Your baby can hear what is going on outside. She can kick, punch, and grab at umbilical cord.

End of Fifth Month
- About 9-12 inches (30 cm) long.
- Weighs 1 pound (454g).
- Eyelashes appear.
- Nails begin to grow.
- Heartbeat can be heard.

What you may be feeling.
- Excited about being a father
- Increased interest in fatherhood
- Your focus is turning inward and you are thinking more about your needs

<u>6th Month</u>
What your woman is going through.

Physically
- Period of great weight gain begins
- Increased sweating
- Increased blood flow will give her major "glow."
- Increased baby activity

Emotionally
- Decreasing moodiness
- Continued forgetfulness
- Feeling as if the day of birth will never come
- Stronger bond with baby
- Continuing dependency on you

Your baby's growth and development
Your baby is now covered w/ a thick waxy coat called a vernix. She is responding to sounds outside the uterus, and her kicks and punches are becoming stronger.

End of Sixth Month
- Can kick and cry
- Might even hiccup
- Has fingernails

What you may be feeling.
- Examining your relationships with the father figures in your life
- A sense of mortality
- Feeling limited in your ability to function.

<u>Third Trimester: 7th Month</u>

What your woman is going through.

Physically
- Increased physical discomfort (general)
- Itchy abdomen
- Some increased clumsiness
- Learning to walk in a new, awkward way
- A normal vaginal discharge (leukorrhea)
- Increased Braxton-Hicks (false labor) contractions

Emotionally

- Decreased moodiness
- Dreaming/ Fantasizing about the baby
- Concerns about the many roles she will have to play (wife, mother, and employee)
- Fears about labor and delivery

Your baby's growth and development
Your baby's lungs have matured and she can dance to the music that plays outside the womb. She is beginning to feel cramped in the uterus.

End of Seventh Month
- Weighs 2.5 to 3 pounds
- Can move arms and legs freely
- Eyes are now open
- Measures 15 inches long

What you may be feeling.
- Increasing acceptance of the pregnancy
- Visualizing the baby
- Speculating on the baby's gender
- Fear of falling apart during labor

8th Month
What your woman is going through.

Physically
- Strong fetal activity
- Heavy vaginal discharge
- Severe general discomfort
- Frequent urination
- Sleeplessness
- Increased fatigue
- Shortness of breath (baby's size puts pressure on neighboring organs)
- Swelling from water retention
- Frequent Braxton-Hicks contraction

Emotionally
- Feeling special-Everyone treats her like a queen.
- Feeling a bond with other mothers
- Feeling beautiful/ugly
- Fears about being a new mother.
- Concerns with her body's growth after childbirth
- Afraid her water will break while out in public

Your baby's growth and development
At this stage, your baby girl has assumed the birthing position. It is a head down-position

that she would maintain for the rest of the pregnancy. The baby can open her eyes and respond to your individual voices.

End of Eighth Month
- About 16.5 to 18 inches (average 42 cm) long.
- Weighs about 4 to 5 pounds (average 1800 g).
- Hair grows.
- Skin gets smoother as a layer of fat develops under it.

What you may be feeling.
- Self-conscious about your woman's physical appearance and the impact it has on the people you encounter
- Panic (the loss of your personal life).
- Nesting (preparing your home for the new baby).
- Sex -Again (a father often has fears about hurting his wife or his baby through sexual intercourse.)

Essentials for Your Nursery

For the baby
- Enough diapers to last for at least a few weeks
- Baby soap and shampoo
- Thermometer (digital is easiest)
- An ear bulb for the baby's nose
- Nail scissors
- Cotton swabs and alcohol for umbilical cord dressing
- 3 or 4 undershirts, sleepers, coveralls with snap, and baby blankets
- Sun and snow hat
- Snow suit (as needed)
- Bottles and formulas -even if breastfeeding, just in case.....

For Your Partner
- Nursing pad
- Any medication for C-section or episiotomy
- Maxi pads (several weeks supply)
- Milk and vitamins (good for nursing mother)
- A good book about a baby's first years of life
- A few pleasure and plenty of comfort food

9th Month
What your woman is going through.

Physically

- Fetal activity -all she can do is squirm
- Increased sleeplessness and fatigue
- A renewed sense of energy as the baby's head slips into pelvis and takes pressure off of internal organs
- Increased pressure and pain ("She's gonna be miserable.")

Emotionally
- More dependent on you and fearful of your commitment to her and the baby.
- Impatient: anxious to complete pregnancy and give birth.
- Short-tempered
- Afraid she will be overwhelmed with responsibilities of loving you and your baby.
- Afraid she will not be ready for labor and birth
- Increasing preoccupation with the baby

Your baby's growth and development
Your daughter is almost ready to push free from the womb. Her fingernails and toenails are very long and she will have a head full of hair.

End of Ninth Month
- 18 to 20 inches (46 to 51 cm) long.
- Weighs 7 to 9 pounds (3 to 4 kg).
- Organs have developed enough to function on their own.

What you may be feeling.
- Confusion. Role of father VS Role of husband.
- Increased dependency on your partner
- Feeling guilty.

Chapter 3: Childbirth

Normal Delivery

Your woman will be pregnant about 280 days. By that time, your baby will have matured to a point when he/she can take over his/her own life functions. Your woman will go into labor and experience uterine contractions that will separate her from the baby.

There are three stages in labor. The first stage is the longest, and it is called the *cervical* stage (or dilation stage). This is a preparatory period involving the complete involuntary opening of the cervix, which is the opening in the uterus through which your baby will pass.

The cervix must open 4 inches (nearly 10 cm) before your baby can go through. Sometimes, during the later part of the dilation stage doctors will give women pain medicine. Pain medicine can make your baby sluggish and interfere with his/her breathing. It can also make it difficult for your woman to help in the birthing process.

The second stage is known as *birth*. This stage begins when the cervix is fully dilated and continues until the baby is independent of your woman's body. Babies are usually born head first. This is called crowning. When a baby is born buttocks first, it is referred to as the breech position. A breech birth requires the skillful hand of a trained professional, like a mid-wife or medical delivery doctor.

The third and final stage is the afterbirth. In this stage, the *afterbirth* separates and is expelled from your woman's body. The two things that make up the afterbirth is the placenta, the amniotic sac with its membrane. This stage will most likely begin about twenty minute after the baby's birth.

The Apgar Test

Your hospital will give routine tests to determine your baby's physical condition at birth. This test is usually given 1 minute after birth and repeated at 5 minutes. Your baby will be rated from 0 to 2 with a total score of 7 to 10 (normal). A lower score may mean that your baby needs special medical attention. The Apgar test will measure your baby's condition in 5 areas.

- Appearance or coloring.
- Pulse.
- Grimace or reflex irritability.
- Activity.
- Respiration.

Cesarean Delivery

When your woman is in labor, her doctor will attach a device to her abdomen that will monitor the baby's heart rate and the intensity of the uterine contractions. This fetal measuring is meant to detect any problems during labor and delivery. In about 5% of births, normal delivery may be dangerous for the mother or baby. Sometimes, women may suffer from diabetes or toxemia, which can have a negative impact on delivery.

If during your woman's pregnancy, the doctor finds that a normal delivery would be dangerous or impossible, he/she may perform a *Cesarean* section. The doctor will deliver your baby through a surgical incision in your woman's abdominal wall and uterus. Your woman's recovery will most likely take longer after a Cesarean section than after a normal birth.

To determine whether your woman will need a Cesarean section, her doctor will use a technique called *ultrasound.* These are high-frequency sound waves, reflecting off the body, and forming a picture of the body's interior on a monitor. Your woman's doctors can see how the cervix is dilating and the baby's position in the womb. It also gives the doctors a heads up on the number of babies your woman is having as well as their growth.

Hospital Stay after Delivery

Hospital-care for your woman and baby will vary depending on the hospital you choose. Their care will come in either traditional care or rooming-in. Under traditional care a pediatric nurse in the maternity ward will most likely care for your newborn.

This is a desirable option if your woman has had a difficult delivery or is in poor health. Babies are usually brought to their mother when he/she needs feeding. If your woman is in good health, your baby will be brought to her at other times as well.

Rooming-in is when your new baby and your woman are cared for in the same room. There are many advantages that come with this particular form of care. One advantage is your woman's ability to constantly watch your baby. This provides a great deal of security for your baby. With your baby in the same room as your woman, you two can get acquainted with your baby while working with a medical care-giver.

The bond between you and your baby will begin immediately. You and your woman will develop great confidence in caring for your new baby. As a father you will have the opportunity to play a significant role in child-care right from the beginning.

Postpartum Care

Different hospital policies may vary but in general if your woman has a normal delivery she will stay in a hospital 2 to 3 days, and 5 to 7 days with a Cesarean Section. This is time would be used for rest and recovery after delivery. It will also give your woman time to learn self-care and the proper care for your new baby. You and your woman can learn about feeding and bathing your baby.

It is in the best interest of your woman and baby that she breast feed. So, you can expect the doctor or nurse to put your baby up to your woman's breast immediately after birth. This action will stimulate the secretion of hormones that signal lactation.

Postpartum Blues and Depression

Once a sperm fertilizes an egg, it brings about a hormonal shift. Levels of progesterone remain high during pregnancy and that will comfort your woman. Her maternal instinct switches into high gear as she prepares for birth.

After your baby is born, her body will go through another drastic change. For a few weeks, the hormone prolactin (milk production) will be produced and progesterone levels will drop. With this normal change comes the postpartum blues. The postpartum blues are brought on by the stress of adjusting to the life of a new mother, as well as the normal hormonal changes after birth.

If your woman has been properly raised, then she knows what to expect from this new change in her life. If she has not been taught to be a woman, then she may feel disappointed in her expectations of being a new mother. She may feel overwhelmed and even guilty about her new role as a mother. All of these things may contribute to the postpartum blues.

Coping with the Postpartum Blues
- She may have fits of crying spells.
- The new baby wets, messes, and spits up regularly.
- Around the clock feedings.
- Her stitches and staples hurt her and the healing process is long and hard.
- Her breasts are painful and engorged.
- Her personal needs as a woman have not changed.
- Her duties to her man have not changed.
- Her duties as a homemaker have not changed.

Most women will shake the postpartum blues with a normal monthly menstrual cycle. For a few women, the postpartum blues will quickly escalate to a problem known as postpartum depression (PPD.). These women will develop severe and prolonged symptoms of depression following child-birth.

Postpartum depression (PPD.) and premenstrual syndrome (PMS) have a lot in common. A major difference is that PMS is cyclical, and occurs just before the menses. PPD., on the other hand, is continuous and does not change with each menstrual cycle. Since PPD. has no cyclical changes or symptoms, it is very difficult to diagnose.

For some young mothers, PPD. will not be diagnosed until their menses begin and their symptoms advance into some monthly pattern. Many times, these symptoms may not evolve for six to seven months. When prolactin levels are very high, progesterone levels are very low. These conditions bring about PPD.

Symptoms of Postpartum Depression:
- Being tired.
- Tearful feelings with low self-esteem.
- An inability to cope or keep up with other people's demand.
- Women may withdraw into herself with the baby, and neglect everyone else.
- Women may neglect the baby, and focus all of her attention on her man.

Atypical depression is one of the main symptoms that help diagnose PPD. A new mother with PPD. wants to sleep all the time. She will feel totally exhausted and will sleep around the clock. They do not necessarily need to sleep; they just want to sleep all of the time (With normal depression, a person can not sleep.)

These symptoms may begin at birth, as a continuation of normal postpartum blues. The symptoms may also begin with the use of birth-control pills. Birth-control pills have progestin and will aggravate any depressed feelings.

New mothers who have PMS prior to pregnancy are more likely to suffer from PPD. PPD. is only diagnosed if the symptoms are continuous, abnormal, and last for a considerable length of time.

Postpartum depression and premenstrual syndrome are treated the same way. Although there is no scientific evidence to validate the treatment, some doctors use natural progesterone suppositories. The best treatment for severe PPD. or PMS is to work with a doctor to make some dietary changes:
- Reducing caffeine.
- Reducing sugar.
- Increasing intake of vitamin B6, vitamin C, and calcium.
- Take appropriate doses of magnesium.

Premenstrual Syndrome

"Premenstrual syndrome is a hormonal deficiency disease that is characterized by a clustering of symptoms in the premenstrual phase and an absence of symptoms in the postmenstrual phase."

Gillian Ford

Women may have symptoms a few days before the menses, while others may complain that their only good days are those that fall between the end of their menstrual period and ovulation. The most important thing in the diagnosis of PMS is the timing of the symptoms.

The Physical Symptoms of PMS:
- Migraines.
- Nausea and dizziness.
- Eye problems-conjunctivitis, sties, and visual disturbances.
- Skin problems-acne, boils, hives, oral and genital herpes.
- Respiratory problems-asthma, allergies, recurrent flu-like symptoms, hoarseness, and tonsillitis.
- Repeated bladder or yeast infections.
- Hemorrhoid or Varicose vein flare-ups.

The Emotional Symptoms of PMS:
- Irritability, lethargy, depression (almost always present).
- Feeling out of control.

- Uncontrollable rage.
- Paranoia and suicidal impulse.
- Violent outbursts.
- Desire to flee and Anxiety attacks.
- Feeling of being a split personality.
- Phobic symptoms: fear of crowds
- Crying jags.

Additional Emotional Symptoms:
- Occasional mental problems
- Feeling worthless
- Feeling guilty.

As a father, you can help your daughter cope with PMS, by assisting her in keeping record of the physical and emotional symptoms. This would help her validate the problem and pinpoint specific symptoms. Finding the right treatment or series of treatments may be a process of many trial and errors. Successful therapy may require your daughter to change her habits and life-style.

A chart and diary can help put your daughter in closer touch with her body. With them, she will be able to more accurately measure what her symptoms are and determine whether or not those symptoms are cyclical.

<u>Personal Touch for Women with PMS</u>

Reflexology for helping Premenstrual Syndrome and Menopause
Give her a complete reflexology workout twice a week, 2 weeks before her menstrual cycle begins. Stimulating her circulation will wash the retaining fluids and relieve the heavy bloated feelings. Have her cut back on salty snacks and that will lessen fluid build up.

The Back of the Foot
- Take hold to her right foot, place 2 fingers or a thumb, in the fleshy part on the outside of the foot, between the ankle and the heel.
- With a press-and-roll technique, massage the entire area around the outer side of her foot.
- Massage to the back and underneath the ankle feeling for special pressure points. (ovary reflexes)
- Repeat with left foot.
(* Caution: If she is having problems with her ovaries, the area will be extremely painful. Use a light touch.)

Inside of the Foot
- Using your fingers or thumb, press into the soft area just under the ankle bone.
- If it is sore just underneath the ankle bone and slightly back towards the heel, be

very gentle. (reflex point for the uterus)

- Gently press into the depression behind the ankle and back towards the heel.
- Press along the sides of her Achilles tendon, moving up towards her calf muscle. Use the press-and-pinch method.
- Do not over massage. A little attention the first few times is better than over stimulating the reflex point.
- Repeat the exercise on the other foot.

A Complete Foot Workout
- Using gentle deep pressure, massage the whole foot.
- Start at the toes and work your way back to the heel.
- Press hard enough to trigger the reflexes beneath the skin.

If you encounter a painful spot on her foot, work it briefly and continue to work the entire foot. Return to the painful areas after you finish working the whole foot. Do not overwork a reflex. You can bruise the sensitive areas. It may take several mild sessions, but the pain will eventually work its way out. The blood will flow freely and flush out poisons bringing her vitalizing, pain-free health.

Overcome Mood Swings and Depression

The Endocrine System is a powerful coordinator of all body functions. These glands regulate body rhythm, and balance chemical and emotional functions. The thyroid gland reflex will be used to influence her mood. When the thyroid gland is not functioning properly, the body feels depressed. These decreases also affect the brain resulting in depressed emotions. (Thyroid reflexes are on both hands and feet.)

In addition to the endocrine gland, focus on the liver (very sensitive), lungs, solar plexus, and brain to fight both stress and depression. The liver cleans the blood, and distributes vitamins and minerals throughout the body. The liver can affect menstrual pain and cause stress.

Work the whole liver area for about seven seconds. Remember, do not over massage the liver area. She should increase body movement to become more limber. She should also take brisk walks, and practice deep breathing exercises. This will relieve stiffness and improve circulation.

Reflex the Urinary System

In order to keep the kidneys, bladder, and urethra strong, you will need to drink 8oz of water for every twenty pounds of your weight. Your kidneys filter waste and maintain chemical balance in the blood. Work the reflexes of the bladder and kidney, and that will stimulate the ureter reflex. The kidney reflexes lie lengthwise below the adrenal reflex in the center of both the foot and hand.

Massage the Kidney
- Place both hands on your hips with thumbs in front and all fingers pointing

towards your back.

- Position hands just above the waist and press fingers tips in a circular motion over the kidneys.
- Continue the circular motion on down to the lower end of the tailbone. Repeat three times. This will relieve tension and get fluids moving away from congested areas.

Relax and Relieve Menstrual Cramps (Relieve tension in the ovaries by rocking your pelvis.)

1st Exercise
- Lie on your back and bend your knees, placing both feet flat on the floor.
- Sway your knees to the left, then to the right.
- Move your knees about eight inches in both directions.

2nd Exercise
- Sit up with your back firmly against the wall.
- Bend your knees, placing both feet flat on the floor.
- Sway your knees to the left, then to the right.
- Move your knees about eight inches to either side.

3rd Exercise
- Simply lie on the left side of your body. The stomach is mostly on the left side of the body. By lying on the left side of her body, a woman takes the pressure off the uterus and that relieves cramps.

4th Exercise
- Lie on your back and take deep breathes.
- Allow your body to go limp.
- Slowly take several deep breathes, while mentally visualizing each part of your body relaxing.
- Inhale a deep breath for seven seconds while tightening your toes. Then slowly exhale relaxing every muscle.
- Gradually work your way up each and every muscle in your body. Tighten toes. Then tighten toes and ankles. Then tighten toes, ankles, and feet.
- Keep going until you have tightened every muscle from head to toe.
- Once your whole body is relaxed. Place your left hand below your navel and press firmly. If the area is tender, gently massage with circular motions for 7 seconds, and then take a slow deep breath.

Castor Oil Packs for Sore Breasts

Relieve minor infections and inflammation.
- Cold-pressed castor oil (substances that increases T11 lymphocyte for healing infections)
- A wool flannel cloth

- A piece of plastic
- Heating pad

Fold the flannel cloth several times and sock it in castor oil (saturate the cloth without dripping). Place cloth on breast or infected area, cover with plastic, and put heating pad over breast or infected area. Set heating pad on high and adjust for comfort. Leave it on for one hour. Use as needed, 3 to 7 and it will draw out congestion. Within a week, she should be free of all inflammation. (* Keep castor oil and used wool flannel cloth sealed in freezer zip lock bag in the refrigerator.)

Cool Her Breasts

Cool Rub. Place your hands in a large bowl of ice cubes and a little water. Gently shake away any excess water from your hands. Cup your hands over her breasts, and gently massage to ease lymph fluids back into the lymph passages. Repeat this several times.

Reflexology for Developing Beautiful Breasts

Your daughter's breasts will be a symbol of her femininity and their shape and size are as important to her as a boy's organ is to him. Reflexology can help her have the healthy full round breasts she desires. It can also help your woman maintain her youthful appearance.

Massaging the Breast
1. Take your woman from behind.
2. Place both hands on her bare breasts.
3. The left hand on the left breast and the right hand on the right breast.
4. Cup each breast with your fingers pointing towards the breast bone and your thumbs pointing upwards. (The nipple should be between the thumb and the index fingers.)
5. Gently massage rotating your fingers up towards her throat.
6. Start with your fingers far enough back that you pull the muscles under the arms
7. Use a forward lifting motion with each rotation.
8. Be gentle. Do not do this often in the beginning. (It will make her breast sore.) Start off light and gradually work up to a comfortable routine.
9.
* Pouring sea salt over the breast before a massage is recommended.

Massaging Reflexes

Massaging reflexes in the neck improves your skin and stimulates hormones for developing beautiful breasts. Breasts are related to the sex glands and your reflex workout for the endocrine glands and gonads will help improve your breasts.
- Kneading and massaging the breasts with the fingers and palms of your hands will enlarge and shape her breasts.

47

Reversing Massage

1st Exercise
1. Place the fingers of the left hand on the breastbone and slide them under the right breast.
2. Work your fingers clear around the breast with an uplifting motion.
3. Do the same thing with the left breast
4. Repeat them both several times.

2nd Exercise
1. Place the fingers of the right hand on the breastbone, and follow the vein under the breast, pressing on the solid bone beneath.
2. Work the fingers along the outer edge of the breast and up into the fore part of the arm.
3. Next time, follow the same procedure but massage up toward the outer muscle of the arm.

* The short lived tender spots that you may encounter are nothing more than stagnated blood. Any unduly tender spots that you find in the breast that do not go away should be checked by a physician.

Some women have been able to dissolve their benign breast lumps by changing their diets. These women removed coffee, tea, chocolate, and cola from their diet. These items contain a stimulant called methylxanthines. Studies show that this stimulant provokes the growth of cystic lumps.

3rd Exercise
1. Place the fingers of the left hand at the nipple of the left breast and slowly massage towards the outer breast in full circles.
2. Gradually enlarge the circle until you have covered the whole surface of the entire breast.
3. Do the right breast the same way.

OR

1. Place the palm of the left hand at the nipple of the left breast.
2. Pressing with the ball of the hand, slowly massage towards the outer breast in full circles.
3. Keep enlarging the circle until you have covered the whole surface of the entire breast.
4. Do the other breast the same way.

Reflexology for Back Pain

The spine is a very important part of a body's general health. Most back problems come from tension in the muscles around the spine. The strain on muscles around the spine, cause the muscles to tighten and pull spinal vertebrae out of alignment.

Lower back is the biggest single medical complaint in the country. With the use of a good chiropractor and a reflexologist that understands the cause of the medical problem, many people find permanent relief. All over the world people have found great reward with the use of foot and hand reflexology to aid in relieving back pain.

Working with Tender Reflex Buttons

The spinal column is located in the center of the body. When looking at the foot from the big toe (the top of the spine) to the back of the heel (the tailbone or coccyx), there is almost a replica of the spine. If there are any weaknesses along the spine, there will be tender spots found along this area. Working any tender reflex in this area will stimulate a renewed energy into that part of the spine.

In the hands we find the same spinal reflexes. If you start at the base of the fore finger, curve down around the thumb muscle to the bones that join the finger and thumb (lower back) to the wrist.

Proper Treatments

When muscles are not relaxed and loose, they can pull bones out of place. Reflexology is used to relax the tension from the muscles around the spine. Once the muscles get fresh oxygenated blood, they can properly respond to nerve impulses. Working reflex points will reopen channels for the flow of life energy to the body's electrical system and free the healing forces to help malfunctioning areas of the body.

Feet and Back Problems

As odd as it may sound, one of the best things for back problems is walking. Walking is a natural method of strengthening all the muscles in the body. A brisk walk sends oxygen to all the cells and tissue of the muscles and internal organs. A brisk walk will do more for the body than jogging or running.

Surveys have shown that jogging proved to be harmful to 40% of those who jog. Instead of jogging, try a "Rebounder" or small trampoline. It will be more beneficial without harming the bone structure of the body.

Stair climbing is also a great way to get the exercise you need with out harming the bone structure. Many types of shoes can cause back pain. 20% of back problems are caused by flat feet. Corrective shoes and reflex massage can correct these back problems. (* Note: Vitamin C has been proven to help many backaches.)

Foot Exercises for Straightening the Back
1. Hold the feet straight out in front of the body. (10 inches apart)
2. Curl the toes of the foot back towards the body as far as possible.

3. Bring feet towards each other so that big toes are touching.
4. Force both feet down, holding toes under as you take 20 steps forward. (Walking pigeon-toed)
5. Relax feet by shaking them two or three times.
6. Stretch and straighten both feet out. Straighten feet by walking briskly around the room. Walk 4 times on your toes and then 4 times on your heel for 20 steps. Then walk 4 times on the inside of your feet and then 4 times on the outside of your feet. These exercises are good for keeping the back straight and strong.
7. Repeat one time.

Proper Diet and Vitamins for Reflexology

Nutritionists recommend that people eat an enormous amount of fresh living foods (raw vegetables and fruit) and plenty of fresh drinking water.

Brewer's Yeast: Healthy Eating
- It contains 17 different vitamins (including all family B vitamins).
- 16 amino acids
- 14 minerals (including trace minerals)
- 36% protein
- Only contains 1% fat (1 tablespoon/ eight grams/ only 22 calories.

(* It is available at neighborhood health food stores. This is not baking yeast. Never eat fresh yeast for baking.)

Blackstrap Molasses or Unsulphured molasses (Good for Internal or External Use)
As a home remedy, it is good when applied to:
- cuts
- abrasions
- as an enema (for a troubled colon)
- as a douche (for troubles in a woman's area)
- toothaches or sores in the mouth

As a healthy part of a daily diet, blackstrap molasses:
- very rich in iron
- rich in vitamin B
- add small amounts to warm or cold milk

(* Only purchase blackstrap molasses from a health food store. Products at traditional store have too much sugar.)

Wheat Germ (keep it refrigerated for freshness)
- vitamins B-1, B-2, B-6
- niacin
- rich in protein
- provides 3x the iron of other sources
- vitamin E (good for the heart)

Yogurt
- helps retain vigor, vitality, and youth
- high quality protein
- good source of calcium and riboflavin (vitamin B-2)

1 Cup of Yogurt with Powdered Milk
- 7% of the calories
- 17% protein
- 50% calcium
- 30% vitamin B-2

Liquid Golden Oils with Vitamin E
- Good source of energy
- It is more slowly digested and absorbed than all other foodstuffs
- It should always be added fresh

Powdered Milk
- No animal fat
- High biological quality of protein
- Rich in riboflavin and calcium
- Easily digested

Garlic
- Vitamins A, B, C, and D
- Rich in sulfur and iodine
- Contains bioflavonoids.

Garlic helps:
- Stimulate liver and kidney
- Eliminate worms in children and pets
- Relieves rheumatic and arthritic and many other ailments.
- Good for high blood pressure.
- Helps regulate body odor.
- Garlic and onions are good blood purifiers

Herbs

There is an important link between a proper diet and good health. Herbs, like fruit and fresh vegetables, herbs play a very special role in our efforts to fight off illnesses. Some people believe that herbs help cure diseases. Herbal teas are good for our health. Do not boil herb tea.

Sage and rosemary tea is good for strengthening your body. Add honey, peppermint, and lemon if desired. Speak to the salesperson at the local whole food health store for detail information on herbs and their different uses.

Deep Breathing and Drinking Water for Reflexology

Water
- 70% of our body is water.
- Our system requires water to function.
- Lubricate joints.
- Regulates body temperature
- Aids in digestion
- Kidneys need water to flush out waste.
- Water in the blood helps carry oxygen and nutrients to body cells.
- Muscles and skin need water.
- Washes out excess fat.

It is better to drink too much water than not enough. When the body dehydrates, it pulls water from the muscle and tissue. Dehydration stresses the body and the muscle and tissue suffers. Reflexology helps the body clean itself of toxins and impurities. The elimination of liquid waste is necessary or balance and body revitalization. The body needs water for both structure and function.

Safe Drinking Water
- Boil water for 5 minutes, let it cool, and then put the fluid in a container and shake it well. Shaking the container will oxygenates the water and improves the taste.
- To add energy to the water, take the container and swirl it in a spiral motion. The water should move in a circular motion. This will regenerate the water natural electricity.

Deep Breathing

Deep breathing will improve immune power and blood pressure. It is good for respiration and the body's cardiovascular system. Proper breathing exercises will also improve circulation and mental abilities. The human body is made up of trillions of cells that thrive on adequate water and oxygen.

Oxygen is necessary to build red cells. Without the oxygen of life, the body becomes weak and loses vitality. Oxygen is important for converting food into nourishment. Oxygenated blood feeds cells, organs, glands, nerves, tissue, hair, teeth, and bones.

Deep Breathing Posture
- Good posture is essential for healthy breathing.
- Sit on the floor with your legs crossed. (If necessary use the wall for support.)
- Lie in bed or on the floor and prop your knees up on a chair in a sitting position.
- Sit in a high back arm chair.

Deep Breathing Exercise

- With proper posture and mouth closed, slowly draw-in a breath. (The breath should be felt in the upper lining of the throat. It should give off a slight hissing sound.) Place both hands on each side of the rib cage.
- Air should be taken into the lower part of the lungs, and there should be an expanding of the lower rib cage.
- When the lungs feel full, slowly exhale with air passing at the top of the throat with mouth closed. There should be another hissing sound in the throat.
- There should be an expansion of the chest and rib cage, and a slight pulling in the stomach. (This does not happen in regular breathing.)
- Still relaxed. Continue to breathe exhaling from the top of your chest and going downward until the lungs are empty.

(* Note: This exercise may be difficult and feel awkward at first, but in time it will become natural.)

The deep breathing exercise should only be done in two breathes the first time. Choose a certain time of the day when you will practice deep breathing. In the beginning, it should only be done once a day. It can gradually increase in the days that follow. It will not be an easy exercise, and will take time to learn properly. Stay focused and the effort will soon change your life.

The Lay Mid-husbandry

A midwife is a person who has specialized training in childbirth. They also give care and advice during the woman's pregnancy and after she gives birth. You can find midwives working at birthing centers, hospitals, and private homes.

Here in the United States, registered nurses can get a certification from the American College of Nurse-Midwives. Some states require nurses who want to practice midwifery to have a special license. In other state, nurses practice under their nursing license.

Midwifery emphasize that childbirth is a natural process. It is the responsibility of the midwife to help the family have a safe and satisfying birth experience. Most midwives only take patients who are going to have a normal childbirth. A midwife must be trained to recognize signs of a difficult birth.

If necessary, a doctor is called, or the birth mother is taken to the hospital. Lay midwives have no formal medical training in midwifery. Some states offer permits to lay midwives. They usually work in rural areas that have relatively few physicians.

Check This Out!
What's In a Name, My Brother?
"A name can be the first step on a journey of a thousand years into the future--an identification of African ancestry that will allow a more clear and vital interaction between we who live in North America and the people of Africa."

African Names for Families (Satellite Productions).

For many years, Blacks in the United States lack the education and self-awareness needed to be concerned with how they were named. Even during the periods of great cultural and social movements, many were not fully aware of the significance a name could play in identifying an individual as part of an ethnic group with a valuable cultural heritage.

Your name is how the people of your world will identify you as a person. A name is one of the few possessions that can survive death. It is sacred and probably the most valuable thing we possess. Some people have the fortune of being able to trace their family name and history back for hundreds of years. As Black Americans, our sacred link to collective African cultures was broken centuries of slavery.

Naming your baby girl can be a major task. In many families, children are named after relatives or close family friends. Sometimes children are named for character traits they have or qualities their parents hope they will grow to have, such as virtues or beauty.

In some Asian ethnic groups, it is common to have only one name. In many Latin cultures, children might be given several names indicating family names on both sides of their families, religious icons, and even their birthplace.

In southern United States, many African Americans have held on to names like Ada, Ebi, Essi. These are a few of the African names that survived slavery and hold some history. Their abductors quickly renamed the African hostages, who were brought to the western hemisphere to be exploited. After Emancipation, many Africans returned to our homeland with European American names. Some of them chose to keep their slave surnames.

All over the world, cultures that have suffered the savagery of European colonial rule are regaining their ethnic identities. On both the continent of Africa and in the United States of Americas, people are reclaiming this link to self-awareness, cultural pride, and self-reliance. Many Islamic and biblical names are of African origin.

Research the names in your family. Learn the language of your name and its cultural origin. Find out if your name has a special meaning and why it was given to you.

Affording the Costs of Making a Baby

Expenses

Having a baby can be expensive. Even with good insurance, the deductible plus the 20% most policies require can still add up to thousands of dollars. In the following section, you will get an idea of what to expect. After reading this section, get out your insurance package and see what it covers.

Pregnancy and Childbirth

Most doctors charge a flat fee for the entire pregnancy. That package includes:
1. Monthly visits during the first two trimesters.
2. Biweekly visits over another month or so.
3. Weekly visits until delivery

The flat fee the doctors charge does not include:
- Blood and Urine Test
- Ultrasounds
- Hospital fees
- Other procedures

Obstetrician/Gynecology

General prenatal care and problem free vaginal delivery will be $2500 to $6500. The doctors usually discuss the services they will provide and their rates. You will need to find out what insurance plans they participate in. Find out whether they will directly bill the insurance company or will they expect a 25% deposit from you for the anticipated bill. You should also know whether they will accept your payments in installments and whether their fee has to be paid before the day of delivery.

Midwife
Average cost of a delivery is about $1200.

Lab and General Expenses
- Blood: Throughout the pregnancy you may spend, from $100 to $700 for various blood tests.
- Ultrasound: An ordinary pregnancy will require up to 3 ultrasounds at $200 each.

Prenatal Testing
- A candidate for amniocentesis or any other prenatal diagnostic test can pay $800 to $1200.
- Genetic counseling $300 to $500

(Any prenatal tests that you have done that are not required may not be picked up by your insurance.)

Hospital Birth
- A problem-free vaginal delivery and a 24 hour stay will cost $1000 to $2500.
- For you to stay overnight with your woman at the hospital add $200 per day to the bill.
- Anesthesiologists charge form $750 to $1500 for an epidural; additional fees for a spinal block, and even more for a Cesarean section.

With/ C-Section
A cesarean section is major surgery that will require a longer recovery time for your woman and your baby. Average costs $15,000.

Obstetrical Clinic (Low-Cost Alternative)
- It is less expensive than the hospital.
- The doctor delivering your baby will be inexperienced or a medical student.
- These clinics often have state-of-the-art facilities

- The students at these clinics are taught the latest methods and have some of the best teachers.

Note: Free and Subsidized Medical Care
- Many state and county health department operate free health clinics.
- Hospital emergency rooms are required by federal law to give emergency care whether you can afford to pay for it or not.

Check the Bill Before You Pay It
You and your woman should check your medical bill closely. Contact a registered nurse or doctor who can go over your bill and make sure that everything you were charged for was actually necessary for any of your medical procedures. After a close look at their medical bill, some people have reported a 20% difference in their bill.

Read your insurance policy and know when the best time to tell them about the pregnancy and the baby's due date. Find out when your baby can be added to the insurance policy.

Chapter 4

The Life Cycle: The Infant Woman (0-2 years)

Parent-Infant Bond

Children have many needs. For a long time, people considered those needs to simply be food, clothing and shelter. Equally important is the physical expression of loving care. Love and nurturing are vital to a child's growth and development. A strong bond between you and your baby is an essential need. So, don't be afraid to hug, kiss and love on both your woman and your baby.

Research has shown that babies that are separated from their mothers at birth due to health reasons and do not get the intimacy they need fail to thrive. Even after the children are given back to their parents and taken home, they do not develop patterns of behavior at a normal rate. Studies also confirm that parents who do not get to care for their babies from the start, experience feelings of inadequacy and guilt. So, it is in everybody's best interest to give love to his or her little baby as soon as possible.

Right after birth, your baby will most likely be quiet and alert. That is the best time for you and your woman to bond with your baby. The first few hours after birth are believed to be the most important time for you and your woman to bond with your little baby.

When you see your baby for the first time, you should talk to her in a calm voice and stand where she can see your face. Put your finger into the palm of your baby's hand and let her grasp it. The more attention you and your woman give your little baby, the more your baby will respond to the two of you. Remember, that your positive actions and reactions affect your baby. Talk to your baby and imitate his/her sounds.

Parent-Infant Interaction	
Stage I.	Infant coos, smiles, babbles, or cries.
Stage II.	The parent's response
Stage III.	Infant shows signs of being consoled and content.
Stage IV.	Parents show signs of pleasure and confidence.

Your baby's attachment to you is your attachment to him/her. In the early months of your baby's life, your response to his/her needs give him/her feelings of contentment and satisfaction. The more your baby learns to recognize you and distinguish you from others, the stronger your bond. Your little baby learns to identify you as the one who gives him/her love and pleasure.

At the age of four, your baby will have developed a strong bond to you and your woman. For this reason, you may find your baby putting up a fuss when you try and leave them with a baby-sitter. Some of the characteristics of infant love are a child's willingness to come to you instead of someone else. A second characteristic will be you and your woman's ability to soothe your baby even when other cannot. Lastly, your baby will show less anxiety in new situations when you or your woman is with him/her.

You want to provide a constant source of support and security for your baby. Don't think that comforting your baby with love and affection will make him/her weak and helpless. You and your woman's comfort will help their growth toward self-reliance. Being a supportive and encouraging parent will help your baby develop confidence through infancy and childhood.

Infant Characteristics

Your baby may seem like a little bundle of mystery for you and your woman, but once you start caring for your baby you will become familiar with infant routines and characteristics. When your baby is new he/she will be small, wrinkled, and oddly shaped. The head may be cone shaped for the first day or two after birth.

Your baby's tummy maybe round and distended, and legs and arms may appear to be very small and thin when compared to his/her baby's head. His/her head will make up almost 1/4 of his/her total body length. At birth, your baby will be about 20-21 inches and he/she will weigh on average 7 1/2 pounds.

At the top of your baby's head is an opening that enables the bones in your baby's head to move around at birth. That soft spot at the top of your baby's head is known as a *fontanel*. By the time your baby celebrates his/her second birthday, those bones would have grown together. Babies are born with blue eyes.

After several weeks, their true color will develop. The natural pressure from birth will make your baby's eyes puffy and red. After a day or two the swelling will go down and your baby's appearance will look more natural.

When your baby is born, he/she will have varying amounts of hair on his/her body. Your baby may have soft down on his/her head, or coarse hair over their shoulders and down his/her back. The excess hair will rub off soon after birth. Both of these patterns are normal.

Infant Abilities

Your baby will begin interacting with the environment at birth. Your baby will have many basic abilities. He/she will be able to breathe, cry, swallow and suckle. Your baby will be able to spit up, cough, and eliminate waste. All five senses are fully functional.

All babies have reflexes that work to protect them. These protective reflexes will continue to function until the baby learns to move voluntarily (Your baby's voluntary movement will be learned at about 3 months old). "If you gently stroke a baby's cheek, he will turn his head in the direction of your finger and open his mouth (*Rooting Reflex*).

Also, your baby will be born with a sucking reflex. All you have to do is put something into your baby's mouth, and your baby will begin to suck. If you hold your baby upright from underneath his/her arms, let his/her feet touch a firm surface, and he/she will move his legs in a walking motion (*Walking Reflex)*.

Your baby will tighten his/her finger around anything that is pressed into the palm of his/her hand. This is called the *grasping reflex*. This particular reflex is so strong at birth that your baby can support his/her body weight with a grasp of your fingers.

The *startle reflex* is when your baby reacts to stimuli with his/her whole body. When your baby reacts to a loud noise, he/she will throw out both legs and arms. His/her fingers will stretch out as trying to catch something. As your baby's limbs slowly draw back to the body, his/her knees bend and fists will clinch. These grouped movement make-up the startle reflex.

-Keeping Your Game Tight.

A Baby's Intelligence

How do you react when you see a little baby? Are you ever surprised at how they respond to you? Babies are highly developed people. They can see, hear, and even learn while still growing inside your woman's tummy. The next time you are "checking out" a baby, pay close attention to her behavior. What things does she seem to be taking in? How in tune does she seem to be with her surroundings? When you get a chance to spend time with your baby, keep in mind that she is a complex being?

Caring for your Infant

Your baby will be totally dependent on you and your woman. He/she will depend on you for food, clothing, shelter, and love. For some parents this can be overwhelming. Be patient. As you and your baby's mother get to know your baby, the two of you will adjust to her demands.

Feeding

One of the most important things your woman will do is breastfeed your baby. Breastfeeding helps babies build immunities against allergies and many diseases. Most women choose natural feeding because it is economical and convenient. Bottle-feeding is costly, commercial formulas vary in mixture, and they requires different amounts of preparation.

Breastfeeding is also good for parent-infant bonding. It is a good way for your woman to express loving care. Your baby and your woman should breastfeed for as long as possible. When your baby enters what some might regard as the "terrible two's," the time she spends breastfeeding will make a big difference in your wife's ability to nurture, mold, and direct her.

You and your woman should discuss the proper planning for coasting your baby from breastfeeding to bottle-feeding. Once your baby becomes depended on bottle feedings, she will become more self-reliant. She will be more mobile and free to explore her world. You and your woman will see a difference in your ability to manage her movement.

<u>A Personal Touch for Children</u>

Reflexology for Children

Reflexology works easiest on children. They are attuned to nature and it is their natural instinct to embrace a natural way of healing. Reflex therapy should be taught to all children. It can be used to remedy various complaints common to children. Children can learn to use the healing forces of reflex therapy to help give relief for toothache, nervous tension, and trauma caused by accident.

All of the techniques taught in this book may be used on children. When you provide therapy to a baby, make sure that you do not apply pressure at the top of the head. The soft spot at the top of a newborn's skull is made up of four bones that have not yet grown together. The soft spot is protected by a tough membrane, which comes together when the baby is 10 to 20 months old. NEVER APPLY PRESSURE to the soft spot of a baby's head.

When reflex therapy is used on a small child, use the same pressure that you would the petals of a rose. Begin with very light pressure, and gradually increase pressure when you find a tender reflex. The child will flinch when a tender reflex is stimulated.

Reflexology may stop a crying baby in minutes. A proper reflex work of the baby's feet and hands can quickly comfort them. A very soft scratching movement on the back of a small child's hand can calm a restless baby. Research has proven that constant contact with small children helps them progress. The use of simple reflex therapy techniques are a good way to make physical contact with a child. It can make both parent and child feel a closer bond.

Reflexology Relieves Digestive Problem
1. Lay the baby on his or her back so that you can see each other's faces.
2. With an open left hand, gently press on the baby's tummy.
3. The reflex point is two inches below the navel.
4. Ask the baby where he or she hurts, and place the palm of your hand over the troubled area. (There may be a pulse of blood over the affected area.)
5. Let the warmth of your hand give a soothing and sedating effect.
6. Give the baby a complete reflex workout focusing on the endocrine glands. Remember, that if one of the endocrine glands is off, there will be disharmony in the whole body.
7. Start with the baby's thumbs and big toes. (Follow the reflexology chart for small children.)
* Note: There may be a period of cleansing as the digestive problem dissolves.

Massage for Babies and Children

Massage helps to reduce colic, constipation or diarrhea, coughs, colds, and irritability. It is a very healthy means of nonverbal communication between parent and child. Massage has been proven to be good for even the most difficult babies. Even children as old as nine years of age who suffer from convulsions have been soothed by something as simple as a stomach massage.

Giving a Massage

There are no special techniques or sequence for massaging babies. Do what comes naturally and let your strokes adapt to the baby's tiny little body. Use fingers and thumbs on areas too small for the palm of your hand, keep all movements slow and smooth, and let your hands and the child be your guide.

Use a light vegetable oil all over the baby's face and body. Almond oil and sunflower oil is easily available and suitable for babies. Do not use baby oil (mineral oil). It is not easily absorbed into the baby's skin.

Face Massage
1. Stroke the baby's forehead from the center to the sides.
2. Stroke from his nose out to the temple.
3. Glide down from the top of the face to the chin.
4. Circle around the eyes, stroking out along the eyebrows and very gently back under the eyes from nose to temple.

Abdomen Massage
1. Stroke from the hips up the front of the body,
2. Glide out to the shoulder and down the arms, stroke from the shoulder down the sides of the body.
3. Work with both hands together, then alternate using one hand stroking up, while the other hand strokes down.

4. Put both hands on either side of the abdomen with your fingers pointing towards each other.
5. Glide your hands gently back and forth across the abdomen in a crisscrossing movement, keeping each stroke light and smooth.

6. Stroke clockwise in a circle around the baby's navel with one hand following the other. As your arms cross, gently lift one hand over the other. (This technique relieves colic and stomach aches.)

Note: Babies should not be too tired or hungry when you use massage to comfort them. The best time is after a bath. The baby can lie on your lap or on a towel on the table or floor. Make sure that the room is at a comfortable temperature and free from drafts.

Arms and Legs
1. Hold out one of the baby's arms and stroke it from shoulder to hand, always massaging away from the heart.
2. Then, squeeze the baby's arms, shoulders, and hands all over.
3. Stroke the back of your baby's hand, and massage the wrist.

4. Stroke the palm of the baby's hand, gently uncurl the fingers, and then gently squeeze and rotate each finger.
5. Repeat the exercise with the baby's other arm, wrist, and hand.
6. Lift up one leg and stroke it from the hip to the foot, massaging away from the heart.
7. Squeeze and stroke the leg all over.
8. Take the baby's foot and rotate the baby's ankle.
9. Stroke the top of the foot and then squeeze and rotate each toe.

Note: Babies are fascinated with their bodies. They will closely watch you gently squeeze and manipulate their hands and feet.

Back Massage
1. Lay the baby on her stomach and stroke her whole back.
2. Start at the feet and work your way up the leg, across her bottom and up her back.
3. Glide your hands off the top of her back, across the shoulders and down her sides.
4. Run your thumbs up her back on either side of her spine,
5. Slide your hands in a crisscrossing motion back and forth across her back.
6. Stroke round each buttock and knead it gently.
7. In a rhythmic manner softly pat and pinch your baby's bottom, using your hands alternately.
8. Finish the back massage with a cat stroke. Gently slide each hand from neck to toe alternating one hand after the other. Repeat this stroke several times.

Note: Babies enjoy having their bottoms gently pinched and patted. Their little bodies are plump and their skin is satiny smooth, they are lovely to touch.

Massage for Children

Massaging children is like massaging babies. Children of all ages enjoy massage. Children tend to get restless so make their massage session short. Keep all sessions spontaneous and enjoyable. Do not massage the abdomen after a big meal. Children do not need to undress. They can be massaged through light clothing.

Face Massage
1. Stroke the child's forehead from the center to the sides.
2. Stroke from his nose out to the temple.
3. Glide down from the top of the face to the chin.
4. Circle around the eyes, stroking out along the eyebrows and very gently back under the eyes from nose to temple.

Note: When stroking the face, use the tips of your index and middle finger to massage the temple and the hinges of the jaw. Slide your finger tips in small circular movements, using gentle pressure.

Abdomen Massage

1. Stroke from the hips up the front of the body.
2. Glide out to the shoulder and down the arms, stroke from the shoulder down the sides of the body.
3. Work with both hands together, then alternate using one hand stroking up, while the other hand strokes down.
4. Put both hands on either side of the abdomen with your fingers pointing towards each other.
5. Glide your hands gently back and forth across the abdomen in a crisscrossing movement, keeping each stroke light and smooth.
6. Stroke clockwise in a circle around the child's navel with one hand following the other. As your arms cross, gently lift one hand over the other.

Note: Children should not be too tired or hungry when you use massage to comfort them. The best time is after a bath. The child can lie on a towel on the table or floor. Make sure that the room is at a comfortable temperature and free from drafts.

Children Giving a Massage

At the age of three children learn to make themselves useful in caring for others. They have a genuine interest in helping their mothers and fathers, and they get great pleasure from making others happy. At the age of five, young children can learn to give a very good massage. They enjoy the percussion sounds that come from chopping someone's back, the kneading because it is like playing with clay, and the stroking because it is so easy to do. Above all children like it because it is fun.

When your child is active and full of energy, let her straddle your back and massage your shoulders and thighs. Let her massage your face and forehead while they tell you about their day. Pummeling your back is fun for a child. The gentle karate chops help release tension in the back and shoulders.

One of the best massage techniques for small children is "A child walking". This is a massage that requires your child to stand on your back and slowly walk from the top of your buttocks to the area at the base of your neck and shoulders. This is a safe technique, because their little bodies are light. (Caution: Limit the direct pressure applied to the spine.)

Note: Children are fascinated with learning new things. They will closely watch you and learn from you how to properly give a massage. Children getting attention from adults and will love the time you spend with them.

Back Massage for Children

Stroking
1. Start with your hands on the lower back, your thumbs on either side of the spine and your fingers pointing towards the head. With relaxed hands, you should stroke firmly up the back. You should lean onto your hands, using the weight of your body to apply pressure.
2. Pull back down on the muscle at the base of the neck. Then, stroke out across the

shoulders and the top of the arms. Allow your hands to mold to the curves of her shoulders, arms, and back. Sweep your hands round the top of the arms and then down the sides of her body.

3. Stroke your hands lightly down the sides of the body, keeping them relaxed and taking care not to drag the skin. At the waist, pull upward and inward. This gives the lovely feeling of having a tiny waist. Repeat ten times.

Daily Infant Care Schedule

The schedule you and your woman set for the first six weeks of your baby's life includes feeding, sleeping, bathing, and playing. Every baby is different, so there is no such thing as an ideal schedule. Most mothers are encouraged to build their schedules around the baby's feedings and sleep time. Whatever you and your woman decide, you should stay flexible. In the first few months, your baby girl will eat and sleep at all hours.

Your Baby Communicates Through Crying

It is natural for a baby to cry. Babies cry when they are hungry or thirsty, too hot or too cold, tired or over-stimulated. Sometimes at the end of the day your baby will cry just to let off steam. When your baby cries for you and your woman, it is important for you to treat it as if your baby is talking to you. Your response to your baby's cry is like answering someone when they call your name. It reassures your baby that you are paying attention to her.

Ignoring your baby girl may cause both short-term and long-term distress. Occasionally, your baby may swallow air while crying. This will cause great discomfort and make her feeding difficult. When your baby cries for a prolonged period, she will suffer exhaustion. This will make it difficult to soothe her.

Over time, if your daughter's cries go unanswered she may learn that her needs are not important and make it difficult for your baby to form deep loving relationships. All babies have their own "crying language." As parents you and your woman will quickly learn to understand your baby's crying language.

Parent Adjustments to Infant-Care

In the first three months, you and your woman will rapidly learn to interpret their baby's needs. These are very difficult months for many new parents. The day you bring your baby home from the hospital will be a happy occasion. It will also be a very exhausting. Do not make the mistake of thinking that it will be a time of rest for you or your woman.

Your newborn baby will rarely sleep through the night. She will have to be cared for no matter where you and your woman is your lives or relationship. In order to make things easier for yourselves, you and your woman will have to adjust your schedules so that you can sleep when the baby sleeps. You two want to share the responsibilities for the care of your newborn. It would also be good if you and your woman can get someone to help out the first few weeks.

The first stages of parenthood can involve a lot of stress. The intensity and number of changes you and your woman will experience when bringing home a new baby is regarded as a crisis. Your woman is going to spend most of her time caring for the baby. When she is not focusing her attention on the baby, she will need to eat and sleep properly, especially if she is breastfeeding.

You may feel as if your woman is neglecting you, but that is not the case. Work with your woman, and help her care for your baby. This will enable you to share the experience and play an even bigger role in your baby's life. This will promote good feelings between you and your woman.

Historically, in many cultures men did not play a major role in the early years of their children's lives. In other cultures, fathers are very active and are as emotionally involved as the mother. Today, fathers are often present at the birth, share in the delivery, and develop attachment to the baby at birth.

Your active participation in your baby's life will help you build a very strong and satisfying parent-child relationship. There are studies that show that eight-month-old infants in play situations sought out fathers more often than mothers. There is no substitute for the nurturing father.

When you and your woman are sharing your parenting duties, you should plan for some alone time away from your baby. The most important part of shared parenting is the mutual support each of you will have. Working together, you and your woman can give more consistent and effective "up bringing". When you and your woman are able to discuss difficulties with your baby, problems can seem a lot less drastic.

First Year of Development

Children grow in predictable patterns. Understanding your baby's developmental patterns means knowing what to expect when your baby reaches certain ages and stages of growth. Remember, there are wide ranges of ages at which children "normally" do different things. Your baby's rate of growth depends on proper food, water, rest and exercise. All of these things are a vital part of your baby's physical development.

In the first year your baby will grow very fast, and in that same time she will probably triple her birth weight. In the first two years your baby's brain and central nervous system will develop and as a result, other abilities develop. Because of the rapid growth, you and your woman will have to pay very close attention to the baby's nutrition and health.

In addition to changes in size and brain development, your baby will learn the coordination needed to perform different skills. In the first six months your baby girl will learn to lift her head, roll over, and even sit-up. At one year, she will be able to move around on her own. She will go from crawling around on her hands and knees to walking along holding on to furniture. She may even be able to walk by herself. All babies develop at different rates.

When your baby is born, all of her sensory abilities should be working. She will hear, taste, smell, see, and feel. These five senses are how she will learn to explore the world. Babies see at birth. They enjoy looking at human faces. They have a natural fascination with the contrasting colors and shapes of an adult face. Babies even enjoy seeing pictures of human faces. They also enjoy looking at checkerboard designs of black and white.

When your daughter is less than two months, she will have a fixed focus on anything within eight inches of her eyes. Between three and seven weeks of age most babies look into the eyes of people holding them. As they get a few months older, babies enjoy looking at brightly colored or moving objects. Because your baby will spend a lot of time in her crib staring up at the ceiling, it would be in her best interest to have stimulating things to observe. Moving her to different locations in the house, or positioning her so that she can see out of the door or window would be very good for her.

The day your baby is born she will know the satisfying feeling that results from sucking. Your baby girl will use her mouth and ability to taste to explore the world. For more than a year your baby will put everything she can grasp into her mouth. Therefore, everything in her reach should have rounded edges, be too big to swallow, and washable. Make sure you and your woman check all toys for removable parts, and keep all small or sharp objects out of her reach.

Motor Development

1st Month	Chin ups.
2nd Months	Chest ups.
3rd Months	Ability to reach and miss objects.
4th Months	Sit with support.
5th Months	Sit on lap and grasp objects.
6th Months	Sit in a high chair and grasp dangling objects w/palms.
7th Months	Sit alone.
8th Months	Stand with help.
9th Months	Stand holding furniture.
10th Months	Ability to creep.
11th Months	Walk when led.
12th Months	Pull up on furniture to stand.
13th Months	Ability to climb stair steps.
14th Months	Stand alone.
15th Months	Walk alone.

Safety Tips for Keeping Your Baby Safe from Common Household Accidents
• Never leave your baby on a high surface such as a table or bed. Make sure the rails on the beds are secure and the sides of the crib are up so your baby cannot roll out.
• Keep your floors free of clutter and your house well lit to remove the danger of tripping when carrying your baby.
• Close off areas of your house that might be a danger for your toddling or crawling baby. (Use safety gates or close and lock doors.)
• Never leave a baby alone in the bathtub. Be mindful of hot water, slippery surfaces and water deep enough to drown in.

When your baby is born, she will feel the prick of a needle, but her sense of texture and temperature will not come until she grows older. Your baby's sense of touch plays a big role in developing feelings of security. Picking up your baby girl comforts her, but holding her up to your shoulder will make her content and alert. Do not give into the nonsense about "spoiling a baby" by picking her up when she cries. People who specialize in the early stages of life have found that picking up your daughter when she cries is actually good for her.

When it comes to your daughter's hearing, she will respond to high-pitched sounds better than any other. Sounds can soothe your baby. The sounds of soft music can help her relax and sleep. In her first months, your baby will find pleasure in the sounds of her voice. As she gets a little older, she will enjoy playing sound game with others. If you hear your baby babble and you mimic the things she says, then she will most likely repeat the same sounds.

Sound will play a huge role in your daughter's learning. Everything from the sound of approaching footsteps to the sounds of familiar voices, are an important part of her growth. Sound will keep your daughter alert and help pave the road for speech development.

It is good for your baby to hear your voice as often as possible. When you are cleaning or feeding her, talk about whatever comes to mind. It does not really matter what you talk about, as long as your tone and your facial expressions are comforting.

Your daughter's sense of smell plays an important role in your baby's sense of judgment. A strong or unpleasant odor will cause your daughter to turn her head away and change her breathing patterns. It will also help her identify people and things that are familiar to her.

Second Year of Development

In your daughter's second year, she will learn to tell you what she wants and express herself more clearly. As you and your woman work with her to explore her world, she will learn to use language skills better. At about twelve months your baby girl will be toddling and her growth rate will slow down.

She will have less of an appetite, so you want to keep her away from junk foods. If you can, serve her small portions of healthier foods throughout the day. Trying to make her stick to three square meals at specific times of day will not always be good for her.

In her second year, she will become better coordinated. She will learn to walk more smoothly, and climbing will become a new skill. Your baby girl will learn to use two hands for pushing, pulling, and carrying things around the house.

You will also find that she enjoys doing activities that require the use of her whole body. Your daughter's motor abilities will improve very fast, so her enthusiasm for exploring new things can be dangerous. Do what you can to encourage your baby's growth, but be mindful of potential hazards.

Safety Tip for Preventing Burns:
• Never leave a young child alone in the house.
• Be mindful of flammable material like bed sheets, blankets, and her clothing.
• Keep matches and lighters away from your baby.
• Turn pot and pan handles toward the back of the stove while cooking.
• Keep hot foods and liquids out of your child's reach.
• Keep hot electrical appliances like, curling iron, clothing irons, and hot coffee pots out of your baby's reach.
• Keep your baby out of the kitchen during food preparation.

In your daughter's second year, she will be a big bundle of energy that is constantly exploring her surroundings. She will always be on the go. Your baby will be full of curiosity. As she explores she will find great pleasure in taking things apart, pushing things over, and moving things around. This will be a major source of entertainment for your new baby.

Some people look at their baby's actions as mischievous, but your baby's exploratory activities are a necessary part of her growth. You and your woman want to do what you can to create safe opportunities for your baby to explore. Things that are potential hazards like chemicals, drugs, sharp and pointed objects should be put out of reach. On the other hand, cabinets with pots, pans, books, and canned goods are a great source for investigation. Give your baby girl the freedom in which to explore and learn.

There will be times when your baby will attempt things that exceed their ability. If your baby scatters things in the floor or has sudden outbursts, it is likely an indication of frustration. Find activities that your baby can do successfully. This is important for her self-confidence.

Your baby will learn a lot through sensory experiences. She will enjoy playing with material she can taste, feel, and take apart. When you give your baby something to explore, remember that your baby will enjoy action toys and objects that move or make sounds because of your baby girl's actions. Toys and objects that require detail finger movement and are two mechanical can be frustrating for her.

In her second year, your daughter's interest in other children is simply a curiosity. She is not mature enough to socially interact. Her ability to play and share with other children will not come until later. As a toddler, your baby has to learn how to connect emotionally with other children. Babies are naturally possessive, and learn early to assert their will with others.

Preschool Development

Between the ages of three and five, your baby will go through rapid changes. If you think you have your baby all figured out, watch yourself. You and your woman are in for a surprise. The preschool years will bring about new and unexpected patterns of behavior. During the preschool years, physical growth is at slow rate. Your baby girl will appear taller, but thinner than before.

Almost all of your daughter's understanding of the present will come from her past experience. She will try to interpret new events by relating to what she has already come to know. As your daughter's experiences increase in variety and quantity, her interpretations will likely become more accurate.

When your baby is in preschool she will learn to understand her world through language. Her vocabulary will quickly increase and she will learn to communicate more effectively through speech. She will learn to use her voice to express feelings and desire. Although she will still express herself physically, words will gradually become her tool for asserting herself.

Your child will often misunderstand familiar words when they are used in a different situation. For your baby girl, meaning will depend upon the ideas or images the word brings to mind. You are taking the time to explain the new meaning to your baby when words occur will go a long way towards helping her develop new ideas, understanding, and language skills.

Your child will always take words literally. If she heard you refer to someone as a "fat head," she would be surprised to see that the person in question has a normal sized head. She will not see the differences between relationship words. In her mind, when it comes to other children, most women are "mommies." She will not understand that the same person can play many roles, like a wife, mother, grandmother, sister, or aunt.

At preschool age, your daughter will ask all kinds of questions. She will quickly become a little "chatter box" answering your every statement with a "Why Daddy?" Answer her questions with honesty in words and definitions. This will help her better learn about her world.

One of the best responses to your baby girl's questions would be to open a book and introduce her to the wonderful world of books. When she asks you a question, try and answer with another question. "What do you think?" "What would you do in that situation?" or "How do you feel about that?" These types of questions will help your daughter think for herself. They also help her develop problem-solving skills. You and your woman will learn to assess her ability to think, plan, and make decisions.

When your baby girl begins to identify with objects of different sizes or shade, she may have trouble telling them apart. She will need an opportunity to work with similar things that differ in color, texture, and so forth. The time you spend working with your baby girl will help her learn to understand relationships among different objects.

During these years your baby girl will learn to better appreciate children her age. With you and your woman's guidance, she will learn to work and play well with children her own age, as well as with other people. Through peer interaction, your baby girl will learn to recognize the rights and needs of others. This development will not happen fast.

Children are "Me" oriented, and they need time to learn the viewpoint of others. With your guidance, she will learn to show consideration for other when she understands how her words and actions make people feel. Only through experience will your daughter learn to share.

The experience will teach her that sharing something does not mean losing it. She will learn that through sharing, other people will learn to accept and appreciate her. Over time and through experience, your baby girl will learn to delay her own immediate wants and consider others.

As an infant or toddler, your baby girl will not control her emotions. She will show very little consideration for other people's feelings. You and your woman can teach her socially acceptable ways to express her feelings. If you learn to recognize her emotions, you can show her a better way of dealing with her impulses. First, you want to acknowledge that you are aware of her feelings, and then instruct her in the way she should behave.

Do not encourage your daughter to deny her feelings by saying things like, "Big girls don't cry!" "Don't be scared!" or "Awe girl, you ain't that mad!" These sayings will not help her learn to deal with her emotions. They will instead make her feel as if anger, fear, and sadness are unnatural feelings that she should not have. This will make her feel guilty or rejected.

All children need a chance to reflect on their feelings, emotions, and behavior. That is how they learn that all feelings, both positive and negative, are natural and manageable. The time you spend nurturing and working with your child during this period of rapid growth will help you better understand her.

Chapter 5

The Life Cycle: The Woman Child (3 years- 9 years)

Meeting your Child's Needs

When you make your baby, you are taking responsibility for the future generations. The responsibility of being a parent begins the day become aware of your ability to procreate. Parenting is a life long commitment that if properly prepared for produces little anxiety, but great satisfaction.

The basic needs of all human beings are food, clothing, warmth, and rest. Your baby girl will respond to all of these needs by crying. Although many parents learn to identify with their children's needs through trail and error, there are many ways to recognize your baby's needs. As your daughter gets older, she will continue to react to her needs for food and rest.

When you observe your baby's behavior, you will notice a change in her manner when she is tired or uncomfortable. To best meet your baby's needs, you may try and schedule both her meals and rest on a timetable, and dress them comfortably. This is one of the ways that your baby girl learns to trust your ability to care for her.

When addressing your baby's emotional need for security comes with your ability to properly provide for her physical needs. Your daughter will feel safe when she knows she is in the company of people who are there to love and care for her. If your baby comes in contact with a stranger or she is left alone, she may feel abandoned and cry out of anger or fear.

To help your baby maintain a sense of security:
• Set a daily routine.
• Communicate with your baby so that change doesn't catch them by surprise.
• Whenever possible make changes slowly
• Be consistent. "Say what you mean, and mean what you say!"
• Always try and be there when your baby needs you.

Your baby needs to know that she is accepted, and that her behavior does not affect the love you have for her. When you compare your daughter's behavior to others or tell her to act like someone else, you are telling your child that she is not good enough. Be careful about your use of the word "bad" when describing your daughter's behavior. The use of such terms will make your baby feelings of rejection and shame. Make sure your daughter understands that you approve of her, but you do not approve of her behavior.

As a parent, you should always show appreciation for your daughter's efforts. When she tries to help you or your woman, you should thank her for her best efforts, even if she does not do as well as you thought she would. Your praises, hugs, and kisses show your baby girl that you enjoy her for who she is and not who she may become.

As a toddler, your baby will be able to move around on her own. She will try very hard to accomplish many things and often want to do things for herself. If you encourage her efforts, she will develop self-confidence. She will develop a sense of worth and capability. As she reaches new goals, and gain new skills, she will foster self-reliance.

When you and your woman give your daughter opportunities for different kinds of learning experiences, you support your baby's initiative, or self-starting ability. If you and your woman invest a little time and money in arts and crafts, your baby can experiment and use her creativity. This will help her further develop self-confidence.

Your daughter's sense of self-esteem is rooted in her personal sense of adequacy and self-respect. Making fun of a child or laughing at her can destroy her self-esteem, so take any abuse your daughter suffers seriously. Even the abuse of other children can have a long-term impact on your daughter's self-esteem. You would be surprised at the number of eating disorders and nose jobs inspired by the destructive behavior of unruly children.

Understanding your Child's Behavior

Your daughter's behavior can be linked to her inborn characteristics, a particular experience, and the emotions she may be expressing. Understanding you baby's behavior depends largely on her motives. The more you understand your baby's personality, the better you will understand her behavior.

Your daughter's behavior can be influenced by your child-raising practices, but her individual personality will have a core impact on her behavior. Consider these basic characteristics:

1. Activity. Your daughter may be passive or aggressive in her action. Some children show great initiative and are always moving, squirming and wiggling around. They are anxious to explore their world and often need close supervision. Children who are more passive may seem comfortable just sitting quietly, showing less initiative. Remember, no one type of child is better than the other.

2. Regularity. Your baby may adjust to a regular eating and sleeping schedule shortly after birth. She may be born of a predictable nature, which would make it easy for you and your woman to arrange your daily routine around her. Or, she could be the kind of child that can never seem to get onto a schedule. As a parent, it may be difficult to predict how long your baby will sleep, or how much she will eat.

3. Adaptability. When it comes to adaptability, your baby girl may accept change and new experiences with enthusiasm. Or, she may shy away from new things, and resist strangers. She may find new situations upsetting.

4. Sensitivity. Your child's level of sensitivity to the environment may vary. One child may sleep heavily and rarely be disturbed by anything going on around them. Another child may find it difficult to sleep. The slightest sound may wake her up. Your child's level of sensitivity will also affect her response to changes in taste, temperature, and pain.

5. Mood. Some babies are generally happy and joyful. Other babies may seem irritable

and cry a lot. These inborn traits are likely to affect your feelings and behavior.

6. Ability to Concentrate. When some children try and focus on an activity, they are easily distracted by the goings on around them. Other children can be involved in a particular activity and refocus their attention. These children may be so in tuned with their activity that nothing else distracts them.

7. Persistence. The amount of time a child devotes to an activity that is difficult for her may vary. Some children will keep working no matter what. Other children are less persistent, and would give up easily.

Your Child's Life Experiences and Behavior

Your daughter's behavior is products of both her personality and experience. As she gets older and faces new challenges, she will alter her behavior patterns. Your daughter will learn from watching and imitating others.

Through observing you and your woman, she will not only learn proper behavior, but she will also learn who should play certain roles. When your daughter's behavior gets a positive reaction, she is likely to repeat it. If she does something that brings about a negative response, she is not likely to repeat that behavior.

Relating to Others

Your daughter will behave differently with different people. She will learn that what works with some people will not necessarily work with others. Your daughter will want and need your attention. Her need for your attention will be so great that she will rather have negative attention than no attention at all. Do not be surprised if you find your daughter acting out when you have company over, or if you are on the telephone.

Young children often feel as if they are not important when someone other than them has your attention. Your daughter needs to know that her place in your life is still secure when she is around others. A new baby in your home will be particularly challenging for your daughter. She will often feel that the new baby is taking away attention that is supposed to belong to her.

Physical and Emotional States

Your daughter's emotions will influence her behavior. If your daughter has a birthday party, too many guests, too many gifts and noise can become a major irritation. If your daughter is ever feeling overexcited, removing her from the crowd and giving her a little quiet time alone with a caring adult will comfort her. When there is too little to do, the party will not keep her attention and your daughter can become bored. It helps if you keep a few things with you that she can play with, like a toy or some clay.

Safety Tips

These are cautions you should take when choosing toys for your baby girl:
• Toys with small parts that could be swallowed.
• Objects with small removable parts.
• Stuffed toys with glass or button eyes.
• Toys with sharp edges.
• Any rubber or plastic ball small enough to fit in your baby's mouth.
(Adapted from "Our Children's World" by the National Safety Council)

Guidance and Discipline

Your daughter will learn more about behavior from observing you, than she would anyone else. When you least expect it, your daughter will be watching and absorbing your attitude, interests, and prejudice. Your daughter will learn certain behaviors that she will not use until later. She will more likely learn from people she trusts, than to imitate the behavior of someone that makes her uncomfortable. Responses like aggression are more likely than others to be learned quickly.

Your actions speak louder than words. If you are easily frustrated, then your baby girl would pickup on that kind of behavior. You cannot teach her to be patient and understanding if you are not a patient and understanding person. Attempting to teach your daughter not to do things that she sees you do all the time, does not work.

As a parent you can teach responsible safety habit through modeling. When your daughter watches you behave in a potentially dangerous situation, she learns reasonable safety precautions. But hold on to your potatoes! Because the same model learning that teaches your daughter certain cautions can also lead her astray. If your baby girl watches you overreact to a spider, superstitions, or other "dangers," she can pick up your fears.

"Practice saying what you mean, and meaning what you say," is the key to teaching responsible behavior. You and your woman must try to be the kind of people you want your baby girl to grow up to be. In this way, your baby will most likely learn to behave the way you want her to.

Practical Tips for Effective Baby-Sitting
• Be familiar with parent rules and guidelines.
• Know important telephone numbers. (Police, Fire Department, Poison Control Center)
• The nearest neighbor telephone and address.
• Have specific hours scheduled for baby-sitting.
• Tour the house and know the location of everything you need.
• Be familiar with emergency procedures and escape routes.
• Learn all special instructions regarding the child's allergies, and medication.
• Lock all doors and window. Never admit strangers.
• After dark make sure you have someone to accompany you to and from home.
• Do not have long telephone conversations.
• Watch children closely and always keep children within earshot.
*Do not allow children under 4 to eat anything that might choke them, such as gumballs or hard candy. Do not let them put objects into their mouth.

When it comes to creating rules for your baby, remember that discipline is more than punishing inappropriate behavior. Discipline is about building a teacher-student relationship, and providing guidance to someone who wants to follow you. Your baby will want and need discipline. Rules and regulations set standards for your daughter's behavior. The best discipline is that which shapes your daughter's life and promotes self-control and self-discipline.

Rules are necessary for effective guidance. Rules must be clear. Make sure your daughter understands what is expected of her. Teach her what is proper. Do not make the mistake of thinking that pointing out her wrongs is the same as telling her what is right. Rules should be fair and age appropriate. Always consider your daughter's level of development and make only realistic demands.

Rules should be necessary. Many people make so many rules that even they cannot keep up with them all. Rules should protect your baby and others. They should protect the rights and property of others. There should always be a good reason for your rules, whether you share those reasons with your child, or not.

Some times it is best to respond to your daughter's "Why?" with a "Because I said so-that's why!" It is important that your daughter understand the reasons for your rules, but it is equally important that she respect the commanding authority that comes with your being her parent. In the event of an emergency, time may not always permit you to explain in detail the reasons for your instruction. Your daughter must learn to instinctively obey your commands.

Caution: If you respond with a "Because I said so!" your baby may at times feel powerless and grow frustrated and resentful. The more your baby learns to trust you the more comfortable she will be when asked to blindly obey your instructions. There are exercises designed to improve trust in relationships. Your daughter will better accept the rules if the reasons for them are clear, but she will only follow those rules when there is trust.

Consistency is essential to discipline. Consistency in enforcing rules under different circumstances will give your daughter a sense of security. Sometimes, you may have to bend the rules a little, but be careful. Do not let your flexibility be confused with inconsistency. If a situation came up that required you to make exceptions to a rule, make sure it is understood that the unusual circumstances make it necessary.

Experiencing the consequences of her actions is how your daughter will learn. Consequences should be reasonable and directly related to the situation. They should also relate to present and future behavior. Always make decisions regarding consequences when you and your woman are calm. Remember, your efforts are to correct her undesirable behavior and teach her a better self-control.

Parenting Styles

Your parenting style refers to the actions and attitudes you show in your behavior toward your daughter. The attitudes and manners you bring to parenting your daughter come from your parents and the models of your childhood. One of the most important things to remember about parenting styles is the affect it will have on the emotional health and behavior of your baby girl.

W. C. Becker was a researcher who considered parental attitudes to fall along three intersecting lines. The first line is warmth and hostility. Warmth is the nurturing, supportive parental behavior. Hostility is the cold or angry attitudes and actions toward children.

The second line permissiveness and restrictive ness. Permissive parents make few demands on their children. Restrictive parents are very rigid and controlling. They place great demands and limitations on their children.

The third and final line is anxiety and detachment. An anxious parent will be overly concerned with the small details of their child's life. The detached parent shows little emotional involvement in their children's lives.

Research has shown that when parents combine warmth with permissiveness, children are more cooperative with others. They are assertive, and friendly. One study showed that warm and restrictive parents are likely to be self-controlled, satisfied with who they were. Parents who are hostile and restrictive, produce children who were anxious and had feelings of guilt. The rejected by the parents lead to feelings of self-rejection.

The children that were raised by parents that were hostile and permissive grew to be less obedient and were more likely to show aggression toward others. If you are overprotective and treat your baby with warmth, she will likely demand her own way and be prone to throw tantrums. At the same time, if she is strictly controlled and overprotected she will grow shy and submissive.

As parents, you and your woman will face situations that produce anxiety, tension, and stress. Your ability to properly guide your daughter begins with your love for yourself. If you do not like yourself and properly know how to care for yourself, you will not be able to care for others. Understanding the way you and your woman were raised will go along way towards your understanding your ability to create the right type of environment for your daughter. You will have a difficult time being a nurturer, if you were never nurtured as a child.

Parenting Tasks			
Parenting Roles	Parents (%)	Mother (%)	Father (%)
Discipline the children.	83	7	9
Go to open school week.	76	22	1
Help the children with homework.	72	20	5
Speak to teachers if children are in trouble.	71	20	8
Decide on children's allowances.	67	9	20
Teach the children sports.	57	4	36
Take children for checkups.	35	63	1
Clean the house.	33	65	1
Shopping for children's clothes	32	66	1
Stay home when children are sick.	26	72	1
Prepare the meals.	22	77	1

[Source: The General Mills American Family Report: Raising Children in a Changing Society. (Minneapolis, Minn.: General Mills, Inc.)]

The Needs of Parents

Many parents measure their love and commitment to their loved ones by the degree of sacrifices they make to properly provide. This has left many men and women to feel the need to be family martyrs. Caring for your baby and meeting her needs does not mean that your needs must be ignored. Parents need satisfaction, and parent care is an essential part of good parenting.

Do not think that your daughter's achievements or limitations are a reflection on your ability as parents. You are responsible for your own well-being, and any feelings of adequacy. Caring for your baby is a developmental process. As your baby girl grows, so will your parenting responsibilities.

Take advantage of opportunities to sit with other parents and share parenting experiences. Sharing with other parents can be a good chance to learn more about child-care. This can be a great comfort to you and your woman.

Raising your baby will be one of the most rewarding things you will ever do, but it will also be one of the most demanding experiences you or your woman will ever know. As parents, "you will need someone at your back." Close friends and family members who care for you and are willing to listen without judgment, can help you put you and your baby's needs into perspective. Your family and friends can support you with child-care assistant and moral support. It is important for you and your woman to choose the proper role that the people in your life will play in raising your baby girl.

Recommended Age	Diptheria/ Pertussis/ Tetanus	Polio	Measles Mumps Rubella	Hemophilus Influenza Type B (Hib)
Childhood Immunization Schedule				
2 months	*	*		
4 months	*	*		
6 months	*	* (optional)		
15 months	*		*	
18 months	*	*		
2 years				*
4-6 years	*	*		
14-16 years	*			

(Source: Healthy People, The Surgeon General's Report on Health Promotions and Disease Prevention, US Department of Health, Education and Welfare, 1979.)

The Working Parent

By 1990, 50 percent of all preschool-age children will have working mothers, and 60 percent of all school-age children will have a working mother. Today, 75 percent of the women working share the financial burden of providing for their families. Other women are career oriented and choose to work.

You and your woman will likely find yourselves juggling many of the home and work responsibilities. One of the biggest challenges the two of you will face is finding adequate child-care. Finding the right day care and evaluating cost and safety will be an important concern. There are community-based organizations that provide resources and referrals for quality child-care. You will find several kinds of child-care settings.

Make the right day care arrangement for you and your baby:
- Is the caregiver warm and attentive?
- How do they use discipline?
- When is discipline used?
- Do they provide interesting activities?
- What is her background and training?
- Is there First-Aid and basic life support equipment available?
- Is the environment clean and well kept?
- Is there a plan for sick or troubled children?
- What type of security does she provide?

Chapter 6

The Life Cycle: The Pubescent Woman (10 years-14 years)

There are two periods in a young woman's life when she will experience a rapid growth. In her first year she will triple her weight and grow 50 % in height! It will be the fastest growth period she will know. The second period of rapid growth will be just before adolescence. This particular change in development will be a sign of puberty.

A New Woman's Time for Growth and Change

Puberty to Young Adulthood

Between 10 and 14 years of age, children go through puberty. Puberty is the early stage of adolescence and is the period of time when males and females become able to reproduce (secondary sex characteristic). Girls on average undergo puberty earlier than boys. Girls begin puberty somewhere between 10 and 12 years of age. Boys begin at 12 to 14 years of age. The entire process takes three to four years to complete.

Physical Change

Your Daughter's feet and hands will grow first during puberty. This can cause clumsiness until the arms, legs, and muscles grow to fill out her framework. Before puberty there are little difference in the size and shape of males and females.

It is important that your son understand that there will be a lot of physical changes and her growth will not be like every other young woman her age. Puberty is a result of hormones and chemical substances released into the body. The male hormone is testosterone, and the female hormones are estrogen and progesterone.

Acne

Acne is a common problem for 4 out of 5 adolescents. It can last for 1 to 2 years, or for 10 years or more. Acne is not a result of eating chocolate or greasy foods. Acne is usually caused by the male sex hormone called androgens, and it is present in both males and females.

Acne Tips
• Avoid oil-based makeup and greasy lotions.
• Keep your hair and face clean.
• Change washcloths every day.
• Do not squeeze or scratch acne.
• Avoid sunlamps.
• If her acne is severe, she should consult a dermatologist.

Summary of the Physical Changes of Puberty

Female
• Growth spurt occurs.
• Hairline remains the same.
• Acne may appear.
• All permanent teeth are in.
• Axillary (underarm) hair appears.
• Perspiration increase.
• Breast develop
• Waistline narrows.
• Hips widen.
• Uterus and ovaries enlarge.
• Public hair appears.
• External genitals enlarge.
• Ovulation occurs.
• Menstruation begins.
• Long bone growth stops.

Male
• Growth spurt occurs.
• Hairline recession begins.
• Acne may appear.
• All permanent teeth are in.
• Larynx enlarges; voice deepens.
• Facial hair appears.
• Shoulders broaden.
• Axillary (underarm) hair appears.
• Perspiration increase.
• Some breast enlargement may occur.
• Changes in muscle develop.
• Pubic hair appears.
• External genitals enlarge.
• Sperm production begins.
• First ejaculation occurs.
• Long bone growth stops.

Mental Changes

During adolescence your son's brain will grow to its full size and weight. His capacity to think and reason will increase. At this stage, your son will better understand cause and effect. He will begin to see different ways of solving problems and making decisions (complex logic and reason).

Your daughter's memory skills improve and memory span increases. This will enable her to retain more information. Make your daughter's thinking more flexible. Introduce her to new ways of thinking, reasoning, and making decision, so that she can gain experience that will help her in life choices.

As he begins to mature, she will discover new interests, career goals, and hobbies. All of your son's changes will not happen overnight. Change will take a bit of time. Teach your baby boy the importance of exploring new things and practicing new thinking and learning skills.

Emotional Changes

Your daughter will experience spurts of strong emotional feelings. There will be times when your daughter will feel as if she is on an emotional roller coaster with feelings going up and down at a moments notice. Close relationships and family support are important, even if she is unable to communicate to others what she is feeling and thinking. Make sure your baby girl understands that the confusion she will sometimes feels is normal. The same hormones that cause changes in her physical and mental development will stimulate emotional changes as well.

Social Change

During puberty and the rest of adolescence, your daughter will experience a great deal of social change. Aside from feeling things more deeply and focusing on the importance of peer acceptance, your daughter will complete a set of developmental tasks.

Check This Out.
*** Cultural Rites of Passage.**

"Age does not depend upon years, but upon temperament and health. Some men are born old, and some never grow so."

Tyron Edwards.

In many societies, there are cultures that publicly recognize a person's change in social status. One such change is the advancement from adolescence to adulthood. In Africa, there is an ethnic group known as the Mbuti. The Mbuti people have a special rite of passage for new adults. For the first time in their lives, mature boys and girls are separated by their society. These girls are joined by friends and live in a special elima house.

During a festival given by the village, these girls sing to the boys who sit just outside of the elima house. The boys respond to the girl's song with a song of their own, and the ritual is a type flirtation where future marriage partners may be chosen. How do you and your family plan on recognizing your daughter's transition to adult status?

Developmental Tasks

A sociologist named Robert Havighurst asserts that there are 9 developmental tasks that an adolescent must master in order to grow into a healthy, mature adult.
- Forming more mature relationships with people her age of both sexes.
- Achieving a masculine or feminine social role.

- Accepting one's physique and using one's body effectively
- Achieving emotional independence from parents and other adults
- Preparing for marriage and family life.
- Preparing for a career
- Acquiring a set of personal standards as a guide to behavior
- Developing social intelligence, which includes becoming aware of human needs and becoming motivated to help others attain their goals
- Developing conceptual and problems-solving skills

(It is believed that each one of these tasks must be achieved before reaching maturity.)

Personal Identity

There are supposed to be factors that make everyone unique. Establishing your own personal identity is an important part of all other developmental tasks and is centered on your self-concept. These are questions your daughter should ask herself when forming her own personal identity.

- Is she carrying out her responsibilities on her own, without someone having to remind her?
- Is she getting her school work/church work/cultural work/social work done on time?
- Is she making decisions without the influence of her peers?
- What does she want to do after high school?
- Is she thinking about what she wants to do after she finishes her education?
- Has she examined her beliefs about the proper behavior for males and females?
- Is she aware of the image she projects as a female?
- Does her behavior reflect a personal set of values and standards by which she lives?
- Does she know what other people like and dislike about her?
- Does she expect to work for what she wants, rather than just having things given to her?

Friends and Peers

Even though your daughter will need to develop healthy relationships with friends and peers, it is more important that she define herself separate from any group. When your daughter builds relationships, she must not allow herself to become friends with people who will challenge her beliefs, or try and make her do something that she knows is morally or ethically wrong. A friend will not try and make her do anything she does not want to do.

Chapter 7

Adolescence Woman
(10 years- 16 years)

"There is nothing enduring in life for a woman except what she builds in a man's heart."

From Adolescence to Adulthood

Adolescence is a time for growth that will be painful at times and a pleasure at others. Your daughter needs to understand that growth does not have to happen without her input. The more she learns about her growth and what to expect, the better prepared she will be for her growth changes.
- She should understand her own behavior and why people react to her as they do
- She should make appropriate decision about who she is and who she will grow to be
- She should learn to behave in a way that reflects her personal values and goals
- She should work to achieve her goal and live up to her responsibilities.

A Time for Your Daughter to Understand Herself

The name you and your woman give your daughter is important, but the name itself does not truly describe who she is. People often try and define themselves by the people in their lives, their appearance, or some talent or skill. This can be a mistake. These things are significant, but they are all just small fractions of the total individual

Her Inner Woman

For young women who are not taught and given proper direction, adolescence is a very difficult and confusing time. Without adequate instruction, your daughter will put unnecessary stress and strain on her, her parents, close friends and other family members. The more you teach your daughter about being a woman, the less anxious she will be about all of the things going on both in & outside of her. What your daughter learns about herself will assist her in making decisions and in achieving personal goals throughout adulthood.

Her Goals

The definite plans your daughter will make in life are her goals. These goals help provide a mental picture of what she plans to do with her, her future, and what she must do to get the things she needs. Planning, organizing, and coordinating her goals will guide her in the best use of her time, energy, and other resources.

Her goals will stem from her needs, responsibilities, and the many challenges she can expect throughout his life. Your daughter's needs and goals are based on what is important to the inner her. The values you instill in your daughter will determine the kind of person she grows to be. Her values will be directly rooted in your family's history, cultural heritage, religious philosophy, and belief systems.

Many people go through life avoiding decisions and letting thing fall where they may. Others are pressured to make decisions that are not in their best interest. They have a hard time setting goals and acting on them. Your daughter should know that if she is going to reach her goals, she will have to give them plenty of thought, make sound choices, and to act on those choices responsibly.

Peer Pressure

Pressures from friends and classmates will be a very common part of your daughter's life. Both pressure and popularity may be a concern for her and her friends. People her age often look to their peers for acceptance and praise. It is common for young people to depend on their peers to learn about themselves.

There will be times when your daughter will feel as if everywhere she looks there is someone calling on her to make decisions. Some of those decisions will be related to her sexual feelings. It is important that your daughter understand that there is nothing she can do to keep these feelings from happening. She must also know that the feelings she will experience are healthy and natural.

You want your daughter to know that her feelings cannot be helped, but how she behaves in response to those feelings can be helped. One of the most important things you will teach her is that her feelings do not have to be acted on. You and your woman should teach your daughter to decide on a code of behavior for sexual situations. She should know before she becomes intimately involved with a man the proper code of conduct for a new woman.

Make sure she knows the difference between sexual feeling and feelings of love. Once she knows sexual feelings, it will be easier for her to make sound decisions concerning them. Your daughter and her friends should know that not being ready for sex is not a bad thing.

They should know that not every person their age is sexually active. Many teens have been taught the beauty of their sexuality and the potential dangers associated with sexual activity. Many have decided to wait until they are married or in a mature relationship before having sex.

Things Your Adolescent Should Consider When Thinking About Having Sex.
- Do I feel any pressure to have sex?
- Where is the pressure coming from?
- Am I trying to prove something to someone?
- Am I trying to save this relationship by having sex?
- Have I talked with my boyfriend or girlfriend about our expectations from this relationship?
- How will having sexual relations might change it?
- Am I ready for the challenges of being parents?
- Have I completed my education?
- Do I have adequate employment and finance for building a life with another person?
- What would I do if I got a sexually transmitted disease (STD)?
- What would my parents and family say if they knew I was having sex?
- What would I do if my sexual partner had symptoms of a sexually transmitted disease (STD)?

- Am I ready for all of the challenges that come with being sexually active?

When your daughter meets a man she should welcome an open and mature conversation about sexual relationship. It is important that she discuss her long term goals and responsibilities when facing a sexual situation. If she does not want to have sex, she should make that clear. She should state that up front without feeling a need to justify her decision.

Teach your daughter that anyone who feels she needs to justify herself has not accepted her decision not to have sex. Any answer she gives will be challenged. Your daughter should know that responsible people do not need a reason not to have sex. She should avoid compromise if she feels strongly about something.

As a woman, all of your daughter's decisions will be made to improve her life. If it doesn't make her healthier, stronger, smarter, or better prepared for all of life's challenges, then it's a waste of her time. She does not need a reason to say no to sex; she needs only the best of reasons to have sex.

Common Pickup Lines for Teens Being Pressured for Sex

Many boys will try and manipulate your daughter the same way pimps manipulate potential prostitutes. These boys learn to prey on your daughter's insecurities. They will attack her level of intelligence, her physical appearance, or her reputation. They will even attempt to use any problems that she may be having with you or your woman.

These boys will try and break your daughter's self-image, and redefine her in ideas that a child may consider adult or romantic. If your baby girl is being pressured to have sex, one or more of these lines may be used:
- "All the kids are doing it."
- "If you ain't gonna do it with me, then I'll find someone who will."
- "If you are in love, then it's OK."
- "You are not a real woman 'til you do it."
- "It's good for you."
- "You won't get pregnant. We'll be very careful."
- "It's good for clearing your acne."
- "Let's just try it once, it won't hurt us."

Not every teen is sexually active. Non-romantic love and a genuine concern for someone mean taking responsibility for them and sharing in their growth and development. Even when taking all precautions a woman can get pregnant or get a sexually transmitted disease.

Teen Suicide

A teen who do not have strong family connections, friends, religious leaders, or a favorite teacher, often find themselves all alone during bad times. Many of these teens turn to destructive behavior that hurts them and those closest to them. In some cases, these teens attempt suicide. Most of them suffer extreme depression and feel completely hopeless. Suicide is the 8th leading cause of death among all people, and the 2nd leading cause of death for teenagers.

There are a lot of things that contribute to teen suicide.
- They experience an extreme sense of social turmoil.
- They become overwhelmed with the competition and pressure to succeed.
- The loss of a loved one (most often event leading to a suicide attempt.)
- The loss of health.
- The loss of social or academic status.

It is difficult for a layman to identify a teen on the path to suicide. That is why it is so important to seek counseling when you see a teen suffering from depression. It is also important to get the family and closest friends involved with the teen and her suicide counseling. Most of the teens that attempt suicide, do not really want to die.

Their destructive behavior is a cry for help. Even if your daughter never attempts suicide, the stress and strain of dealing with teens that are can have a bad impact on your daughter's life. It is important to remember that watching over your daughter, sometimes means looking after her friends.

<u>Teen Pregnancy</u>

Over 1 million Americans teens become pregnant each year. About half of them give birth. Out of every 100 teenage females, 10 will get "knocked up", but only 6 will actually birth a baby. It is believed that 5 out of 6 teen pregnancies are unplanned. The teenage females that think having a baby will make them feel more grown up, give them more control of their lives, or give them someone to love make up the 1 out of 6 that are planned.

It is important that your daughter and her friends understand the scope of pregnancy and childcare. She should be taught to consider the long-term financial, emotional, social, and educational costs to herself and her children. 50 to 80 percent of teen mothers drop out of high school. Many of them will live in poverty.

Those that have babies at 15 and 16 years of age are likely to have a second child before their 20th birthday. Many of the children born to teen mothers, end up in foster care, abused, or neglected. There are several programs available for teen mothers that help them stay in school. A teen mother who completes her education is more likely to "wait until she's grown", before she has another baby.

The special risks of adolescent pregnancy:
- Her pelvis may not be large enough for the passing of a full-grown baby.
- Her body may not be mature enough for the great physical stress of pregnancy.
- Her nutritional needs for her growing body as well as the nutritional needs of her unborn baby maybe to high for her to meet.
- Teenage mothers are more likely to have babies born with low birth weight.

Teen Pregnancy and Parenthood

Your daughter's adolescent growth will be a full-time job. An unplanned pregnancy, birth, and care of a child would make her life very complicated. She should understand that making a baby is life time of change that many teens learn the hard way.

Your daughter and her friends will be pressured to have sex and they should be ready for the responsibilities and challenges of saying "NO". You should teach your baby girl to keep herself fresh and clean.

Saving Up For Your Daughter's Education

Finances

In 18 years your little baby will be going off to college. Between 1975 and 1995, college tuition and general expenses rose about 5 to 8% a year. It is projected that college costs will continue to rise 6 to 7% a year. This means that by 2035 a single year at a public college will cost more than $70,000; at a private college, costs will exceed $150,000.

The scope of this book will focus on the most common alternative investment choices. After you read this information, contact your stockbroker or financial planner and make sure your choice fits your educational needs. It would also help if you contact your accountant and get his or her feed back.

Zero Coupon Bonds are bonds that you purchase for a fraction of what they will be worth when they mature. These bonds are offered by both the government and independent corporations. You could by a bond for $200 that will be worth $1000 by the time your daughter starts college. The price you would pay today would be based on current interest rates the higher the interest rate, the less money you pay. When the bonds mature, the longer you hold them the less you pay.

The advantages of zeros are:
- You pick your maturity date, from one year to thirty years.
- You can lock in current interest rates.
- You will know the exact value of your bond when it matures.
- The market for zero bonds is active and it can be sold for whatever it is worth at the time.
- Government-issued zeros are not at risk of default.

The disadvantages of zeros are:
- If interest rates increase after you buy the zero, you can not take advantage of the increase.
- You have to pay income taxes on the money earned from your zero every year. (Buying tax-exempt zero coupon municipal bonds will eliminate this problem.)
- If you do not hold on to your bond until it matures, you may lose a percentage of your principal.

Series EE Savings Bond is a type of zero coupon bond issued by the U. S. Government (like a zero bond) that you purchase for less than its face value.

The advantage of EE bonds are:
- They pay an adjustable rate of interest if you hold them at least 5 years. (They pay a guaranteed 85% of the average market yield on 5 year Treasury securities)

- No taxes are due until the bond is cashed.
- They may be entirely tax-free depending on your purpose for cashing them in.

The disadvantage of EE bonds are:
- Your maximum investment is $15,000 a year in EE bonds.
- There is no market for these, so you can not sell them. You can only cash them in. (You won't have to pay a commission)
- If your income exceeds $60,000 a year, the IRS will adjust the amount every year for inflation. (The tax-exempt rule does not fully apply.)

Mutual Funds

There are more than four thousand different mutual funds available. These funds range from high-risk to low-risk, enabling you to choose the one that is right for you. In the last ten years, mutual funds have increased about 13% a year.

Insurance

Life Insurance

This is a time for you and your woman to focus a little attention on life insurance. It is important for you to consider the life of your child after the untimely death of you or your woman. The right life insurance policy on you and your woman will make a huge difference in the event of a tragedy. It is important that you or your woman be able to adequately provide for your baby in the event of a death.

Life Insurance for Children

When you get insurance on your baby, it should be a policy that builds cash value.

Disability

Long-term disability coverage is very important. A long-term illness can be more devastating than death. If your employer has a short-term or long-term disability plan, look into it immediately.

A Safe Search for a Financial Planner, a Stockbroker, or an Insurance Broker
- Ask trusted family members and friends for recommendations.
- You need someone who will teach you everything you need to know about investing your money.
- You need someone who will sit down with you and explore the unique circumstances of your family's needs.
- Check the background of your person and look closely at both personal and professional references.
- Note: Do not give weight to private organizations and fancy social clubs. Those organizations only mean that the person paid a fee to join.
- Connect with someone you can see at least once a year for any changes in your financial situation.

<u>The Emotional Side of the Menstrual Cycle</u>

Menstrual Cycle

Menstruation marks the fertile years of a woman's life. It is the monthly shedding of the inner lining of the uterus, accompanied by bleeding, that occurs when a woman who has not become pregnant. Menstrual periods usually begin at puberty and continue until menopause.

Most of the time a woman's body is well adjusted and happy with her lifer, but throughout the month there are changes in her hormonal levels. There are rises and falls in her hormonal levels that will affect a woman's moods, emotions, and personality. A woman's hormonal change is as predictable as the ocean's tide, but as unpredictable as the ocean's weather.

The Surging Tide
This marks the ocean's incoming tide and the rising water levels that follow. The seas come to life and stir with energy as the rushing water come a shore. The first week of a woman's menstrual cycle, her estrogen advances and fills her body in preparation for ovulation. During this period, she will experience great passion and energy.

First Week: Rising estrogen levels
- Self-directed, disciplined
- Assertive: tries to motivate family and friends
- Independent
- Optimistic
- Self-confident, positive
- Outgoing, extroverted
- Has high self-expectations; manic-like busyness
- Task oriented
- Overly ambitious

(Some women have feelings of gloom that stretch over from the fourth week, and a sense of well-being follows quickly.)

High Tide
At this point, the tide is in. The water level is high with a pulsating moan that seems almost overwhelming. In the second week of a woman's cycle estrogen reaches its peak and levels off. Her pace is more moderate and she has a confidence and determined to reach her every goal. She driven, ambitious and centered on specific projects.

Second Week: Estrogen levels off and declines slightly
- Blue skies with plenty of sunshine
- Not depressed
- Inner strength w/ a sense of well-being
- More realistic than the week before
- Less assertive
- Creative, with positive energy

- Optimistic
- More tolerant
- Idealistic dreamers
- Sensitive to beauty in the environment

The Fertile Waters

During high tide, before the waters recede, the ocean is fertile with life and ideal for the professional fisherman. The waters are calm but in no way still. There is a growing tension as the seas prepare to leave the shore. Ovulation begins after nearly two weeks bringing noticeable changes. This distinct phase will bring about an emotional state of peace and well-being.

- Passive, introverted
- Passive receptive (submissive, patient, accepting, open minded)
- Sexual readiness (rising estrogen and progesterone together produces high levels of sexual behavior)
- Strong maternal feelings
- Romantic and sentimental feelings
- Tolerant of minor irritations
- Sense of being unified or whole

The Ebb Tide

In the third week of a woman's cycle, the estrogen levels rise slightly. Progesterone surges rise and gradually dominate her body. By the end of that third week, the two hormonal wrestle for control and restlessness will invade the woman's body. During the week, a woman's days will be energetic at times and dull at others. Her life is like the tropical seas that experience an eerie calm just before a hard storm.

Third Week: Rising estrogen and overriding progesterone (subject to variable feelings: some happy and sad)

- The doldrums
- A sense of doom
- Apprehensive for no apparent reason
- Feelings of self-doubt
- Discouraged
- Losing sense of well-being
- Impatient and losing interest.

The Outgoing Tide

In week four of a woman's cycle, there is a brief countdown before menses. The progesterone and estrogen levels are receding quickly like the ocean's tide. There is tension building as the seas pull away from the shore and empties into the depths of the churning ocean.

Fourth Week: Premenstrual (estrogen and progesterone levels fall)

- Very reactive, irritable, touchy, and nervous

- Moody, unstable
- Sensitive to noise
- Unpredictable, outburst of emotions
- Quarrelsome
- Unreasonable
- Lack of self-confidence
- Not ambitious
- Melancholy, withdrawn
- Awkward and shaky
- Food binges (sweets and spices)

Low Tide

The primal waves move in quickly to cover the shore. In low tide the seas draw back and appear to be still, but they are by no means calm. Some women find the few hours before their periods begin, a very uncomfortable time. They find themselves struggling with great pain and stress.

The Changing Tide

The seas grow slightly weak, then swell and roar as they flood the shores. A woman's internal tide will flood her body with hormones, and change her emotionally. A woman's hormonal changes will rise and fall in an ancient cycle. Along with the waves of estrogen and progesterone passing through her system, you will see how your woman's emotional life is affected by her chemical changes.

The symptoms vary from one monthly period to another, and will vary woman to woman. Some women may not feel any emotional changes at all. The above list will help you be more aware of a woman's changes. Understanding her hormonal changes will make you more aware of any emotional disturbances and mood swings she may experience. Your knowledge of the menses will help you cope and gives hope to your woman.

Chapter 8

The Young Adulthood Woman
(17 years- 32 years)

"Of all the rights of women, the greatest is to be a mother."

Lin Yutang

Your daughter is a woman. From the moment the sperm meets the egg, on through old age and death, your daughter will be all woman. Each stage of her life is about her growth and development as a woman. Her preparation before each stage, the instruction she receives during each stage, and how she learns to analyze and evaluate her experiences after each stage is what will enable her to get the most out of each life cycle. This level of focus will ensure that her experiences during each stage will have the most positive impact on her life as a woman.

The life cycle has different stages and the early stages of infancy, childhood, and adolescence last only a short while. With the life expectancy being somewhere around 76 years of age, after adolescence your daughter has her whole life a head of her. When we look at the life of your daughter, we focus on each stage of her life from before the cradle to beyond the grave. This is not common in all cultures. For many, the life cycle does not begin until birth and for the most part is over after adolescence. Adulthood had not been considered a time for major growth.

Most of our development tasks come about as a result of physical and mental maturation, the cultural pressures of society, and personal goals of the individual. Like every other stage, adults have to complete various developmental tasks that lead to maturity.

There are 5 major aspects on which these special tasks focus.
- occupational role
- individual identity/personal self-reliance
- relationships with other people
- relationship to society
- acceptance of growing older and of the reality of death

Young adulthood may begin between the ages of 17 and 20. This stage begins when individuals are able to take care of themselves without requiring a great deal of help from parents and other family members. These young adults are able to support themselves by working and they are able to make important life decisions and take full responsibility for all of the decisions made.

Most young adults are at their peak in physical development. They have matured mentally, and are capable of carrying a lot of stress while adjusting to new situations. During this time your daughter will continue to sharpen skills and gathering information that will make her more self-supporting and secure. She will become a healthy component of the community and contribute to our society.

This is a period of choice. She will likely choose an educational and professional career. This stage involves committing to others. Many people will build their closest friendships during, build bridges over troublesome gaps in family relationships and choose intimate love affairs.

It is important that your baby girl complete developmental tasks at each stage in her life in a timely fashion.

Chapter 9

Middle Adulthood Woman
(33 years- 55 years)

"A woman's guess is much more accurate than a man's certainty."

Rudyard Kipling

In many societies the life expectancy was around 40 years of age. In more advanced societies the life expectancy is much longer. At the age of 40, your daughter will be able to see for herself that she has reached the midpoint of her adult years. She will know that more than half of her life is gone. At this stage, your daughter may see her life in terms of time left to live rather than time since birth. Looking back on her life, she will find that mid-life brings new insight and self-perspective.

With the exception of making a living, one of your daughter's chief concerns will be what she will do with the next half of her life. There will be many factors in your daughter's life that make her feel that time is running out. This is not uncommon. During the mid-life, there will be many changes. Some of them will be good for her; others may be bad. Career changes, the death of a loved one or close friend, marriage, and possible grandchildren are all changes common at this stage.

Some people might find it difficult to accept the passage of time. Those who do may make drastic changes in their behavior and way of life. This is what some people call a mid-life crisis. Your daughter can progress through middle adulthood without serious problems. Teach her how to adjust her hopes and goals and adapt her life-style to her newly experienced feelings of being in touch with herself. One of the things she can do is make a career change that is more personally satisfying.

Caution: For many families, parents reach middle adulthood at the same time some of their children are reaching adolescence. As a result, your personal needs as a parent may clash with your daughter. Because both you and your teen are going through a major life change tension and conflict may increase. You and your daughter learning about each other's developmental tasks and becoming more aware of each other's needs will go along way towards keeping parent-child conflicts at a minimum.

There are a number of transitions you and your woman need to be prepared for in this stage of life. One transition facing you as a middle-aged adult is your children entering adulthood and needing to leave home. This particular transition is known as the "empty-nest syndrome." Another recent transition involves the return of adult children. After a divorce, or a loss of income, many adults are moving back home with their parents. The term for this is the "cluttered-nest syndrome."

Food for Thought.....
90% of Ovarian Eggs are produced by the Age of 30.

According to a study published by the University of Saint Andrew and Edinburgh University in Scotland, 95% of all women will have less than 12 % of their ovarian egg reserve left by age 30. By age 40, their ovarian egg reserve will be somewhere around 3%. A woman is most fertile between the ages of 18 and 24. Her ovarian egg production stabilizes until the age of 30. As she enters mid-life malaise, her ovarian egg production takes a nosedive until menopause. The general message for women is, "Plan to make babies early!"

Mid-Life Malaise

Malaise is the sensation of discomfort that women experience through mid-life. During this period, a woman may feel uneasy, slow and droopy.

A Mid-life Slump

These are a few questions that may give you a little insight into the emotional changes that a woman will experience in middle age. The mid-life slump takes place in the early stage of peri-menopause.
1. Is she experiencing a drop in her energy level?
2. Has she lost interest in sex?
3. Is she losing interest in her hobbies or simple pleasures?
4. Is she experience depression unrelated to her menstrual cycle?
5. Does she speak of foreboding feelings?
6. Is she touchier than usual or having crying spells?
7. Is she having a difficult time making decisions?
8. Is she having memory lapse?
9. Does she ever feel unwanted or useless?
10. Does she often express an excessive amount of failures?

These are the most prevalent symptoms of the mid-life slump:
- Drops in energy level
- Decreased interest in sex
- Morbid or sadness (unusual feelings of sorrow)
- Loss of interest in hobbies or favorite activities
- Depression
- Doldrums (feelings of doom or future destruction)
- Touchiness and over-reactive
- Crying spells
- Crazy days (feeling out of control)
- Increasing dependency
- Memory lapses
- Feeling unneeded or useless
- Feeling unloved
- Romantic notions or daydreams (an escape mechanism)
- Wanting to escape or get away

- Recapitulation (a review of past decision that bring about regret or worry for past deeds)
- Introspection "Woe is me!" (self-examination)

There are 5 stages to a woman's reproductive life:

Pre-menarche
These are the developmental years before puberty.

Menarche
A woman's first period beginning the menses. It is a specific point in time.

Menstrual
These are years of ovulating, menstruating and menopause.
- Post-menarche is a time in early menstrual years when irregularity is common.
- Menstrual is for years 20 to 40 and refers to years of regular cycles
- Peri-menopause is the time around menopause when there are declines in estrogen and cycles may vary slightly. It includes pre-menopause, which is the period when symptoms are obvious. Climacteric is the lay term for the entire menstrual process.

Menopause
This is the moment that menstruation ends. It is often used to include the range of time when definite symptoms of estrogen deficiency are present.

Post-menopause
These are the years after menstruation has completely ended.

Check This Out!
One Step Closer to a Much Healthier Life Style: An Anti-Aging Diet.

According to the US Department of Agriculture, the following anti-aging dietary guidelines may help your daughter.
- Eat foods rich in vitamin E, vitamin C, and beta-carotene.
- Do not get more than 30 % of calories from fat.
- Eat low-fat food rich in calcium.
- Get at least 25-40 grams of fiber every day.

Chapter 10

Late Adulthood Woman
(56 years- ?)

"A beautiful lady is an accident of nature. A beautiful old lady is a work of art."

The attitudes and values regarding health, proper diet, and nutrition have resulted in longer life expectancy. It is believed that the average person will live to be 85 years of age with a maximum duration of 115 years. Advancements in medicine, diagnosis and treatment of diseases have increased life expectancy.

The Measure of Age

Aging is predictable, but it varies from person to person. Gerontologists focus on three measures of age.

- Chronological age (number of birthdays).
- Biological age (how well different parts of the body functions). They observe physical fitness, heredity, life-style, health habits, emphasizing diet and exercise.
- Social age (how well we master developmental tasks at each stage of life.)

Physical Process of Aging

As a person grows older the process of cell division slows. Cells capable of dividing and producing new cells decrease in number. Slow cell division results in a build up of waste within the cell. As waste builds up, cell function slows and cells gradually deteriorate.

These are physical changes that come with aging.

- Skin loss its elasticity and begins to thin and wrinkle.
- Facial and body hair turns gray.
- Toe and fingernails become brittle.
- Hearing and vision problems may likely develop.
- Bones lose calcium (they become brittle). Joints become less mobile.
- The basal metabolism slows.
- The kidney function slows.
- The hormonal secretion decreases.
- The body's immunity system weakens.
- A loss of lean body mass, with an increase of fatty tissue. Muscular strength weakens.
- Vital capacity for air in lungs decrease.
- The heart is less efficient in pumping blood.
- The body's use of glucose changes and less energy is produced.

Your daughter should know that changes that are characteristic with aging are inevitable, but a person's overall life-style can make the difference in her health and life expectancy.

The Menopause

Menopause is a very healthy and natural part of a woman's life. For many women, menopause is a symbol of growing older. This can be a time for great fear and depression. Although contrary to popular belief, menopause is not the end of a woman's life. It is only the end of her childbearing years. For many women all over the world, life after menopause is a time for personal growth and change.

There is a lot of literature floating around doctor's offices with information helping women better prepare for the final stage of their reproductive lives. Help the women in your life gain a balanced understanding of what to expect with menopause. Do not allow your women to be misled by the negative information found in literature that over emphasizes the negative aspects of menopause.

It is not inherent that women go crazy during their special change of life. A study done by Dr. Larry Galton revealed that 50.8% of women reported no acute discomfort with menopausal symptoms. 89.7% of the women that reported difficulties continued living normal lives with no interruption. Only 10.3% of women surveyed were incapacitated at intervals.

The average age of menopause is 52 years. 30% of women will have menopause by 45 years of age. 68% of women will have had menopause by the age of 55. 75-80% of women will suffer from estrogen withdrawal. Pre-menopause may start as early as 33 years and end as late as 60.

Peri-menopause or climacteric is a gradual process taking 4 or 5 years. The process begins around 38 years of age and ends around 45. As a woman's reproductive system begins to shut down, the ovaries will produce less estrogen. Over time, the physical and emotional signs of estrogen deficiency will appear.
Theses are exceptions to the peri-menopause time table:

- Premature menopause is the complete cessation of the menses before the age 40.
- Surgical menopause is menopause brought on by the removal of both ovaries.
- Menopause after the age of 60. Women who experience the menses after 60 are likely to develop endometrial cancer.

During peri-menopause, the adrenal gland and ovaries produce a weak male hormone called androstenedione. A woman's body fat converts androstenedione into additional estrogen. Even with the added estrogen the woman's body suffers a deficiency.

Physical Symptoms of Menopause
1. Erratic menstrual cycles
2. Hot flashes and flushes
3. Insomnia and consequent tiredness
4. Vaginal dryness
5. Bladder changes
6. Loss of fatty tissue and decreased muscle tone
7. Dry skin
8. Breast changes
9. Unusual skin sensations

Other Symptoms (estrogen related)
1. Dizziness
2. Weight gain
3. Bloating
4. Gastrointestinal disturbances such as diarrhea and constipation
5. Calcium deficiency

The Emotional Side of Menopause
- Feeling less attractive
- Feels less feminine
- Decreased interest in sex
- Anxiety and tension
- Low self-esteem
- Depression
- Touchiness and over-reactive
- Crazy days (feeling out of control)
- Increasing dependency
- Memory lapses
- Feeling unneeded or useless
- Feeling unloved
- Romantic notions or daydreams (an escape mechanism)
- Wanting to escape or get away

Reflexology for Menopause

Lydia Pinkham Liquid is good for mood swings, insomnia, and hot flashes. All ways check with your doctor when trying a home remedy if your symptoms continue. Give your woman a full foot and hand reflex workout.
- You will want to focus on the endocrine system to balance her blood sugars.
- Work the reflex areas for the brain and spine. (Both are found on either side of the feet and hands.
- Feel the bony instep on the inside edge of your feet or down the length of the index finger.
- Hot Flashes can be soothed by working the thyroid glands (regulates metabolic rate) and lymph glands. This will releases waste fluids from lymph glands.
- Do not forget your breathing exercises and proper hydration.

The bones and spine can be worked for great lengths of time, but reflexes to organs and glands must be limited to a few seconds at a time. Do not over work reflexes to organs or glands.

Life after Menopause (Post-menopause)

After menopause:
- Reproduction has completely stopped.
- The vagina has shrunk to near pre-puberty size.
- Ovaries produce very small amounts of estrogen.
- There are no follicles produced for fertilization.

There was a time when people believed a woman's life was over after menopause. Before modern medicine and hormone replacement therapy, menopause left women withered and sickly. In the 1300's, the life expectancy for a woman was 33 years. Many women did not live long enough to go through menopause.

In the 1900's, the life expectancy had risen to 48 years. Women rarely lived long enough to experience life after menopause. Today in modern societies, a woman's life expectancy is 70 to 80 years and menopause falls in the midpoint of a woman's life.

These some of the things a woman can expect during this liberating stage in her life:
1. There is a rise in her energy level.
2. A woman's general health is good.
3. There is an increase in sexual enjoyment
4. There will be more freedom and self-reliance.
5. They will have new desire for learning and socialization.
6. She will have a greater capacity to learn and grow.
7. There will be a greater capacity for love and sharing.

Check This Out!
Some Get Older, While Others Get Better.

In many cultures, the older a person is, the wiser that person is considered to be. Young and middle age people seek the instruction of their elders. In these cultures, the aged are treated with great respect. Children are raised to know that their elders have a lot of experience and history to share.

In mainstream America, there is little respect given to the aged. Because we live in a world that makes use of only the newest technology, the older people in our world contribute very little to society. In a world where technology changes rapidly and represents the advancement of a people, the elderly and the "out dated ways of doing" may not be valued.

In societies that values age, the elderly play very important roles. However, in our society the aged are often separated from daily group activities. What value will your daughter learn to put on aging? How will you teach the value of aging?

Breaking the Age Barrier in the Name of Friendship

In our society, young people rarely have the opportunity to mix and mingle with the elderly. Help your daughter build healthy relationships with the elderly people in your lives. They will both have a lot to share with one another.

If you do not have a significant relationship with a senior citizen, develop one. Try and plan engagements that will enable you to spend more time with your elderly relative. If the elders of your family live far away, try corresponding with them the best you can.

You and your daughter can build a relationship with an elderly neighbor. Or volunteer your time at an agency that pair young people with older adults. If you and your baby girl invest a little time enriching the lives of the elderly, you may find the experience rewarding.

Helping Your Baby Girl Find a Mentor.

Helping your daughter find a person who is an expert in an area in which she will excel can be very good for her. A mentor can be a great source of support and information. All throughout history great people have had mentors. These days you can find mentor programs at schools, churches, and social out-reach programs. Help your baby girl explore her creative side and find a talent or craft that she would like to learn, improve or develop.

Find someone who is competent in that field, and see if they would be willing to work with her. Your daughter will be expected to play the role of an unpaid assistant or errands girl for that person. That will compensate the person for his or her time and guidance. This could be one of the most rewarding experiences in your daughter's life.

The Last Part of the Life Cycle

Death and Dying

Facing death is always challenging. Many people often avoid talks about death. People fear death and dying. Despite our efforts to understand death, we have no firsthand experience and our normal inclination is to fear the unknown. However, part of your daughter's mental health depends on her ability to accept death.

Death
Clinical death occurs when the systems of the body shut down. Clinical death can sometimes be reversed and life can be restored. Brain death is the loss of all brain and brain stem functions. In this case, people cannot be revived and life cannot be revived.

Many people only experience the death of a friend or loved one late in life. For many people, death is a foreign or distant experience. Some people do not often get an opportunity to learn how to cope with death. Other people see death as a result of illnesses that are prolonged and emotionally draining.

Several factors influence our understanding death. 1.) Personal experience. 2.) Spiritual beliefs. 3.) Family attitudes. 4.) Values. 5.) Person's age.

Under the age of 2
Children are not aware of death. They only recognize that some who was once there is

no longer around.

From ages 2 to 5 years of age
Children recognize death, but do not understand that it is permanent. Children may see death as a type sleep.

From ages 5 to 9 years of age
Children see death in the form of an elderly person, a fairy princess, an angel, etc. Death is real to children at these ages and it is recognized as permanent. However, they do not see death as something that can happen to them.

By Age 10
Children see that death is final, but do not recognize that anyone could die at anytime. It is not until adolescence that people learn that death can come at anytime.
(Each stage of development varies. Their experiences with death and the things they have been told will have a major impact on their acceptance of death.)

Grief
Losing someone you love, or watching someone you care about grieve is difficult. Consider these tips.
- Everyone grieves in their own way, according to their own timetable and style.
- Anxiety attacks and having physical symptoms are all normal reactions to grief.
- There is no short cuts to grieving. The grieving process takes years, not months.
- Open-ended conversations about death and discussing the person who died helps everyone cope with death.

Stages in Accepting Death

These five stages in the acceptance of death have a lot in common with any major loss. Although reactions to death will vary in degrees, there are general guidelines for accepting the process of dying and death.

Stage 1: Denial. It is an attempt to avoid reality. They treat their fatal illness as if it is a dream. They behave as if it is all a big misunderstanding. Sometimes a patient will often feel isolated and helpless.

Stage 2: Anger. This is the why me stage? Anger and resentment is a natural reaction. People at this stage often vent their anger through envy towards those who have a long life ahead of them. Their family and friends may see the patient's attitude as ingratitude. As people pull away, patients feel isolated and rejected.

Stage 3: Bargaining. People begin to think that there is something they can do or say that will give them more time on earth. They will attempt any medical treatment, prayer, and major promises to change their lives for the better.

Stage 4: Depression. This is a time for people to grieve for all they have lost and everything that will be lost. This is commonly a time for silence and withdrawal. Their feelings are one of great loss. People at this stage should be encouraged to grieve.

Stage 5: Acceptance. This is a stage for facing the reality of their illness. Acceptance leaves a person feeling helpless. People are not happy or unhappy. They are at ease and ready to make proper preparation for their departure. The period of depression and anger is over.

The primary emotion that operates throughout these five stages is hope. People hope for a cure or a remission and they hope that death will not occur.

Appendix I: Herbal Medicine and Womanhood

Herbs for the Female Reproductive System

There are several herbs that may benefit the female reproductive system. Many herbs for the female reproductive system come from American Cultures. These cultures native to the Americas have a deep connection between them and Mother Earth. This ancient relationship produced a life of deep healing and aid for women and for the birthing process.

Uterine Tonic
The uterine tonic is good for toning and strengthening the whole reproductive system. It is good for the tissue of the organs as well as their function. Each herb has a unique associated action that should be explored to find the one that is most appropriate. Remedy herbs for the whole reproductive system:

- Black Cohosh- is a versatile relaxing nervine used to normalize the female reproductive system and to aid uterine activity in labor.
- Blue Cohosh- is a good uterine tonic that eases false labor pains. It also helps ensure a less complicated delivery.
- Chaste Tree- aids in normalizing hormones. It is good for menopausal changes, relieving dysmennorhea, and curving premenstrual stress.
- False Unicorn Root
- Life Root
- Motherwort
- Raspberry- is used to tone womb tissue, assist with contractions and check hemorrhage during labor.
- Squaw Vine

These herbs are used as holistic healers when there is no specific acute disease. They are used when weakness of the sexual organs has a negative affect on the whole body.

Emmenagogues stimulate and promote a normal menstrual flow. Some emmenagogues do not care for the whole system. There are also emmenagogues that may be used to stimulate to the point of irritation, which can be useful in some treatments. Choosing the proper herb for a specific treatment should be determined by considering their associated actions. The most useful emmenagogues in an almost endless list:

- Blue Cohosh
- False Unicorn Root
- Life Root
- Motherwort
- Parsley- is an effective emmenagoue but should not be used in medicinal dosage during pregnancy. It may excessively stimulate the womb.
- Pennyroyal
- Rue

- Southernwood (also known as Lad's Love) - can be used to stimulate delayed menstruation.
- Squaw Vine
- Yarrow

Herbs that Promote Normal Hormonal Output

These herbs make up an important group that balances the functions of the endocrine glands which control the proper functions of the reproductive system. Chaste Tree is the most important in the herb of this group. The Chaste Tree remedy normalizes estrogen and progesterone activity. It is useful in every aspect of menstrual dysfunction and menopause.

Astringents
Astringents are used in respect to the female reproductive system and these herbs have a special affinity to it:
- American Cranesbills
- Beth Root
- Burr-Marigold
- Lady's Mantle
- Periwinkle- may be used internally or externally as an astringent and may treat excessive menstrual flow.
- Shepherd's Purse

Demulcents
Demulcents are often used to provide for the mucous membranes. The urinary demulcents are often a good source and these herbs are:
- Bearberry
- Blue Cohosh
- Corn Silk
- Golden Seal
- Irish Moss
- Marshmallow

Antiseptics
Antiseptics can be for something specific like the urinary system, or it could be for general purpose:
- Bearberry
- Couch grass- is useful for treating urinary infections like cystitis, inflammation of the prostate and inflammation of the urethra.
- Echinacea
- Garlic
- Juniper
- Wild Indigo
- Yarrow

Alternative and Lymphatic Tonics

Problems with the reproductive system can have a negative impact on the whole body. For this reason, it may be appropriate to use alternative tonics and lymphatic tonics. Some of these herbs are:

- Blue Flag
- Burdock
- Cleavers
- Enchinacea
- Poke Root
- Sarsaparilla

* Note: Damiana has a tonic action on the hormonal system and also has a reputation as an aphrodisiac.

Nervines and Others

The purpose of these herbs is to maintain healthy nerve activity for the female reproductive system. Changes in the reproductive system may lead to a build-up of water. A diuretic may be needed to flush the excessive fluids from the body. Several of the emmenagogues have nervine activity. These are some of the relaxing herbs:

- Cramp Bark
- Skullcap
- Valerian

*Note: Nervine tonics like Damiana and Oats will also make a nice addition.

<u>Patterns of Reproductive Illnesses</u>

In this section, we will view the diseases of the female reproductive system as they are associated with the menstrual cycle, pregnancy, childbirth, menopause, and associated infections.

The Menstrual Cycle

Uterine tonics may be used regularly or just for the time leading up to the onset of the period to ensure a healthy and easy menstrual cycle. Herbal tonics may treat pre-menstrual syndrome, menorrhea, dysmenorhea, metrorrhagia, menorrhagia, and amenorrhea.

Amenorrhea is the absence of menstruation. For an adolescent, a uterine tonic can help establish a natural rhythm. The best herbs are Blue Cohosh, Chaste Tree Berry, False Unicorn Root, Rue and Southernwood. If menstruation is delayed in an adult woman, the uterine tonic may help her body's withdrawal from the use of contraceptive pill and find its way back to a natural rhythm.

Make a tea and drink it three times a day. The tea mixture should be 2 parts Chaste Tree Berry, 2 parts False Unicorn Root, 1 part Blue Cohosh, and 1 part Rue will be beneficial. An old remedy for delayed menstruation is an infusion of equal parts of Pennyroyal and Tansy. This tonic should be drunk 3 times a day until the period begins.

* Note: Make sure your woman is not pregnant before you use certain herbal tonics. The emmenagogues are potentially dangerous if used to induce abortion. If she is not pregnant, these herbs are safe when used as directed.

Menorrhagia is when period flow is stronger than normal. Excessive flow can be regulated by astringents without crippling the normal process. If her flow continues to be excessive each month, than she should see her physician to make sure that it does not indicate a more severe problem.

A basic astringent treatment could be based on a tea that is 1 part American Cranesbills, 1 part Beth Root, and 1 part Periwinkle. This tea should be drunk 3 times a day the week before the period begins and during the flow itself. If it is an on going problem, the tea should be drunk once or twice a day throughout the cycle.

Metrorrhagia is unexpected bleeding that occurs in the middle of the cycle. Use a uterine tonic to help in a more basic way. Use Chaste Tree Berry to balance out the hormones. The herbs used for menorrhagia will also be useful. It is important that she balance her loss of blood with a diet rich in iron. (Green Leaf Tea is a great source of natural iron.)

* Note: Pennyroyal (Mentha pulegium) is taken to basically strengthen uterine contractions and as an emmenagogue. Pennyroyal should not be used during pregnancy.

Dysmenorrhea is a condition where periods are accompanied by intense cramping pain. The uterine tonics, anti-spasmodic tonics, and nervines may be very beneficial in pain relief. A mixture of 2 parts Black Haw Bark, 2 parts Cramp Bark, and 1 part Pasque Flower should do the trick. This herbal tea should be drunk 3 times daily when needed.

Some of the other herbs to consider are Black Cohosh, False Unicorn Root, and Wild Yam. Consult a good herbal book to choose the most appropriate herb or combination of herbs for her individual needs.

Premenstrual Syndrome

PMS is brought on by hormonal changes in a woman's body. Some of her response to her menstruation is physical in respect to those hormones and some of her response to these changes may be psychological. A woman my view her cycles as a curse, or she may learn to see menstruation as a beautiful and exciting time in her life. A woman's culture and up bringing may have a major impact on how she receives her menstrual cycles.

An infusion of equal parts of Skullcap and Valerian can be taken as often as needed. If there is cramping, she may use Cramp Bark and Pasque Flower. For water retention, add Dandelion to the mixtures.

Contraceptive Pills

The contraceptive pill is based on a woman's hormones. The extensive use of contraceptive pills poses important questions about the effects of long term use. When a woman stops taking the pill, her body takes a while to balance and regain its natural harmonic functions. Endocrine and uterine tonics may help bring balance to her systems.

An herbal tonic with 1 part Black Cohosh, 1 part Chaste Tree Berry, 1 part Licorice, and 1 part Motherwort. Drink this tea three times a day for the first two weeks after coming off the pill, twice daily for the third week and once a day for the fourth week.

Licorice helps the adrenal glands. Black Cohosh and Chaste Tree Berry will support the uterus and those glands responsible for producing sex hormones. Motherwort eases false labor pains in pregnant women, eases the discomfort of menopausal changes, and suppresses the tension over delayed menstruation. For women who are no longer using contraceptive pills, Motherwort supports the nervous system and will help her regain emotional balance.

* **Note**: Tansy (Tanacetum vulgare) –may be used as an emmenagogue to stimulate menstruation, but it should never be used during pregnancy.

Pregnancy and Childbirth

Pregnancy is a very special time that should be treated with great reverence and awe. The baby's peace and security while in the womb comes from the woman's lifestyle the lives of the people around her. Herbal remedies, proper exercise, and a good diet are important, but so are your love, understanding, and involvement in every aspect of the pregnancy. I recommend that you and your baby's mother read a book on natural childbirth.

There are an abundant number of plants that a woman may use throughout her pregnancy. Some may be taken daily where others are good for specific times. The best of these herbs are Raspberry Leaves and Squaw Vine. These are toners and may be taken individually or mixed together. A cup a day should be taken for the last three months of pregnancy, but would be better used throughout the pregnancy. Nettles are a good source of iron and will help with both nutrition and general bodily functions.

Herbs to Avoid During Pregnancy

Like some of the emmenagogues herbs, a number of herbs stimulate the uterus. These herbs can be useful during certain times in a woman's life, but during pregnancy an externally stimulation of the uterus can bring about a miscarriage. The most common of these stimulating herbs are:

- Autumn Crocus
- Barberry
- Golden Seal
- Juniper
- Male Fern
- Mandrake
- Pennyroyal
- Poke Root

Rue is mainly used to regulate menstrual periods, where it is used to bring on suppressed menses. It may relax smooth muscles in the digestive system and relieve spasmodic coughing.

Sage can be used as a compress to promote healing. It may also be used as a mouth wash and gargle. It is good for treating laryngitis, pharyngitis, and tonsillitis.

- Southernwood
- Tansy
- Thuja
- Wormwood

The action of these herbs can be attained by other herbs, so there is no need to risk the health of a woman's pregnancy by using these herbs.

Threatened Miscarriage

Miscarriages are sometimes the body's way of dealing with a natural reproductive problem. However, miscarriages may also be the result of inadequate diet, excessive stress or trauma. When these situations threaten a healthy pregnancy, herbs can provide the extra vitality needed to avoid an unnecessary miscarriage. General uterine tonics that are good for supporting pregnancy and protecting against miscarriages are:

- Black Haw Bark
- Blue Cohosh
- Cramp Bark relaxes the uterus, thus relieving the painful cramps associated with periods and protecting the body from miscarriage.
- False Unicorn Root
- True Unicorn Root

A combination of toning, anti-spasmodic, and nervine relaxant: 2 part Blue Cohosh, 2 parts False Unicorn Root, and 1 part Cramp Bark. Drink this tea 3 times a day.

Morning Sickness

A safe and specific remedy that can be used as needed is Black Horehound, Irish moss and Meadowsweet. Some helpful nervines are Chamomile, Hops and Peppermint. Use a mixture of 2 parts Meadowsweet, 1 part Black Horehound, and 1 part Chamomile. It should be drunk three times a day. The better her diet, the less she will need it.

Labor

Drink a tea with Raspberry Leaves and Squaw Vine the last three months of pregnancy will aid in childbirth. If during delivery a woman needs to stimulate her uterus, use a safe oxytocic herb like Golden Seal.

Milk Production

Mothers may improve their breast milk production with the use of Aniseed, Blessed Thistle, Caraway Seeds, Fennel Seeds, Fenugreek Seed, Goat's Rue (perhaps the most powerful), and Vervain. The tea can be drunk three times a day as an infusion made from 1 or 2 tablespoons per cup of water.

These seeds are rich in volatile oils and can be combined to make a very good tea. Mix 2 parts Caraway, 1 part Fennel, and 1 part Aniseed or 2 part Fenugreek, and 1 part Aniseed. Either tea would be made by crushing the 2 tablespoons of seeds and putting them in a cup of cold water. Bring the water to a simmer and remove from heat. Let it stand 10 minutes and cover the cup to preserve natural oils. Drink a cup three times a day.

If the flow of milk needs to be stopped for any reason, drink Red Sage or regular old Garden Sage made into a fusion. Drink the tea three times daily until desired results are attained.

The Menopause

The following mixture will help balance the body and adapt to the menopausal changes. It should be taken for a few months until all symptoms are gone and her change in completed. A useful mixture is 2 parts Chaste Tree Berry, 2 part Wild Yam, 1 part Black Cohosh, 1 part Golden Seal, 1 part Life Root, 1 part Oates, and 1 part St. John's Wort. Drink this tea three times a day.

If heart palpitations, high blood pressure or tension are present, use Motherwort in place of St. John's Wort. In case of associated anxiety or depression, add Skullcap or Valerian to the mix.

Herbs and Sexuality

Use herbs to bring vitality, and put the body at ease. Damiana, Ginseng and Saw Palmetto make herbal tonics that are believed to have strong impact on the reproductive glands. A tonic made from Lime Blossoms, Oats or Skullcap may help with tension and stress that may lead to sexual problems.

Nervine tonics and nervine relaxants are combined to reduce sexual energy. The herbal tonics would be made with Passion Flower, Valerian or Wild Lettuce. Hops are especially good for reducing sex drive.

- Valerian can be used where nervousness, anxiety, and tension trigger asthma attacks.
- Hops can help soothe anxieties that may trigger an asthma attack.

Appendix II: Eastern Zodiac

The Grand Cycle of Life: The Twelve Signs of the Eastern Zodiac

Rat

1900, 1912, 1924, 1936, 1948, 1960, 1972, 1984, 1996, 2008, 2020, and 2032

The Rat is a curious character with a mixture of generosity and harsh frugality, charm and ambitious arrogance. There is no doubt that the Rat is "driven," seldom able to fully relax. Rats are always "on the move," racing back and forth, trying to put new projects together, going to party, or just dropping by to spread the latest gossip. They not interested in a simple quiet evening at home. If they ever step out of the metaphoric rat race, they get bored quickly and become sullen and irritable.

The Rat is not a devious type and likes to reach his/her goals by fair means. Rats have a very good sense of the value of people and objects around them. They are shrewd and it is difficult to pull the wool over their eyes. Rats are ambitious and believe in putting in a hard days work. They value high-quality items and will go to great lengths to hold on to the things they have.

Rats have to be careful not to over work themselves. It is very easy for the Rat to get carried away with the thought of making more money or closing one more big business deal. Despite their generosity, the Rat has a greedy side to them that can lead to major troubles.

The Rat is a real family creature, caring for loved ones and offspring. They will show great warmth and sensitivity and are not likely to show the cutthroat mean streak that lurks beneath the skin. The Rats are generous to fault to those they truly love.

Ox

1901, 1913, 1925, 1937, 1949, 1961, 1973, 1985, 1997, 2009, 2021, and 2033

Above all, the Ox personality is ruled by the need for stability in all things. This type does not like change, preferring to travel the well-paved road of conformity and convention. The traditional values of hard work and stable family life are what appeal most to the Ox.

The Ox is generally calm and quiet on the outside, but deep down he has a serious temper that is rarely seen. If Ox ever loses his temper, it is best to stay clear. An Ox on the rampage is a dangerous beast! Oxen enjoy material things and are willing to work very hard to achieve the life style they require. They love good food and drink, and lounging around in luxury, while at the same time believing in discipline, duty and industry. They can often go over board with authority, but their innate kindness can always be appealed to when they go too far.

The Ox is stubborn and will not be pushed into doing something he does not want to do. He is not quick witted or big on humor, but he is steadfast and reliable. The Ox is a committed creature standing by those he loves. Some would describe the Ox as boring, others are grateful for his dependability.

Tiger

1902, 1914, 1926, 1938, 1950, 1962, 1974, 1986, 1998, 2010, 2022, and 2034

In China, the Tiger is regarded highly and is a very charismatic creature. He is regarded as a protector of the home and family keeping ghosts, fire and thieves at bay. Having a Tiger in your life can bring you great power and energy. They can also bring about changes that could prove dangerous.

It is the nature of the Tiger to be dynamic, energetic and fun, but they are also more than capable of making impulsive decisions that prove to be unwise. Tigers take failures very hard and might find it difficult to break out of a depression. Tigers always give one hundred percent in everything they do. They are highly sociable and love to have a good time.

Tigers are enormously sentimental and love family life. They enjoy holding very small children who are dear to their hearts. The Tigers are like over grown children who are as enthusiastic in their elderly years as they were as young children. The Tiger is youthful and clever making him a very endearing character to know, but if you get involved with one, be prepared for a roller-coaster ride.

Rabbit

1903, 1915, 1927, 1939, 1951, 1963, 1975, 1987, 1999, 2011, 2023, and 2035

Rabbits are peaceful and loving creatures that will go to great lengths to avoid upsetting their well-oriented lives. It is the nature of the Rabbit to sidestep conflicts, but it is not wise to consider the Rabbit weak. Rabbits are great negotiators and will fight ferociously to defend what theirs. Their resistance to change makes them conservatives and conformists.

In China, the Rabbit is regarded as a creature of extreme fortune and a symbol of longevity. They are fond of life's comforts and simple pleasures, and their ability to avoid danger means they enjoy life's pleasures well into old age. Because Rabbits are in many ways passive, they live in a world centered on artistic and esthetic sides of life. Their homes will have the nicest paintings, furniture, movies and music.

The Rabbit will get great pleasure from their home life. They prefer the comfort of family and a few close friends over going out for entertainment or being at work. Because of their trouble free lives of convenience and comfort, Rabbit personalities tend to be superficial and timid when facing challenges. It is in their nature to create a world of luxury for themselves safe from the grim outside world.

Dragon

1904, 1916, 1928, 1940, 1952, 1964, 1976, 1988, 2000, 2012, 2024, and 2036

According to Chinese Tradition, the Dragon is a sacred creature and the luckiest of all the zodiacs. Dragons are royalty and are equated with the emperor. Dragons are a restless, but an interesting lot that must be always doing something. Starting new projects, going on big adventures, and exploring a new love, is the way of the dragon.

Dragons are successful in almost everything thing they do. However, it is not uncommon for them to abandon projects before they are completed. The lives of Dragons are a roller-coaster ride full of serious ups and downs, both in love and finance. Dragons are extremely arrogant and consider their opinions to be superior to all others. Their inability to listen and take orders from others, make them natural leaders.

Dragons assume that it is their divine right to lead and that all of their orders are to be followed. Although they may have many followers, they have very few friends. However, the friends they do make they will keep for life. Dragons are difficult and obnoxious, but reliable in times of trouble.

In the face of adversity, they are able to rise above pettiness and deal with things effectively. As leaders they demand a great deal, but they are always fair and they lead from the front. Dragons are people of action, and the word "can't" is not in their vocabulary.

Snake

1905, 1917, 1929, 1941, 1953, 1965, 1977, 1989, 1901, 1913, 1925, and 1937

The Snake is a very self-contained kind of animal, and those born under the sign of the Chinese Zodiac are not given to putting their business in the street. Thus they can be very good in matters of confidentiality. Snakes are shrewd, keeping most information to themselves and choosing the right moment to strike.

Snakes make powerful enemies in both business and personal affairs. They also have very good memory and an ability to feel a depth of dislike that other signs can only wonder about. Snakes can hold a grudge for a very long time never acting on it, all the while waiting for the perfect opportunity to exact some form of revenge.

Snakes are very sophisticated and intelligent, and considered psychic according to Chinese tradition. They love life and pleasure, and are highly sociable.

Horse

1906, 1918, 1930, 1942, 1954, 1966, 1978, 1990, 2002, 2014, 2026, and 2038

The Horse is by nature a very sociable animal and those born under the sign are usually popular with a great number of friends, and always the life of the party. They are the symbol of freedom and strength for most culture around the world. Independence is most important to those born in the year of the horse. They need their freedom to come and go as they please.

The Horse's preoccupation with their freedom often means ignoring the needs of others. They are likely to be late to functions that cater to others and will rarely keep promises. Although Horses are naturally honest and faithful, they will often let their imaginations lead them into making plans they will quickly forget all about. Horses are rarely petty.

However, they are high strung and excitable, which in times of trouble make them more of a disturbance than anything else. Some people might think that the Horse is fickle and shallow due to an equines inability to concentrate for any given period of time. The Horse needs to be constantly on the move, seeking out new experiences, and meeting new people in order to feel happy.

Sheep

1907, 1919, 1931, 1943, 1955, 1967, 1979, 1991, 2003, 2015, 2027, and 2039

The eighth sign of the Chinese zodiac is the Sheep. They are very sensitive and apt to take very personally the most innocent of comments, seeing them as some sort of insult. This sensitivity also makes them very artistic and imaginative.

The Sheep are warm-hearted and compassionate creatures that must be careful not to be made victims by people of a more ruthless nature. The Sheep has a close relationship with the Western sign Cancer, which means that Sheep are essentially family oriented. Sheep go to great lengths to maintain a comfortable home life.

They work hard to avoid confrontations and overt disagreements, but it is unwise to assume that the Sheep is a pushover. They are strong and determined fighters when backed into a corner. The Sheep may look helpless, but they are patient when at work and by stealth will get what they want.

Monkey

1908, 1920, 1932, 1944, 1956, 1968, 1980, 1992, 2004, 2016, 2028, and 2040

The Monkey is ruled by the planet Mercury and has a lot in common with the Western zodiac Gemini. The planet Mercury is considered the clever yet deceitful trickster. Like Mercury, the Monkey is an intelligent quick-witted type of animal that is also given to trickery.

People born under the sign exhibit a complexity of nature that encompasses and mirrors almost every behavioral trait found in humankind. Monkeys are lively and can make the most of any venture. They learn very fast and have a deep need to exercise their minds. When the Monkey is not challenged, they can very easily get into mischief.

Only jobs that are intellectually challenging would fit those born under this sign.

The Monkey is naturally quick, sharp nature, and very competitive attitude. Despite their success, they can easily suffer jealousy and envy. Monkeys are very charming and amusing who tends to have a large circle of friends.

Rooster

1909, 1921, 1933, 1945, 1957, 1969, 1981, 1993, 2005, 2017, 2029, and 2041

Roosters are flamboyant creatures who love to be seen. Their romantic love for themselves, make them highly susceptible to flattery. Those born under the sign of the Rooster like to be noticed and their desire for attention are meant to mask a lack of true self-confidence.

The Rooster has a lot in common with the Leo of the Western zodiac. They both share an unwarranted pride and a tendency to mask their weakness with arrogance. Roosters are generally efficient and well-organized, and characteristically like to keep everyone playing by their rules. They are sharp minded and argumentative.

Those born under this sign would not work well in jobs that require diplomacy, and they should be careful not to take on more than they are prepared to handle. Roosters do not take criticism well. They are easily offended and once their feathers are ruffled it is not uncommon for them to fly into rage.

Dog

1910, 1922, 1934, 1946, 1958, 1970, 1982, 1994, 2006, 2018, 2030, and 2042

Those born under this sign are essentially very honest and direct people who don't care for mind games. Dogs need to know the facts of any matter and they believe in being straight with others. The Dog is most concerned with justice for all. It is not only important that justice be done, but that it is seen to be done.

Dogs are active philanthropists always trying to make sure that fairness and equality saves the day. Those born under this sign are slow to make friends. They prefer to hold their own counsel and leave grand gestures and the hearty approach to others. The Dog sees the world in the most simple of terms. For them, everything is either black or white. People are considered either right or wrong, good or bad, and that's final.

If the Dog is on your side, they will support you in every way. However, if they are against you, they will treat you with disdain. The Dog has a sharp mind and a lively tongue. That tongue can be used effectively in support of their causes.

Boar

1911, 1923, 1935, 1947, 1959, 1971, 1983, 1995, 2007, 2019, 2031, and 2043

The Boar is considered the diamond of all Chinese zodiacs. They are always open, upright, and honest. Those born under this sign are immensely popular people. The Boar simply does not know how to be a cheat or con others.

They prefer to deal with all matters in an honest manner. Because of their good nature, some might consider them simple and try to take advantage of them. The Boar believes that all people are good and should be treated with respect.

They are very hard working and believe in building a life a great pleasure and comfort. Those born under this sign embrace the idea that "my house is your house." Their generosity goes a long way.

Appendix III: Western Zodiac

The Four Seasons of the Western Zodiac

Spring (March 21-June 21)

Zodiac Position (0 Degrees Aries-0 Degrees Cancer)
Quadrant First/ Human (Age 0-21)
Cusp Concepts (Rebirth, Power, Energy)
Signs (Aries, Taurus, Gemini)
Rulers (Mars, Venus, Mercury)
Symbols (The Ram, The Bull, The Twins)
Elements (Fire, Earth, Air)
Motto- I Am, I Have, I Communicate.
Dominant Faculty- Intuition

The astrological year begins in the spring (vernal equinox-rebirth) when the days and nights are equal in length. In the northern hemisphere March 21 represents the first day of spring. The first days of spring in the southern hemisphere are around September 23. Spring is the first quarter (90 degrees) of the year cycle. It begins with the spring equinox ending with the summer solstice.

Spring time is traditionally a period of new growth. Once the winter has past and there is no longer threat of freezing weather, the spring rains and swelling rivers provide a perfect place for crops and vegetables. The return of animals, colorful flowers in full bloom, and all kinds of birds and insects bring new life to this time of the year. As the days grow longer and the temperature increases people spend more time outside enjoying the weather.

The Signs and Life Periods

The Spring can be broken down into three astrological signs. These three are the cardinal fire sign Aries, the fixed earth sign of Taurus, and the mutable air sign of Gemini. These signs represent the first twenty-one years of life when people go through the infancy, childhood, adolescent, and young adulthood stages in life. People in the first stages in life experience many of the same processes as does the earth in springtime.

The first quadrant of the year is a waxing period, and it is governed by the faculty of intuition. During the early growth of both people and springtime there is objective external growth, but very subjective internal growth. Astrologically, Aries is ruled by the planet Mars. Taurus is ruled by Venus, and Gemini is ruled by Mercury. All three planets are considered inner (personal) planets. These planets are relatively small and close to the earth and sun.

The first stages of life are highly subjective (personal) orientation. Children see the world as an addition to him or her. Any fears of life would be powered by the unconscious and colored by intuition. Children naturally absorb and imitate what they see in the outside world. Sometimes, young people can be overwhelmed by the world around them, and behave in ways that are irrational.

The Springtime Personality

Most people born in the springtime have a great enthusiasm for life. They are good at new projects, and their ability to adapt and survive major change is noteworthy. People born in springtime are often more out going and have an impact on their environment. What might be considered a downside to people born in springtime is their capacity to stick to things. Their willingness to stay with an activity that requires them to wrestle with a situation is poor.

People born in this quadrant, enjoy sharing their thoughts and creations. More than those born during other times of the year, the springtime personality needs a regular show of appreciation. People born in this season need their freedom and rarely functions well with restrictions imposed on them. They need to grow, expand and find their place in the world.

Those born in the spring have a positive outlook on life. They have very little patience for negative people and are put off by people with serious attitudes. Generally, spring people have a child like air. Common characteristics of springtime people are innocence, adventurous, and spontaneous.

Summer (June21-September23)

Zodiac Position (0 Degrees Cancer- 0 Degrees Libra)
Quadrant Second/ Human (Age 21-24)
Cusp Concepts (Magic, Oscillation, Exposure)
Signs (Cancer, Leo, Virgo)
Rulers (The Moon, The Sun, Mercury)
Symbols (The Crabs, The Lions, The Virgin)
Elements (Water, Fire, Earth)
Mottoes (I Feel, I Create, I Serve)
Dominant Faculty (Feeling)

The Summer Solstice occurs on June 21 or 22 in the northern hemisphere (In the southern hemisphere it occurs on December 21 or 22). At this time days are longer and nights are shorter than any other time. As summers pass the days grow shorter and the nights grow longer. The summer makes up the second quarter of the year and runs from the summer of solstice to the fall equinox.

Summers are a period in nature when plants mature to full bloom and animals slow down in movement due to the heat. People are traditionally active in the morning and the afternoons become a time for relaxation. For many people this is a time for vacations. More and more people are enjoying outdoor activities. All of the abundance in our Mother Earth's nature is revealed. Life, in this quadrant is slower and more sensual. People tend to eat less and drink more, and wear fewer clothing. This is supposed to be a time when life is most easy going.

The Signs and Life Periods

Summer is made up of three astrological signs. The first is the cardinal water sign Cancer. The second and third signs are the fixed fire signs Leo and the mutable earth sign Virgo. These three signs represent the period in human development between the ages of 21-42 (Young adulthood through middle adulthood). This is a period of time when both people and our Mother Earth share certain processes in our growth. It is a time of flowering and producing.

The second quadrant is governed by the faculty of feelings. It is a period when external growth is clearly defined, but internal growth is more abstract. From an astrological perspective the signs Virgo, Leo and Cancer are ruled by The Sun, The Moon and Mercury. All three of these heavenly bodies are said to be "inner"(personal) in the solar system. That means that they are close to our Mother Earth and require only a month to a single year to completely circle the zodiac.

This period of life has a highly personal outlook, but overtime develops great wisdom. Unlike the child and adolescent stages of life, the maturing adult can separate the outside world from his/her internal self. The unconscious and intuitive drives are not as great as before. During this period of growth people are still highly social, but ego and personalities are not as open as they once were. People are more rational and more conscious in their manner. They are no longer crippled by their subjective selves.

The Summertime Personality

For the most part, summertime personalities are more critical in their thinking and have deeper insight into their response. At this stage in life, they are more focused on completing projects than initiating them. They can be both shut off and open with people and their feelings play a much bigger role in coloring the world around them. People born during the second quadrant are inclined to help and share the burdens of others. Summertime people may develop an emotional connection with the environment as well as any projects.

People born in the second quadrant of The Grand Cycle of Life need to be needed. They are not driven by recognition for their work. They are not driven by adventure or freedom. Summertime people live to serve others and need to invest time in the lives of those they serve.

Fall (September 23- December 21)

Zodiac Position (0 Degree Libra- 0 Degree Capricorn)	
Quadrant Third/ Human (Age 42-63)	
Cusp Concepts (Beauty, Drama and Criticism, Revolution)	
Signs (Libra, Scorpio and Sagittarius)	
Rulers (Venus, Pluto and Jupiter)	
Symbols (The Scale, The Scorpion, The Archer)	
Elements (Air, Water, Fire)	
Mottoes (I Weigh, I Control and I Philosophize)	
Dominant Faculty (Sensation)	

September 23 (In the northern hemisphere) marks the fall equinox. In the southern hemisphere the fall equinox occurs on March 21. At this time, the days and nights are equal in length. As the season passes the days grow shorter while the nights grow longer. This is the third quadrant of the year. It begins at the fall equinox and flows through the winter solstice.

Fall represents the last days of harvest. It is a time when mulch and leaves cover the ground. Plants and vegetation dies and becomes fertilizer for the earth. The temperature is cooler at night and brings frost to early morning. The leaves on the trees change colors and some animals go into hibernation while others began their travel southern climates.

Fall is the third quarter of the annual cycle, is fast pace, and all about survival. Animals and people eat heavier focusing on high-energy foods. Falltime people are waning and life for them is growing more difficult.

The Signs and Life Periods

The three astrological signs for the fall season are the cardinal air signs Libra, the fixed water sign Scorpio and the mutable fire signs Sagittarius. These three signs represent the human years of 42-63. The fall of the year is like the stages of middle adulthood. Middle age was a time for a conservation of power and movement. It's a time in life when survival skills are sharpened.

The faculty of the fall quadrant is sensation. It's considered a period of waning that is subjective with a conscious orientation. The aging in nature and man are visible. Libra, Scorpio, and Sagittarius are ruled by Venus, Pluto, and Jupiter respectively. Venus is a personal planet that lends social and sensuous influences. Pluto and Jupiter are outer or universal planets and are not in close proximity to planet earth. Jupiter takes 12 years to circle the zodiac. Pluto takes 248 years to travel around the zodiac.

The Autumnal Personality

Autumnal people are not usually as enthusiastic as those born in the years first and second quadrant. Fall personalities have a deep need to control their surroundings. Autumnal people are more preoccupied with their world and are more interested in maintaining what they have than starting something new. Feelings are controlled and social activities are taken more seriously. Autumnal people need to directly contribute to any work relationship. They seek mature and very serious relationships.

Autumnal people are subtle in their reaction to things, but feel everything deeply. They are more centered on the things going on around them than most giving self-control and self-understanding high priority.

Winter (December 21- March 21)

Zodiac Position (0 Degree Capricorn- 0 Degree Aries)	
Quadrant Fourth/ Human (Age 63- 84)	
Cusp Concept (Prophecy, Mystery and Imagination, Sensitivity)	
Signs (Capricorn, Aquarius, Pisces)	
Ruler (Saturn, Uranus, Neptune)	
Symbol (The Goat, The Water Bearer, The Fish)	
Elements (Earth, Air, Water)	
Mottoes (I Master, I Universalize, I Believe)	
Dominant Faculty (Thought)	

The Winter Solstice begins around December 21 in the northern hemisphere (June 21 in the southern hemisphere). Winter is the last quarter of the year running from winter solstice to the spring equinox. This time of the year is cold and stiff. Nights are shorter and days are longer than any other time of the year.

Winter is traditionally a time for snow and freezing temperatures. It's a time when people and animal find shelter and begin making use of stored goods. On the surface the earth is cold and still, but deep within the earth all kinds of major changes are taking place in preparation for a new spring. That which appears to be dead is only sleeping and awaiting the changing season.

The Signs and Life Periods

Winter is made up of three astrological signs. They are the cardinal earth sign Capricorn, the fixed air sign Aquarius and the mutable water signs Pisces. These three signs represent the life of humans between the ages 63- 84. This is a spiritual period of life that spans from late middle age to death. This period in life has a lot in common with the winter. It is a time when everything moves with a curious stiffness.

The faculty of the last quadrant is thought and it is considered a period of waxing. The winter personality is least concern with outward change and more concerned with thoughts, philosophy, and religion. Both nature and people have subjective changes taking place on the inside. It has practically replaced any outward growth or change.

Capricorn, Aquarius and Pisces are ruled by Saturn, Uranus and Neptune. These three planets are considered outer planets. They are very large bodies that are far from the earth. They take almost 28, 84 and 165 years respectively to make their orbit around the sun.

Adults at this time are leaning away from competition and making a place for themselves in the world. The days of building a family or making children are behind them. They are preparing for the end of their lives.

The Winter Personality

      Wintertime people focus on the big picture. They dominate their space with confidence, but are flexible. Winter people are very spiritual and are usually the quiet type. They often gain great excitement through their thoughts, work and ideals. One of their most distinguishing features is an active imagination that they objectify and make a source of creativity. Winter people have a great allegiance to the world of ideas.

      People born at this time are less concerned with the world they see everyday and are more concerned with what the world should be. Winter people usually have a healthy interest in political and economic justice and reform.

The Twelve Signs of the Western Zodiac

Aries (March 21-April 20)

Element: Fire	
Quality: Cardinal	
Ruler: Mars	
Symbol: The Ram	
Mode: Intuition	
Motto: I Am	
Aries Stones & Uses: Diamonds enhance self-confidence. Ruby raises fighting spirit. Emerald helps communication. Amethyst relieves headaches.	
Aries Colors: All shades of red	
Aries Body Areas: Head, face, upper jaw, cerebrum, cerebrospinal system.	
Aries Plants: Poppy, thistle, fern.	
Aries Attractions: To Gemini, Leo, Libra, and Scorpio.	

Aries is the first of the twelve signs of the zodiac. It is most rich in elements and represents the beginning of all things. It is primal in nature and represents the ego and will in its purest form. Aries is a symbol of the human soul descending to earth. It also represents the birth and infant child.

Ruled by Mars, the Rams is fiery. It wishes to exist for the sake of itself. This positive entity strives to be simple and pure. Aries does not take kindly to being misunderstood or mistaken for something else.

The Aries Personality

Aries signifies the first seven years of life when a human needs to nurtured in order to survive. Aries undergoes rapid changes that help it to understand its surroundings. This is also the stage that a new being connects with its environment. It will gain language, perception, socialization and other survival skills. Aries tends to be spontaneous, frank and open, but also self-centered and willful.

In their own innocent way, they approach the world with awe and wonders. The urge to be the center of attention is strong, but equally is the impulse to explore. Aries for the most part don not seek the approval of other, but they demand that people pay attention to them. Aries are sure about their abilities. Self-doubt is poison to them, but unless they learn the value of introspection they run the risk of breakdowns when their high self-confidence is undermined.

Aries need to explore their physical limits in order to develop properly. Aries prefers a head on approach to a situation. They may think about a situation at length, but will always act promptly. Aries do not like to be delayed in their efforts. They may have to learn to withdraw from life periodically in order to gain objectivity and study a problem from a distance.

Aries often display a strong desire to lead, but often lack the leadership skills to do so. This will frustrate Aries make them prone to self-pity. At their best Aries can be truly original and idealistic pioneers but at their worst only novelty-seeking, unfeeling egotists.

Taurus (April 21- May 21)

Element: Earth
Quality: Fixed
Rules: Venus
Symbol: The Bull
Mode: Sensation
Motto: I have.
Taurus Stone & Uses: Rose Quartz soothing inspires imagination. Emerald promotes learning: enhances self-confidence. Lapis lazuli deepens activities on the material plane.
Taurus Colors: All shades of blues and deep green.
Taurus Body Area: Ears, vocal chords, neck and throat, palate, salivary glands, cerebellum.
Taurus Plants: Daisy, dandelion, lily.
Taurus Trees & Shrubs: blackthorn, willow, hawthorn.
Taurus Attraction: To Libra, Scorpio, and Capricorn.

Taurus is the second sign of the zodiac. It is the first earth sign showing the fully incarnated spirit putting down roots. Taurus is the nurturing aspect of the ego emphasizing the caring, managing and maintaining stages of life. In human terms, it symbolizes a person's steady growth from childhood to adolescence.

Ruled by Venus, Taurus seeks harmony and is concerned with its surroundings beautiful. Taurus is deeply involved in the material world. Having possessions and establishing security are vital to its existence. Taurus is both fixed and an earth sign it is usually pictured as stubborn and combative, but can be flexible when necessary.

The Taurus Personality

Taurus signifies the human ages 7-14 years. The Taurean is like a child learning to control his environment. They are learning about the importance of having their own possessions, and they are learning how to use and care for their things. The Taurean learns the importance of maintenance and sharing their things. They also learn how to trade and barter. This stage is about learning to do for self. It is important that the Taurean learns that they are not the center of the world and must learn their place in social circles. One of the most important things the Taurean must learn is how to skillfully cooperate with others.

Like a child, Taurean has a deep interest in physical matters. Their strength is in setting up and developing new projects, but they do not crave constant activity. They greatly enjoy their comfort and periods of relaxation. Taurean is good for studying others and advising them in their actions. Planning, organizing and creating strategies for a project is their strength. With the Taurean there is always the danger of procrastinating and losing their drive for action.

Taurean can be team players, but must be given a degree of autonomy. Their individuality and dominant urges make it difficult for them to stay long in the role of a follower. With the Taurean stubbornness, associates at worker may often find themselves facing a "my way or no way" attitude. The Taurean is considered selfish and he/she will always protect his/her interest first. But ultimately they have the best interest of those around them. They are very loyal and live for those they love.

Gemini (May 22- June 21)

Element: Air	
Quality: Mutable	
Ruler: Mercury	
Symbol: The Twins	
Mode: Thought	
Motto: I Communicate	
Gemini Stones & Uses: Citrine lends sunshine to communication. Amber grounds high-flying imagination. Tourmaline helps concentration.	
Gemini Colors: Yellow and Light Green.	
Gemini Body Areas: Hands, arms, shoulders, nervous system and upper respiratory system.	
Gemini Plants: Tansy, yarrow, privet.	
Gemini Trees & Shrubs: Hawthorne, Oak, Heather, Cedar, and Linden.	
Gemini Attractions: To Virgo, Libra, and Sagittarius.	

Gemini is the third sign of the zodiac, representing effortless communication and quick thinking. It has a mental orientation and the first air sign. It is a symbol of the expanding mind of the adolescent as he/she grows to adulthood.

Ruled by Mercury, Gemini is centered on details and is concerned with the link between thought and verbal expression. Variety and change in both experience and atmosphere are vital to the lively Gemini. The Twins represents the Gemini and indicates a need for companionship. This sign holds the capacity for adoption and for sudden changes in direction.

The Gemini Personality

Gemini represents the third period of life (ages 14-21). The Gemini personality is like an adolescent taking his or her steps towards young adulthood. This is a period in life when the adolescent strives to mix socially while working to break away from parents and societal authority. Gemini are out spoken, but they are not rebels.

Gemini revels in their individuality and value personal freedom. They are attracted to excitement and change. Gemini are not home-bodies. They instead, prefer to get out and find their excitement. Few things give a Gemini more pleasure than traveling with friends. For Gemini, trouble means adventure. They are daring and innovative people who find pleasure in recounting their exploits while embellishing a few details.

Usually Gemini is driven by nervous energy to burn. Gemini are attracted to those activities that give them a lift, a sense of exaltation. Many forms of travel appeal to Gemini, but when faced with a long haul may just as soon prefer to give up or change direction.

Gemini likes being part of a group, but they may not readily accept the responsibilities of group membership. They are often accused of being superficial, but in their view changing one's mind is no crime. Living with few attachments is very important to Gemini.

Cancer (June 22- July 22)

Element: Water	
Quality: Cardinal	
Ruler: The Moon	
Symbol: The Crab	
Mode: Feeling	
Motto: I Feel	
Cancer Stones & Uses: Moonstone balances moodiness, relieves stomachaches. Pearl soothes sadness and depression, lessens loneliness, strengthen bones. Peridot bolsters optimism, lends inner strength, and resists emotional instability.	
Cancer Color: Pale colors, cream, white.	
Cancer Body Areas: Breast, diaphragm, stomach, skin.	
Cancer Plant: Water lilies, rushes.	
Cancer Trees & Shrubs: Heather, cedar, Linden	
Cancer Attractions: To Pisces, Scorpio, and Aquarius	

Cancer is the fourth sign of the zodiac and it is a water sign. It represents a deep feeling of being protective and the home. This is a stage in life when a person establishes a home base and he/she learns to use introspection as a means to understand life. Cancer is the stage of evolution and refinement of emotional experience in the young adult. Having children of one's own for the first time brings out strongly protective instincts.

Cancer is ruled by the Moon. It is associated with highly personal emotions, and also with the life of the subconscious. Dreams are integral to the world of Cancer. "If the ocean, whose tides are controlled by the moon, maybe said to represent the universe of diffuse feeling, then The Crab itself can symbolize the crystallization of those emotions in a single being." The hard shell of The Crab protects the extremely vulnerable interior from the outside world.

The Cancer Personality

Cancer represents the period of life, age 21- 28. The Cancerian personality is that stage in life when young adults are seeking to create homes, career and a family for the first time. The Cancerian is protective and knows how to wait, but it is a mistake to think of them as passive people. They can be aggressive when trying to get what they want, but not demanding.

They prefer that others know their diverse moods, passions, and needs. An emotional bond of empathy with others is more important than one of logic and reason. They require deep emotional connections with others as well as the needs to trust and share. Cancerians need a personal bond of mutual understanding to work well with others.

They are often viewed as unusual and are well aware of what makes them different from others. Cancerians have a talent for non-verbal communication. Things like sexual expression and the sharing of affection must be made private, regular and satisfying. This will give the unusual amount of psychological support the Cancerian needs.

Those born under this sign can make a quiet evening alone with a friend an ecstatic experience. Yet, some Cancerians periodically need to express certain unusual aspects of their personality in public. They are particularly persuasive in the private sphere, where they best work their creative juices. Those born under the sign of Cancer value the freedom of expression and release more than anything else.

Leo (July 23- August 23)

Element: Fire
Quality: Fixed
Ruler: The Sun
Symbol: The Lion
Mode: Intuition
Motto: I Create
Leo Stones and Uses: Yellow Topaz restores inner calm, eases stress. Tiger's eye grants vitality. Ruby strengthens heart energies. Milky yellow amber grounds visions.
Leo Colors: Ocher; golden hues.
Leo Body Areas: Heart, back, spine.
Leo Plants: Sunflower, chamomile, lavender.
Leo Trees & Shrubs: Holly, hazel, almond, apple.
Leo Attractions: To Scorpio, Capricorn, and other Leos

Leo is the fifth sign of the zodiac, and is the second fire sign. Leo is powerful and energetic. The Lion represents the need of the ego to make an impact on the world. People born under this sign are ambitious and self-confident.

Leo is ruled by the Sun and represents the fully realized expression through powerful and directed action. Leos like to lead those who follow out of respect. Leos like to guide with warmth. Even though the Lion rules with warmth and sharing, they will not hesitate to go into battle for truth, justice and morality.

The Leo Personality

Leo represents the fifth stage in life when the mature adults bring the full force of his/her power on the world (Age 28-35). The Lion wants to make his presence known. Leos dislike meanness and pettiness, and prefer to overlook things that are not worthy of their attention. They give all or nothing and operate on their own terms. To The Leo

128

their word is bond and they are committed to paying their debts.

Leos need to be appreciated for their efforts. They enjoy being put on a pedestal and revel in qualities of good leadership. Although Leo has no problem with praise, they prefer to work without fanfare. Leos work to convey a high confident, and a secure image.

To those born under this sign, home is a special place. Leo has to be proud of where they live, and when happy they enjoy sharing their hospitality with others. Leos are faithful and will defend those close to them. Their loyalty is legendary, but fixed attitudes and attachments to arrangements worn thin can stand in the way of their growth.

Virgo (August 24- September 22)

Element: Earth
Quality: Mutable
Ruler: Mercury
Symbol: The Virgin
Mode: Sensation, Thought
Motto: I Serve
Virgo Stones & Uses: Amethyst grants freedom from everyday concerns. Carnelian alleviates worry, stomachaches and bad dreams. Pyrite strengthens self-confidence and vitality.
Virgo Colors: Silver, indigo, dark violet.
Virgo Body Areas: Abdomen, small and large intestines, pancreas, spleen, metabolic system.
Virgo Plants: Wintergreen, sage, privet.
Virgo Trees, Vines & Shrubs: Hazel, almond, apple, grapevine, blackberry, white poplar, aspen.
Virgo Attractions: Gemini, Pisces, and Taurus

Virgo is the sixth sign of the zodiac. It is the second earth sign after Taurus and the second sign to be ruled by Mercury with The Gemini. The Virgo is analytical and very careful.

Virgo symbolizes that time in life when all life needs a systematic approach to daily concerns. It represents the life of the adult ego and the efforts one make to give structure and purpose to life. The Virgin is a serious image that is highly selective of most forms of human experience

The Virgo Personality

The Virgo is the sixth period of life representing the age 35- 42. The Virgin compares to a middle aged person steadily making their way through life inevitably meeting and solving problems of mid-life crisis. Virgos are particular in what they share with others.

The inner Virgo does not live in a romantic inner world. Their world is taken up analyzing, solving, assessing. The Virgin is future oriented and focused on personal plans and working toward goals. For example, the careful considerations one makes when planning to take time from work and go on a nice vacation. The very careful and detail packing is the hallmark of the Virgo.

The Virgin can be spontaneous, but there is always the underlying need for structure. They live to serve others and make excellent family members and worker associates. Virgos contribute well to group efforts (sometimes to a fault).

Virgos enjoy word play and wit. They have a tendency to see things in literal terms and expect people to keep their promises. Virgos often communicate with people in a non-verbal fashion. They expect their needs to be met without having to communicate them verbally.

Traditionally, the Virgin is regarded as modest and conservative, but most Virgos can step out of the conventional moral stance and express their passion for life without restraint. This is a freedom they allow themselves that they rarely accept in others.

Libra (September 23- October 22)

Element: Air	
Quality: Cardinal	
Ruler: Venus	
Symbol: The Scale	
Mode: Thought, Sensation	
Motto: I weigh	
Libra Stone & Uses: Opal frees up energy, enhances judgment. Jade helps kidney functions, bolsters courage to make compassionate decisions.	
Libra Colors: Primary colors, shocking pink, night blue.	
Libra Body Areas: Kidney, lumbar spine, ovaries, descending colon.	
Libra Plants: Pansy, primrose, violet, strawberry.	
Libra Trees, Shrubs & Vines: white poplar, aspen. a grape vine, and blackberry. Ivy.	
Libra Attraction: To Aquarius, Aries, and Taurus.	

Libra is the second air sign and the second sign to be ruled by the planet Venus. It is the seventh sign of the zodiac and is the most socially involved of all the signs. Venus represents the need of the mature human being to take his/her place in society. In addition to that Venus is like a coach who knows the role of every player in the game of life

The Scale represents the need for balance in life. Indeed, weighing out life decisions can go very far in Libra. It may lead to well-considered opinions, or result in indecision and uncertainty. Libra focus is on fair treatment for all, but can at times be overly judgmental.

The Libra Personality

Libra represents the period of life from age 42- 49. The Libra personality is like the mature adult going through the mid-life period and embarking on a journey of new beginnings. The second half of life for Libra involves redefining social roles. The Libra is a great admirer of beauty and social harmony, but their controversial behavior and attitudes can create a great deal of arguments. Libra is generous by nature, but are often out of touch with the desires of other.

Libra needs to see both sides of any problem, indeed to explore every aspect of it. Because of this need, it is not uncommon for the Libra to procrastinate. When pressured to make up their mind about most anything, Libra can become very stubborn. Adequate breathing space for Libra is a must. Without it, the Libra will feel nervous and pressured. However, when they feel that they are acting in the best interest of the group, Libra has no problem pressuring others.

Libra has more energy and stamina than many of those born under other signs. It is important that they keep social situations light and have fun. They must learn not to impose their strong opinions on others, and stay up beat. Libra should take feelings of depression seriously. Physical beauty is very important to Libra. For that reason, they must beware of becoming obsessed with their appearances. The second major priority for Libra is fairness. It is important that Libras find the middle ground and avoid becoming to judgmental or overly accepting.

Scorpio (October 23- November 21)

Element: Water
Quality: Fixed
Ruler: Pluto
Symbol: The Scorpion
Mode: Feeling
Motto: I Control
Scorpio Stones & Uses: Ruby supports inner faith and courage needed to face the world. Garnet balances sexual drives. Carnelian keeps one's feet on the ground. Black Pearl grants calm and solace in troubled times.
Scorpio Colors: Black, blood red, charcoal gray.
Scorpio Body Areas: Nose, genitals, blood, urethra, bladder.
Scorpio Plants: Root vegetables, hemlot, and black poppy.
Scorpio Grasses & Vines: Ivy, reed.
Scorpio Attraction: To Capricorn, Leo, and Pisces.

Scorpio is the second water sign and the eighth sign of the zodiac. Scorpio is primarily ruled by Pluto and supported by Mars. Scorpio is a symbol that demonstrates the power of middle age to direct and control the life around it.

Scorpio has two symbols. The most common is the defensive scorpion. The less common symbol is the soaring Eagle. Scorpio has a far-seeing nature that can ascend to great heights and descend to great depths. The Scorpio has the capacity to pull away from people and focus on serious matters and tend to them in a purposeful fashion. With the influence of the planet Pluto, Scorpio has very strong sexual energies and insight into the mysteries of inner human transformations.

The Scorpio Personality

131

Scorpio represents the age 49 -56 and the eighth period of life. This is the onset of middle age and a period in life when individual's attempt to achieve full power within his/her social circle. This may include being a dominant force in the family, community or workplace. It may also include reaching the high point in one's creative achievement. Scorpios are often serious peoples, but are not usually confrontational. They prefer to keep their weapons reserved until threatened.

No other sign under the zodiac has been unfairly labeled than Scorpio. They have been commonly labeled as underhanded, wicked and over-sexed. Scorpio has a deeply intimate connection to the unconscious world, and the themes of death and rebirth play a very big role in their lives. For this reason, it is a difficult and sometimes agonizing transformation in the personality of Scorpio is not uncommon.

Scorpio has an instinctive knowledge of the serious and tragic nature of life. Therefore, despite their great sense of humor and appreciation for the ironies in life, they are suspicious of half-baked philosophies, superficial attitude and undue optimism. Scorpio has an addictive personality and must beware of self-destructive tendencies and overly controlling behavior.

__Sagittarius__ (November 22- December 21)

Element: Fire
Quality: Mutable
Ruler: Jupiter
Symbol: The Archer
Mode: Intuition
Motto: I Philosophize
Sagittarius Stones & Uses: Turquoise protects against catastrophe. Amethyst promotes mildness and understanding. Citrine acts as agent between lower and higher selves.
Sagittarius Colors: Denim blue, beige, bronze.
Sagittarius Body Area: Hips, thighs, liver, veins, the muscular system.
Sagittarius Plants: Asparagus, chestnuts, soybeans.
Sagittarius Trees & Grasses: Reed, elder, yew.
Sagittarius Attractions: To Gemini, Aries, Taurus, and Virgo.

Sagittarius is the third and last fires sign of the zodiac. It is the ninth sign of the zodiac and is ruled by the plant Jupiter. The ninth zodiac represents the growing philosophical outlook of the human spirit. This outlook is expansive with the capacity to see the full picture.

Sagittarius is the archer, a wise centaur who is half-horse and half-man. Its focus is always to the heart of any matter. Sagittarius may deviate towards excess going too far, too fast, but will always encourage others not to limit themselves to petty or base actions. Its energies urge itself and others to see the positive side of things.

The Sagittarius Personality

Sagittarius symbolizes the period of life between the ages 56-63. The Sagittarius personality is that fully empowered individual who has advanced to a stage in life when he/she is focused on personal or universal concerns. They place honesty of intention and beliefs above other things.

Sagittarius lives with strong ethical principles that they apply to themselves and others. The Sagittarian always has a positive outlook, but can easily find themselves in dispute over their idealistic views. They have amazing energy, but may lag when crucial self-motivation and self-confidence declines.

Sagittarians are eternal students, and have a deep interest in nature and animals. Their love for knowledge keeps them constantly seeking to know more about the world. Many Sagittarians learn to ultimately reject many of society's views in favor of a higher truth. They must be careful not to push their beliefs on to others.

The centaur's love of travel is legendary, but once it finds its comfort zone, Sagittarian can be content to stay in one place. In their home, Sagittarians are free to explore their thought and come up with new and challenging projects. Because Sagittarians are constantly looking for new ways to express themselves, they are rarely ever bored.

Capricorn (December 22- January 20)

Element: Earth
Quality: Cardinal
Ruler: Saturn
Symbol: The Goat
Mode: Sensation
Motto: I Master
Capricorn Stones & Uses: Diamond raises self-confidence, enhances ambition. Falcon's Eye augments visionary power, sparks intuition. White sapphire combines discipline with friendliness.
Capricorn Colors: All shades of brown, orange.
Capricorn Body Areas: Teeth, skeletal system, knees.
Capricorn Plant: Hemlock, burdock root, black poppy.
Capricorn Trees: Yew, elder, birch.
Capricorn Attraction: To Taurus, Scorpio, and Leo.

Capricorn is the third and last earth sign, the tenth sign of the zodiac. They are ruled by the fateful planet Saturn. Capricorn is also the first of three zodiac signs that might be called the universal signs (with Aquarius and Pisces). Capricorn represents the serious perspective of maturity and how the spiritual individual connects with the universe. Economy, the conservation of energy, and a responsible approach to everything typify the Capricorn attitude.

The Capricorn Goat grazes for a time, but eventually seeks a higher place on the mountains above. It is characteristic of Capricorn to strive to the top and stay there. They are fateful to nature, but never forget the important of free will and assertiveness.

The Capricorn Personality

Capricorn is meant to represent the tenth period of life ages 63-70. It is that stage of life when mature people need structural support and security. It is also a stage in life when thoughts and ideas might be described as complete or crystallized. Their focus is serious, responsible and a desires to limit rather than expand. Capricorns are conservative, but that does not keep them from trying to reach new heights. They function in a persistent manner. Capricorn is not preoccupied with time tables. Their focus is on persistence and hard work.

Capricorn is the most difficult sign to characterize. Those born under this particular zodiac are very diverse. The one thing they all share is a sense of fatalism. Their acceptance of hard times, trial, and suffering as a part of life gives them a rare acceptance of things. Capricorns may grow uneasy when things are going too well. They are accepting of their roles in life and lack the flexibility needed for change.

Capricorn has an instinctive knowledge of power, and must beware of any developing dictatorial behavior. Generally, Capricorns are how to people. They can tell people how to do things and surprise people with their in depth understanding of things. Capricorns place a great deal of faith in their experiences and embrace their ideas religiously. If they make a mistake or go in the wrong direction, it may take a lot of time and effort by their opponents to show them their errors in judgment.

Aquarius (January 21- February 19)

Element: Air
Quality: Fixed
Ruler: Uranus
Symbol: The Water Bearer
Mode: Thought
Motto: I Universalize
Aquarius Stone & Use: Amazonite opens up inspirational faculties. Aquamarine releases emotions, combats depression. Hematite helps ground Uranian influences. Amber calms restlessness.
Aquarius Colors: Electric blue, silver gray, fluorescent color.
Aquarius Body Areas: Lower Legs and ankles, circulatory system.
Aquarius Plants: Dandelions, resins, frankincense, myrrh.
Aquarius Tree: Birch, rowan or mountain ash, ash.
Aquarius Attractions: Aries, Gemini, and Libra.

Aquarius is the eleventh sign of the zodiac, the third and last air sign, and along with Capricorn and Pisces increasingly universal in orientation. Aquarius is ruled by Uranus and it symbolizes advanced thought that transcends our physical state and permits us to view the infinite in all things. Aquarius is all about acceptance of every point of view, and shows the universal wisdom inherent in actions and thoughts.

The Water Bearer brings truth and a well of wisdom for all to share. Its energy must be disciplined and properly guided without weakening its impact. Aquarius teaches the value of science and extrasensory powers for higher awareness and spiritual transformation.

The Aquarius Personality

Aquarius is the eleventh period of life age 70-77. It is characterized by an increasing detachment from the earthly life. Restrictions and limitations are easily transcended by the accepting nature of Aquarius. Their personalities are unpredictable and eccentric. They often have a reputation for idiosyncratic behavior. Aquarius needs their freedom to express themselves and use their imagination. Aquarians should have as few restrictions as possible.

Joy is essential for Aquarians. They are far more accepting than most and they are often bewildered by rejection. Water Bearers are happy and understanding, but when under attack they can fly off the handle or withdraw from others.

Aquarians strive to maintain objectivity and might be regarded as cool or without emotions. They have the ability to skate through life measuring situations and reacting quickly. As a paradox, despite their happy and free spirited ways, Aquarians are often attracted to the extremely dark sides of others.

The Pisces (February 20- March 20)

Element: Water
Quality: Mutable
Ruler: Neptune
Symbol: The Fish
Mode: Feeling
Motto: I Believe
Pisces Stone & Uses: White opal enhances awareness of illusion. Jade balances kidney function, allays fears. Pearl offers soothing consolation. Amethyst protects against addictive influences.
Pisces Colors: Mauve, purple, aquamarine.
Pisces Body Area: Feet, toes, lymphatic system.
Pisces Plants: Mosses, ferns, seaweed.
Pisces Trees & Shrubs: Ash, alder, pomegranate, dogwood, furze, gorse, wild olive.
Pisces Attraction: Aquarius, Cancer, Scorpio.

Pisces is the ultimate water sign and the most evolved of all zodiac signs. It is controlled by Neptune and to a lesser degree Jupiter. Pisces is the merging of the human soul with the Cosmos and the highest powers of the universe.

The symbol of Pisces is two fish swimming freely in a cosmic ocean teaching us the value of fellowship. It also represents the capacity to see deeply into the life of things. Pisces teaches us not to be afraid of death and that our transformation from the earthly into the spiritual is just the beginning.

The Pisces Personality

Pisces is the twelfth and last sign of the zodiac and it represents the twelfth and last period of life age 77- 84. It symbolizes a spiritual step away from the earthly and advancement towards the cosmos. Pisces is a dreamy, spiritual and deeply emotional personality. They are not known for their practicality. Those born under the sign can be typed as dreamers and when presented as a gift makes a very fine gift. Pisces are generous givers and make very good companions, but they also need their space and plenty of alone time.

Pisces are very sensitive and that can make it difficult for them to build an easy social life. They take a risk of becoming loners. Pisces is known as a sign of sorrow and suffering. They can be vulnerable to depression and sometimes suffer from self-pity.

Pisces are very impressionable and often have good memories. They are true believers and are inclined to devote themselves to others. Those born under this sign are highly empathetic and respond to people in need with great compassion. Pisces must be careful not to let people take advantage of their generosity.

Bibliography

Gay, Harriman, Hendrick, Kreinin, and Leavenworth, *Family Living*, Englewood Cliffs, New Jersey: Prentice-Hall Inc, 1991. (A Simon & Schuster Company)

Don and Mary Merki Ph.D., *Health: A Guide To Wellness*, New York, New York: Glencoe, 1994. (Macmillan/MacGraw-Hill)

Chirs Marshall, *The Complete Book Of Chinese Horoscope*, New York, New York: Stewart Tabori & Chang, 1996.

Jack W. Wright, *Resume's For People Who Hate To Write Resume's*, Livermore, California: Shastar Press, 1994.

Gary Goldschneider and Joost Elffers, *The Secret Language Of Birthdays*, New York, New York: Penguin Studio Books, 1994.

Charles G. Morris, *Psychology: An Introduction*, Englewood Cliffs, New Jersey: Prentice-Hall Inc., 1990.

Joceline K. Alexander, *Texas Lay-Midwifery Manual*, Austin, Texas: Texas Department of Health, 1985.

Armin A. Brott and Jennifer Ash, *The Expectant Father: Facts, Tips, and Advice For Dads-to-Be*, New York, New York: Abbeville Press, 1995.

Jean Lush and Patricia H. Rushford, *Emotional Phases of A Woman's Life*, Old Tappan, New Jersey: Fleming H. Revell Company, 1987.

C. Norman Shealy M.D. Ph.D., *The Complete Guide To Alternative Medicine: An Illustrated Encyclopedia of Natural Healing*, Rockport, Massachusetts: Element Books Limited, 1996.

David Hoffmann, *The Complete Illustrated Holistic Herbal: A Safe and Practical Guide to Making and Using Herbal Remedies*, Rockport, Massachusetts: Element Books Limited, 1996.

Clare Maxwell-Hudson, *The Complete Book Of Massage*, New York, New York: Random House, 1988.

The Making of a Moor Woman: A Father's Guide for Raising His Daughter
Volume I: Book Two

Section 1: Adolescence/Puberty (7)

The Five to Seven Year Gap

Six years of age to the age of eleven

Around the age of six, your daughter should begin learning her life as an infant-woman and woman-child. She should be acquiring a comprehensive education in the proper care of a preadolescent heart, mind, body, and soul. The proper care of her heart should include both those experiences that brought her pleasure, as well as those experiences that brought her great pain. One of the most important things your daughter will learn at this stage in life is the art of bringing the good things of the world in balance with the bad.

She should be learning the nature of her personality and character, and how her personality places on the universal scope. At this stage of your daughter's development, she should be receiving a deeply rooted introduction to the woman she will learn to be for the rest of her life. Your baby's mother and the other women in her life will likely play a very important role in her learning.

She should learn as much as she can about her time in her mother's womb, and the actual delivery. Her life as an infant and woman child should be discussed in great detail. Your daughter should be well versed in her manner, attitudes, fears, and pleasures. Her behavior during infancy and childhood will teach her a lot about herself and her early relationships with the people in her life.

Twelve years of age to the age of seventeen

For your little angel, puberty will begin as early as 10 years of age. By the time she celebrates her 12th birthday, she may have already began her first menstrual cycles. The hormones that are flooding her body and rolling in and out like the ocean's tide will have a big affect on her physically and emotionally. It may also have an interesting affect on her personality.

When your daughter begins her menstrual cycles, she will cross the threshold of womanhood and enter a world of much greater womanly needs and responsibilities. This stage in her life will mark a very special time in her development. Adolescence and the menses will open doors of understanding and awareness that will connect her with the other women in her life. These new experiences will bring about emotional maturity and growth that will put her life as a woman in high gear.

Although our society will try and pair her with boys her age, she will be on a spiritual, emotional, and social level much higher than the boys her age. At about 13 years of age, your daughter will establish a deep connection with womanhood and womenhood that will separate her from her male counter part in almost every way. She will establish a natural bond with woman and the role of a woman at the ages 13 and 14. Her male counter part will not know such a connection to men and the many roles of manhood until the ages of 18 and 20.

The better your baby girl learns to walk in the footsteps of the women before her, the better prepared she will be for all of the challenges that come with being a woman, wife, mother, grandmother, and godmother. The time she will spend with the women that represent the responsible women in your family, and the pillars of your community will be priceless. Work with the women who will interact with your daughter and make sure that their curriculum for womanhood is comparable to your own.

At this stage, your daughter should begin learning the proper way for a woman to care for her heart, mind, body, and soul. This is where she learns the major differences between the life of an adolescent woman and a woman child. She should learn to comprehend the valuable bridge (puberty) that links child to woman. These years should be spent exploring the different stages of womanhood and all of the internal and external changes that she will know throughout her life.

As your daughter learns to function well as an adolescent, she will advance quickly to young adulthood. By the time she is 17 years of age, she should have the maturity and awareness to begin accepting the invitation of a gentleman caller and potential marriage (life) partner. At the age of 17, your daughter should be prepared to receive men who have the "4 M's of Man" fully intact. Expect your daughter to attract mature men 5 to 7 years older with their live in high gear.

These men should be at least 22 to 24 years of age, and they should be ready, willing and able to perform the duties of a man in you and your woman's absence. They should be prepared for the role of a man who will one day be the counselor, teacher, master, and coach of a developing young woman.

Eighteen years of age to the age of twenty-four

Between the ages of 17 and 21, your daughter should be focused on building a strong relationship resume. She should be mastering the lectures of the women who are teaching her how to be a woman, and learning to apply that information in relationship exercises. The lectures and labs should be designed to help her complete the adolescent stages of development and begin her young adult learning.

This formal education will teach your daughter to be a good and proper "help meet" in a man's life. This is a very important advancement for your daughter. Much of her future development of a woman depends on her connection with a good and proper man. She should learn to serve him responsibly and know her place in his world.

One of the most important things your daughter will learn at this stage of her life is the sexual power she will command as a new woman. She must learn the value of her virginity, youth, and innocence. Your daughter must learn the scope of her relationships with the people in her life, and understand the importance of properly managing those relationships.

Your baby girl must not be taught that she is no longer an infant woman or woman-child. She must understand that each and every stage of womanhood is hers to have for the rest of her life. She should be taught to embrace each age and season of her life as pieces to a puzzle. Everything your daughter will learn throughout her life as a woman will be used and reused in many different ways. She should know that everything she learns throughout her life will be relived through the lives of her children and grandchildren.

At 21 years of age, the object of your daughter's affection should be a man at least 28 to 32 years of age. The ideal range for your daughter to make her spiritual connection with a man is 20 to 24 years. At these ages, she will have adequate time to meet a man and build a solid relationship with him before making him some babies.

The Preservation of Innocence/ the Breaking of the Flesh

The day your daughter is brought into the world, she will be born fresh and innocent. As a beautiful baby girl, she has never had sexual intercourse or suffered the ill affects of any sexual perversion. She is unused, untouched and pure. One of the most important responsibilities you will share with your daughter's man is the preservation of her innocence. He must be a man who is prepared for the special responsibility of leading your daughter in the right direction.

Purity Consists of....
- A man must be a commanding force that will rule your daughter with charity and love. That charity must be from a pure heart with a good conscience, and a faith that is genuine and sincere.
- A true man must know what it means to be an institution of life. He must have an understanding of the whole man (A man is a person, place, thing and idea.) He must know that to walk in the light of truth is to walk in the company of a greater power.

Means to Purification....
- The rules established by the major and minor prophets should be observed as righteous and meant for a heart felt rejoice. Our Heavenly Father's commands for responsible living are pure and enlightening. A man's fear of the lord is clean and enduring.

A Gracious Union
- When a man claims a woman, they will reason together. He will want her to be at home with his life and the world he will share with her.
- A responsible man who has spent years preparing to properly receive the love of his life will want to make sure that the curriculum you have provided for your daughter's development matches his own. He will want to know that she has successfully completed the prerequisite learning a woman needs to be a good "help meet". (See The Making of a Moor Woman Volume 2, Book 1)

A Pure Faith/Religion
- A true man is committed to a pure religion, pure faith, and is undefiled in his service to His Excellence on high. A man lives to aid widows and fatherless children. He is also committed to keep himself free from the unclean ways of the world.

The Word of His Highness
- The basis of a man's love for the wisdom of His Highness is its purity.

The Visions of the Purified
- "Blessed are the pure in heart: for they shall see the Creator." Mathew 5:8

- A true man is the son of our Creator and made in his likeness. Although no man is perfect, we strive to be whole in his sight. In the day of his glory, we will see him for who he is and we will know him as he is.

A responsible man, who is serious about the nature of his intimate relationships, and the proper growth and preparation of his woman, will be very careful in choosing his life partner. He will want a woman that has never been tarnished or spoiled. When a man chooses a woman, he is not only looking for a life companion, he is choosing the mother of his children, the caregiver of his elders, and a foster mother to the other children in his extended family. He will be very careful not to choose a female who might compromise his future or the future of his grandchildren

Part of preparing your daughter for her life as a woman, is teaching her the importance of preserving her state of virginity. Your daughter's maidenhood begins with puberty and adolescence and continues until a properly skilled man pledges his loyalty to the preservation of her honor. A true man will not be inclined to build anything long-term with a female who is inadequately prepared or less than a woman.

A Virgin Maiden

A virgin maiden is like a new born baby. She is a bundle of energy that is happy and affectionate. She responds to love, warmth, and understanding. Like a little baby, she love to learn new things and are always open to explore and experiment with new things. Her heart is pure and sincere, her mind is like a sponge, her body is new to touch, and her soul is rich with substance.

As a virgin your daughter will be like the primary color white. She will be fresh, clean and colorless. She will be a reflection of light always bright and cool. White is a primary color that when new looks smart and crisp, but if you are not careful it can be easily soiled. White tends to pick up stains and it is often difficult to preserve.

Every step you take to preserve your daughter's innocence should be taken very serious. It is one of your daughter's most precious gifts. A daughter's innocence is to the human spirit, what fertilizer is to the root of a growing tree. Purity and innocence enriches the soul. It helps to produce an abundance of energy and contribute to the health growth of her heart, mind, and body.

Your daughter should be taught that the life of a virgin maiden is like an untamed prairie that is natural and free. When man who has no vision passes through, a prairie is just another group of rolling hills, an empty field of wild grass and clusters of shade trees. They are unable to see the land's potential.

However, when a man of vision encounters that same untamed prairie, he sees something totally different. He would see the possibilities of his developing a beautiful farm of fresh fruit and vegetables, and a working ranch with a wide variety of healthy livestock. Such a man might in vision his building a big beautiful farmhouse, a proper greenhouse, and a barn with a barbeque pit or smokehouse.

A responsible man who has spent his entire life in preparation for the role of a lover and provider, a counselor and teacher, a minister and medicine man would look at your beautiful little, "Virgin Mary" and see things that any ordinary man would not likely see. A true man who sees the potential in a maiden woman will not limit your daughter to a relationship that makes her feel good, he will work to build a loving relationship that is good for her.

A Chaste Woman

A chaste woman is like a talented artist or master craftsman. She is a powerful and disciplined woman who is morally responsible, honorable, and whole. She is a manifestation of true love, with all of its warmth and understanding.

Such women are resourceful and enjoy learning and exploring new things. A chaste woman is likely open to responsible challenges and ready to morally fight the good fight. Her heart is pure and sincere, her mind is strong and sharp, her body is fertile, and her soul is rich and powerful.

As a chaste woman, your daughter will be like the primary color Black. She will be calm, all embracing and full of color. She will be the absorption of all light, and always whole and penetrating. Black is a primary color that is always full and rich. Unlike white, it is not easily soiled. Black absorbs all color and it preserves itself naturally. White is a new and fragile, but black is mature and whole.

Where a virgin maiden may be compared to an untamed prairie, a chaste woman would be best described as that professional developed farmland that is not only very beautiful in its design and function, but made to produce an abundance of wealth.

New Luxury Cars

A man pursues a virgin or chaste woman the same way a careful person may shop for a new luxury car, buy a tailor made suit, or order a custom built home. Consider the thoughts and desires of the average consumer. He is not looking for a car that is old or misused, because he does not want all of the troubles that come with someone else's headache.

A man buys a new luxury car so that he can be the only one who has ever really driven it. If he buys used, he will focus his attention on classic vehicles. Investing in a collector's item means purchasing an automobile that is considered innovative and top of its line. Classic cars represent a major advancement in automotive design, and they grow more valuable over time.

When a man invests in an automobile, he wants to know that the only limitations are those of the original design. The last thing he needs is to invest a lot of time and money on something that someone else has damaged or neglected. A man wants a new car that is fully equipped with everything he might want or need.

He wants all of that without the fears that come with going behind an irresponsible owner. Investing your hard earned money is like investing both your life and love it is not a little thing and must always be taken seriously. Any responsible man will take his purchases very serious.

Tailor Made Suits

When buying a new suit, a consumer wants to get something that wears well with everything he owns. He wants to look and feel fabulous. A man of means may buy his suit tailor made to fit. This will enable him to work with an experienced fashion designer who will help choose the fabrics, color, style and fashion that are ideal for him.

A professional tailor will carefully take body measurements, and sow the suit to fit his every curve. This type of shopping is popular for those who want the polished, well manicured look of a celebrity. Many people buy off of the rack of commercial clothing stores, but relatively few of them get the same quality clothing as would a person shopping with a professional tailor or seamstress.

A virgin maiden is ideal for a man who wants more than just another suit from the rack. Her innocence makes her fresh and new with plenty of room for growth. This is perfect for a man, who needs a woman tailor made to fit as an ideal "help meet".

As her first major step into this aspect of womanhood, a virgin has no bad habits or baggage from unhealthy relationships. There are no irrational fears or faulty thinking due to the time wasted with irresponsible men in pseudo-intimate relationships. Her innocence is an immeasurable treasure and serves as a very important factor when giving shape to a woman.

Tailor made suites are made with the best quality material and fashioned by people who specialize in that craft. A man can hook up with all kinds of women, but there is nothing like a new and virginal woman who is especially made for him and tailored to fit. Teach your daughter to value the life and the love of a true man.

Custom Built Home

When a man purchases a home, he is looking for something that compliments him in every way. It has to be able to accommodate him and any future life decisions he makes. A man's home is his sanctuary, his school, his work place, and his refuge. His home is where he will build his life and care for his future wife and children. Choosing a home is probably one of the biggest decisions a man will ever make.

When a man of means purchases a new home, he is likely to shop for a custom home builder. Custom builders specialize in unique home designs. With the expertise of a highly skilled custom builder, a man can buy a new home built to his exact specifications. If he needs larger rooms, lower ceilings, a hobby room or an extra den, changes can be professionally made with ease.

Teaching a young woman to be as accommodating as a custom built home is important for a responsible man of vision. A man wants to be able to give his woman proper orientation to his life and instruct her in the way that he needs her to function as his companion. One of the benefits of bringing a virgin maiden into a man's life is that there is no conflict of interests. She has never been deeply in love with anyone other than her father, and she has never been compromised by pseudo-intimate experiences with other men.

The Consummation

Ritual Sacrifice

A sacrifice is a religious ceremony in which something is given to a higher power. Sacrifices are usually given to earn favor, and achieve a proper relationship with the sacred authority. Sacrifices have included food, animals, and human beings. Many religions include a symbolic ritual of sacrifice. There are a number of theories about the origin of ritual sacrifices:

- Sacrifices are divinely inspired.

- Sacrifices are a reflection of inner conflict or uncertainties.
- Sacrifices are a result of guilt and remorse.
- Sacrifices represent a connection between humanity and sacred beings.

The Last Supper (Hebrew Nazarene Jesus)

Jesus arrived in Jerusalem for Passover week. For several days, Jesus spent part of his time teaching in Jerusalem and the rest of his time in the town of Bethany. He had a final meal with his disciples. This meal is known as the Last Supper and was a symbol of ritual sacrifice. During his last Passover meal, Jesus told his disciples to take bread and let it be a symbol of his flesh and wine as a symbol of his blood. The Christian ceremony of Communion is based on the Last Supper.

The Crucifixion/Resurrection/Ascension (Hebrew Nazarene Jesus)

Soon after the Last Supper, Jesus was accused of Blasphemy (insulting Yahweh) by Jewish high priests. Later, he was also charged with treason against Rome by the Roman governor of Judea, Pontius Pilate.

Roman soldiers mocked Jesus for claiming to be a king by dressing him in red robe, crowning him with thorns, and a reed in his hand. Jesus was whipped, beaten and nailed to the cross. Some authorities read that Jesus carried his cross to the hills of Golgotha. Others read that the Roman soldiers made a man named Simon of Cyrene help carry the cross.

Jesus was hung on the cross and positioned between two criminals. After Jesus died, the disciple Joseph of Arimathea took Jesus body to a new tomb and sealed it with a stone. The tomb was later found with the stone rolled away, and the body of Jesus gone.

According to some authorities, Jesus revealed himself to a number of different people around the time the empty tomb was discovered. After the resurrection, Jesus stayed with his disciples for 40 days and taught them. When his teaching was complete, he rose into the heavens. The rising of Jesus into the heavens is often called *The Ascension*.

Sacrament (Communion)

In Christianity, sacrament is a practice that represents the faithful worshiper receiving the grace of God. The different Christian churches recognize a number of different sacraments.

Roman Catholics and Eastern Orthodox churches have 7 sacraments and consider it an aid to salvation:
- Baptism
- Confirmation
- Eucharist
- Penance (confession)
- Anointing of the sick
- Holy Orders
- Matrimony

Protestants share sacrament in large groups, but recognize it as an individual thing between a person and God. Most Protestant churches recognize two sacraments:

- Baptism
- Communion (also called the Lord's Supper)

Quakers consider all life a sacrament, and do not observe outward forms.

When a true man takes a woman for himself, the two of them go through a process of building their relationship. From one stage to another, he will teach her how to care for him in everyway, and he will learn the proper way to provide for her. After they advance to the highest level in their relationship and she has proven her self a good and faithful servant, they will consummate their fellowship through sexual intercourse.

Sexual intercourse is a form of blood sacrifice. The bed or bed roll represents the sacred altar, the true man is the high priest, and the virgin maiden is the offering. The Communion of Christ was the breaking of bread and the spilling of wine. The Crucifixion of Christ was the sacrifice that tore the flesh without breaking bone or damaging any major organs. The Resurrection of Christ was the rebirth of life after death.

The bond between a true man and a virgin maiden has to be presented before His Majesty in honor of the sacred "hoop" established between them. When a man and his woman make love, he will pierce the hymen of her vagina breaking her flesh. The continuous penetration will spill her blood and other vaginal fluids. This is the breaking of the flesh and the spilling of her blood, and it is done without breaking any bones or the contamination of the flesh by the puncturing of any major organs. This is known as the "Blood Sacrifice".

The sexual orgasm represents the little death the two of them will experience at the height of copulation. Sexual intercourse represents the ceremony of a couples union and the communion that will be shared throughout their love affair. The consummation of your daughter and her man is a very special thing. She should be taught to give it great honor.

The Woman as a Sexual Object

Are Women Sexual Objects?

Every woman is naturally a sexual object. According to Webster, sexual is anything of or involving sex, the sexes, or sexual organs. The word object is defined as a person or thing to which an action, feelings or emotions are directed. With this in mind, it would be difficult for anyone to observe men and women interacting on a daily basis and not know the sexual impact a woman has on the average man. Woman has always been a man's greatest passion and the object of his sexual desire.

The body of a woman is a work of art. The deep feminine curve of her figure, the texture of her hair, small bones, and the smooth feel of her skin makes her the center of attention and always on display. The beauty of her sexuality includes her ability to birth and nurse a child. The raw physical beauty of a woman and her powerful role in procreation makes her sexuality the center of life and the object of human sexuality.

"There is no greater aphrodisiac, than a woman craving to be enjoyed."

There are a lot of Black American men and women that think that there is something inherently wrong with a woman being viewed as a sex object. The reason for such faulty thinking is the way we are taught to see sexuality in our society. In the United States, there is a great deal of pressure to embrace a multicultural view of the world. From the time we enter school as children to our first professional jobs in corporate America, we are under a great deal of pressure to be accepting and as politically correct as humanly possible.

Although there are many cultures, nationalities, and religions in the United States, none are more influential than those of European origin. The collective cultures of Europe have always had a considerable amount of influence in the political and social circles that direct our society. When we look at our institutions of socialization like our schools and the mass media, one would be hard pressed to find a public school system or media source that is not influenced by them in one way or another.

The negative images of human sexuality in the United States are primarily the result of the strong European influences on our society. The negative ideas that have always been popular in Europe regarding women and sex are the main source of sexual tension in America. In these cultures, women have always been considered weak and useless, and sex was often regarded as wicked or immoral.

In these pagan oriented cultures, sex took on a lot of different forms that in many societies would have been considered perverse. From Greek toga parties to Roman orgies, pagans had their share of sexual depravities. Overtime, people in European cultures began to travel and migrate to other parts of the world where they interacted with societies with superior social mores and advanced religious beliefs and practices.

When the pagans of Europe began adopting the ideologies of Middle Eastern and African cultures, they began to see the need for healthier and more responsible sexual practices. As Europeans compromised and in some cases abandoned their pagan sexual rituals to the pagan goddess Aphrodite and the god Eros, they began to turn their hearts and minds to their European interpretations of Judaism and Judo-Christianity.

With the birth of the Roman Catholic Church, came a whole new set of ideas regarding the role of the women and human sexuality. The church made sex a sinful, dirty thing that led to feelings of great fear, shame, and self-hatred. With the woman being the object of human sexuality, she became the object of those fears and shame. She became the source of that self-hatred.

European women were divided into two classes. One class was the Madonna. These were the women who came to represent the churches romantic ideas of both the Virgin Mary and the mythological queen of the goddess, Hera. These women were not allowed to communicate openly about sexuality, and were taught that decent women are not supposed to explore the joys sexual intercourse.

The second class of women was the whores or women of low account. The whore was any woman who dared to express her feelings about sex or sexuality. She did not have to necessarily engage in a sexual act to be considered a whore. If she discussed her menstrual cycles or openly expressed her attraction to a man, she would be considered immoral and unrefined.

Men in the Catholic Church were also told not to engage in sexual relationships, but they were not treated with the same level of disdain when they had sex. When a man had sex, they received more of a slap on the wrist. When a woman surrendered to temptation, she would be treated as if she had been food left to spoil. These anti-feminists ideas were common for most of the churches history, and in many ways they still have a considerable influence in the church today.

Men, who engaged the Madonna woman, were expected to treat such a woman with exaggerated courtesies and praise them as they would the Mother of Christ. Men, who married such a woman, would sometimes develop sexual issues brought on by the fear that an impure sexual act, attitude, or feeling was morally wrong. When men and women of the Catholic religion experience these feelings, it was often referred to as, "Catholic Guilt".

Throughout European and European American history sexuality was used in many negative ways. When kings of very powerful nations would go to war and take over another people, it was common for soldiers to rape the women of the conquered people in order to humiliate that culture. Soldiers would violate and impregnate the women of their enemies to create a mixture of their blood.

The women who are violated and gave birth to the illegitimate child of the enemy would sometimes be mistreated and rejected by members of her own clan. She would suffer that abuse for allowing herself to be raped by the enemy. Her child would be considered a half breed and also treated like an outcast. Many men felt it was beneath them to raise a child that had the blood of their enemy. In these situations, a woman's sexuality was actually used to hurt her entire race and culture.

In the Victorian Age, the social mores of many European cultures required women to wear clothing that covered the whole body. Not only were women expected to wear clothing that covered them neck to toe, but the clothing worn was never close fitting. Women were not allowed to wear clothing that showed the contours of their figures.

When men and women spoke of the human body, custom dictated that certain parts of the body not be descriptively named. If people made reference to a woman's arm, thigh, or leg, they would often use the word limb. Making a direct reference to a particular part of a woman's body was considered immoral. It was considered wrong to make reference to a woman's body with words that were thought to be sensual or sexual.

In early European American history, there was a distinct difference between a proper woman and a prostitute. There was a difference in both their manner and dress. A proper woman would wear a full length dress that covered her body. A prostitute would dress provocatively. Her choice of clothing would expose her legs, shoulders, and at time her breasts (or cleavage). Prostitutes wore lingerie, and certain colors that were considered inappropriate.

In the colonial days of American history, the Europeans created religions that were considered Christian. The doctrine and practices of those religions were overtly sexist. Like the societies in Europe, the early settlers created a world for little tolerance for sexual expression. The standards for sexual conduct were very strict for women and very relaxed for men. Their lack of respect for women was visible in customs, art, literature, and legislation.

If a man and woman were unfaithful to their spouse, the man would be forgiven his weakness. Many times, the woman would be blamed for the sexual misconduct of the man. When a woman was found being unfaithful to her husband, she would be pushed aside and treated worse than an animal. In some cases, she may have had a letter or mark placed on her to tell everyone that she was no good.

In modern America, these ideas are still common in many social circles. Even with all the advancements in civil rights, there are still a lot of destructive ideas and images plaguing the minds of people in our society. Despite their many accomplishments, women in the United States are considered less competent than men. Our society still considers femininity inherently less valuable than masculinity. Masculine strength is considered greater than feminine strength and necessary for certain leadership roles.

The feminist movement has worked very hard to combat the negative images of women and women's sexuality. The images of sexuality among Europeans have for many years been a dirty thing. It was the one thing that no one was ever supposed to talk about. The idea of a woman being a sexual object still carries with it the negative social stigmas and negative cultural stereotypes.

In our society, sex has always been that house on the far end of town where men secretly went to take of their pleasures. It was the back streets of the warehouse district where the women of the night went to collect their rent money. Sex was that dirty little secret that a father kept in the bottom of his underwear drawer.

Women represented the so called sinful sexual desires of their men. The men had no respect for women, and their hang-ups about sexuality made a woman's sexuality a very ugly thing.

In the United States, teaching sexuality is controversial and not considered an important responsibility. It is not traditionally taught in schools, churches, community, or cultural organizations. Sexuality in America is something that men and women are introduced to in their youth with little or know formal instruction. Adolescent males and females are left alone to explore sexuality carelessly with no supervision.

The professional information about sexuality that is made available to most young people exist only in pamphlets given out in clinics, and the cookie cutter sections in the text books of their local high school. These sources primarily teach the basics in anatomy and physiology with some mention of sexual transmitted diseases. All of them tailored to fit the political agenda of the local government. Last, but not the least; there is the popular religious spookism taught at the local churches about the evils of sexually transmitted disease and there relationship to the devil and horny sinners.

In main stream America, sex education has not always been considered a priority for healthy living. Our daughters are not taught the skills of a Geisha, and our sons are not taught the art of Karma Sutra. Despite the research and opinions of professional doctors, sex in main stream America is still treated as a foreign part of our lives.

Young women in the United States are basically left to follow in the footsteps of the people before them. When it comes to sex, many parents leave their children at the mercy of their peers, and the mass media. Young women are left to stagger into relationships and wonder what is good for them. For many young women, who are exploring sexual relationships in this manner, it has proven to be a very dangerous thing.

In Our Culture as African Americans

When exploring the values and norms of those African ethnic groups that are humane, we find that the attitudes regarding sexuality, womanhood, and procreation take on a much healthier tone. Women are not made to be ashamed of their bodies. Women are not made to feel that there is anything wrong with being the object of human sexuality.

In mainstream America, exotic dancing is mostly regarded as a negative thing. It is considered to be disrespectful and degrading to women. In many African societies, exotic dancing takes on a whole new meaning. Dancing in a manner that is sexually suggestive could be considered part of a mating ritual. In these cultures, such erotic styles of dancing is a time honored tradition and part of a marital ritual in which a woman performs for the pleasure of her man.

In parts of east Africa, women will dance for the man she desires to have as a husband. She will draw him in to her, they will dance, and through that ritual they will be with each other for the rest of their lives. In many of these societies, lust, love, sexuality, and marriage are all considered a healthy part of building an intimate relationship between man and woman.

In the primitive culture in Africa, sexuality, procreation, the fertility of a man or woman are considered sacred. Many of these cultures have idols that symbolize the sacred relationships mankind has with higher powers. Sexuality and the ability to reproduce are regarded as a major physical and spiritual connection to our Creator. Sexuality and the power fertility are honored as spiritual deities. They are viewed as sacred and holy. These gods and goddesses are given the highest respect.

In a society of people that embraces sexual intercourse, pregnancy and childbirth as something miraculous, the women who wear the title "sexual object" are treated with great reverence. The term sexual object takes on a meaning that differs greatly from those of European cultures. When we praise an African (or African American) woman as a sexual object, we are recognizing them as our sacred link to a fellowship with the Creator and the lesser gods of his court.

Almost all of His Majesty's creatures have some kind of mating ritual. In ethnic groups not crippled by irrational fear and religious superstitions, a woman's ability to erotically titillate and tease a man to a natural high is a very natural and beautiful thing. In such societies, men are not considered weak when possessed by love and healthy lust for women. They are not taught to fear the sexual power of a woman, or feel intimidated by the feminine strength of a woman. These men are taught to know and respect a woman's place in their world.

The African woman, like her African American sister, is taught to see the physical beauty of her body and respect the power she wheels as a woman. Nudity in many African ethnic groups does not carry the negative stigmas common to European cultures. These women are not taught to see femininity as a short coming. These women are taught to appreciate their skin color, the strong and distinguish features of their faces, and the curves of their hips and breasts.

These women are powerfully built and have great athletic ability. They are taught to have a high level of respect for their physical strength and athletic talent. As a culture, we must teach our Black women to see their bodies as a temple of His Highness and vessel of life. Such teachings are essential for the healthy growth and development of the Negro woman.

Among the more primitive societies, there is a premium placed on virginity, and the practice of polygamy was more than a matter of tradition, it was a matter of survival. Young men learned to take responsibility for more than one woman, and young woman learned to work together for the good of them and their extended families. Women, who share the responsibility of caring for her husband and child with her husband's other wives, are not made to feel inadequate.

For the wives who shared the responsibilities of the family, sharing the love of the husband is a beautiful thing. Being apart of a family and sharing the pressures of motherhood and the responsibilities of a spouse, is understood to be their honor and privilege.

Let me make one thing perfectly clear. I am in no way asserting that African societies and cultures are perfect models for life. I am merely pointing out some of the more positive aspects of certain African culture in respect to our topic.

The truth is there are many customs and traditions practiced on the African continent, and a lot of those practices are wrong and unsettling. When studying African culture it is important to know the difference between what is and what was. Some of the traditions and practices learned in African studies are authentically African, and some are both the welcomed and un-welcomed influences of foreign cultures.

Like the races or collective cultures of any continent on the globe, there is a history of both good and bad in Africa. There are over 800 ethnic and linguistic groups, and at least 3000 religious practices of African Tradition. There are many moral and social issues between the men and women of Africa, and there are influences from all over the world working to improve them.

"There is nothing sexier than a beautiful woman craving to be enjoyed, and nothing more natural than a loving man doing all he can to please her."

The Menstrual Cycle Training Session/ Breathing Method

Menstruation is the periodic cyclical shedding of the blood-filled lining of the uterus that occurs in a woman who has not become pregnant. Menstruation represents the fertile years of a woman's life. It begins the first day of blood and ends before the next menstrual cycle. Menstrual periods begin at puberty and continue until menopause. Menstruation is the end of a complex series of hormonal interaction.

The periodic shedding of the endometrium and the unfertilized ovarian egg will occur 14 days after ovulation begins. Through uterine contractions a woman's menstrual discharge will be expelled through the cervix and into the vagina. Blood loss is usually 2 fluid ounces (60 millimeters) and usually lasts between 1 to 8 days. (The average period of bleeding is 5 days.) Menstruation last between 24 and 35 days in 95% of women. (The average menstrual period will last 28 days.)

Pregnancy is the period from conception to birth. There is an average weight gain of 28 lbs (12.7 kg). Much of the weight increase will take place in the last 20 weeks. Just before birth, the fetus weighs about 7.5 lbs (3.4 kg), the placenta and fluid about 3 lbs (1.4 kg). The remaining weight is fat stores and water retention. About six weeks after delivery, the woman usually returns to her pre-pregnancy weight.

A healthy pregnancy requires the desire to have a baby, and a strong healthy body. A pregnant woman needs a balanced and nutritious diet. There should be no smoking or alcohol, and drugs should only be used with the doctor's permission. A pregnant woman needs proper exercise. A pregnant woman also enjoys plenty of sex during pregnancy, as long as there is no bleeding and her water does not break.

Menopause is the cessation of a woman's menstruation. It is the time in a woman's life when certain physical and psychological changes occur as a result of reproductive and hormonal reduction. Menopause usually occurs between 45 and 55 years of age. In 70% of women there are signs and symptoms of menopause.

Hot flashes and night sweats are the most common of those symptoms. Vaginal dryness is a major symptom of menopausal women. The skin becomes thin and the body no longer produces natural oils. Psychological changes also occur as the result of hormonal changes, and the physical symptoms that will affect her daily routines.

There are metabolic changes that accompany menopause that may have a negative impact on her future development. Bone disease, heart conditions, and fatty deposits in the arteries will be come more common problem with women after menopause. Each one of these problems can lead to very serious health issues.

In order to gain some perspective on a woman's menstrual cycle and the important role it will play throughout her life, we will take a look at the United States Army Reserve. As we learn to better understand the important role of our Army Reserve, and its soldiers, we will see a parallel between the reserve duty training and the special training of an expectant mother. We will be able to better appreciate the unique needs and challenges that a woman faces with the menses.

The Army is a branch of a country's armed force that is trained to fight on land. An Army consists of ground troop, military base, and their weapons and equipment. Money plays a big role in the type of armies a nation builds. Countries with great wealth have armies with tanks and armored personnel carriers, helicopters and even ships. Countries with little wealth make use of armored vehicles, a light infantry, and ground attack aircraft.

Potential threats also shape a country's army. If a country has few potential enemies, it may have a reserve of men who may be called to serve in their national militia. Nations with political agendas that make them responsible for other countries have large armies and a considerable war chest.

Countries also differ in how they raise and maintain their armies. Some nations have drafts, some have volunteers, and others have a universal military service calling on everyone in a particular age group to serve. Most nations divide their army into regular or "active duty" army and an army reserve.

Members of regular army are always receiving training and are always on active duty. There job is to always be ready for combat. In support of the active duty units and to be ready for any crisis, many countries maintain an extensive National Guard or militia. The reserve units train citizen for immediate active duty in the event of an emergency.

The soldiers in the Army Reserves begin their training the same as regular army. After basic training and their selected advanced individual training, these reserve soldiers are assigned to a reserve unit. These soldiers will receive training one weekend a month, and additional field training two weeks a year. Members of a reserve unit live at home and work traditional jobs as inactive duty soldiers.

In addition to the Army Reserve, we will also look at the Ancient Egyptians and the important relationship they shared with the seasonal flooding of the Nile River. The more we learn about the Ancient Egyptians and the respect they had for the natural developments of the Nile River, the more we will respect the natural occurrences of a woman's body. We will better understand our woman and her need to listen to and obey the constant changes of her body.

Ancient Egyptian was the birthplace of one of the world's first civilizations. This advanced society began over 5000 years ago in the Nile River Valley. Ancient Egypt was a long, narrow strip of land through which the Nile River flowed.

The Nile River flows from central Africa through the Egyptian desert to the Mediterranean Sea. The rolling desert land lay east of the Nile valley, and mountains rose to the west. The Nile River was the lifeblood of ancient Egypt. Every year it overflowed and deposited about 6 miles of rich black soil along each bank.

The Egyptians named their country Kemet, after the black soil. The fertile soil was used for farming. The Nile River started flooding in July, when the rainy season began in central Africa. As the river flowed northward, the rainfall would cause the level of the river to rise. These flood water continued for about 3 months until the month of September when the flood water would decrease.

The Nile River was also used for irrigation, main trade and transportation routes. Ancient Egypt was known by some as the gift of the Nile. The Nile River's course through Egypt was about 600 miles (1000 km). Just as the river flowed north of what is now Cairo, the Nile River split into several channels forming the Nile Delta.

Average Menstrual Cycle

1st Week of Cycle- Surging Tide/Rising Estrogen Levels
2nd Week of Cycle- High Tide/Estrogen levels off and declines slightly
3rd Week of Cycle- Ebb Tide/Rising estrogen and overriding progesterone (subject to a Variety of feelings: some happy and sad)
4th Week of Cycle- Outgoing Tide/ Premenstrual (estrogen and progesterone levels fall)

I have often heard older Black women say that there is no reason for a woman to live through the discomforts of the menses. Many of them believe that the physical pain that women experience while on their period serves no purpose what so ever. I have even heard some of them refer to their period as "the curse".

These older women could not be more wrong. The purpose of a woman's monthly cycles is not to disrupt her life; it is meant to improve her life. A woman's menstrual cycle is meant to bring her more in tune with herself and the nature of her creation.

The purpose of a woman's menstrual cycle is to prepare her for both pregnancy and childbirth. For the life of a mother, a woman has to be prepared in her heart, mind, body, and soul. All of the changes a woman will experience are meant to prepare her for the stress and strain that comes with the adventure of pregnancy and childbirth. Just as the reserve duty soldiers prepare once a month for war or a national emergency, a woman is to prepare once a month for the 9 months of pregnancy and the many challenging hours of delivery and labor.

A woman is supposed to go through the cramping, hampering, and pain. She supposed to experience the changes in her body weight and shape. The blood and fluid that her body is flushing from her system during menstruation plays a very important role in her preparation. A woman should be taught to build-up her endurance for the pain she suffers monthly, so that she has a greater tolerance for pain during labor. Her menstrual cycle is her reserve duty training for the natural battle of giving birth.

The Nile River and its seasonal flood are like a woman's menstrual cycle. It floods for a period leaving everything man needs in order to plant the seeds of life and reproduce. In early civilizations, man did not have the technology to control their environment. In order to produce food, man had to learn about the Nile River and discipline themselves to work with the earth and her changing seasons.

Just as a woman learns to respect the natural processes of her own body, it was essential that the early Egyptians learn to respect the life and the natural flow of the Nile. A woman and her man should know her monthly development like the back of their hands. When a man takes a woman to make her the mother of his children, he is like a farmer taking responsibility for the banks of the Nile River.

The better he knows the woman's current and the health of her flood, the better he can care for her and share in her development. The same discipline and skills a woman learns during her monthly changes, she will use during the mid-life malaise, pre-menopause, and menopause. The more a man understands his woman's training and disciplines, the better he can support her in her developmental changes.

The entire 28 days of hormonal changes can be directly compared to pregnancy, and childbirth. When a woman is pregnant, she takes prenatal vitamins, learns special breathing techniques, uses a special diet, and learns healthy and proper postures. She may also learn concentration and meditation techniques, closely monitor her fluid in-take, monitor her body weight, closely observe the changes in the shape of her body, and get as much sleep as possible.

All of the exercises and techniques a woman would like to use when making a baby, should be learned, developed and practiced on a monthly basis. The same breathing exercises a woman will use for contractions during childbirth, she would want to practice with her monthly contractions. Listening to her body and learning how nutrition and fluid intake affects her monthly cycle, will help her prepare for the special diet she will need during pregnancy.

The physical fitness exercises needed to strengthen those muscles for childbirth should be practiced regularly. She should also practice Sivinanada or Yoga to learn proper postures. These postures are used to improve blood flow and may be used to take pressure off of the uterus during cramps.

If a woman has PMS, then she is more likely to suffer from PPD. The more time she spends listening to her body and learning what to expect from the whole pregnancy and birth experience, the better prepared she will be. For a woman with PMS or PPD, it is that much more important for her to make that intimate connection with her body and her monthly cycles. When it is time for a woman to make a baby, she will find her experiences from her menstrual cycle training most valuable.

Living in a high speed world where everyone needs to work, get an education, and help carry the load of providing for their families, a woman may have a difficult time trying to function with the hampering pain of the menses. If a woman needs to use medication to give her the peace of mind necessary to function, then by all means she should use it.

Women should know that there is no shame in using medication to deal with a troublesome menstrual period, but they should know not to go over board. It is not good for a woman to be taught to blanket her period with drugs. Masking the pain and the changes going on inside of her will do her a great injustice. A woman should use medication moderately and only when necessary.

The Nature of Relationships (For-profit or Non-profit)

"Love is always a privilege and responsibility, never an opportunity."

Nature of Relationships

One of the most important things your daughter will learn is how to build healthy relationships with others. As a young child she will have playmates that will help her learn the importance of sharing. When she is a few years older, her relationships will become more challenging, and she will learn what it means to function as part of a group. Whether she is building relationships with individuals or a group, there is something she should understand about the nature of relationships.

There are two types of relationships:
- For-profit relationships (exchange) intending for profit, or intended to gain an advantage.
- Non-profit relationships (charity/volunteer) not intending or not intended to earn a profit.

All men and women are social beings. As social beings, we have the responsibility of learning how to build healthy relationships. Whether those relationships are short term, long term, intimate, or casual, it is important for everyone to know the nature of those relationships. There are two types of relationships. One is for-profit and the other is non-profit.

A for-profit relationship, enable people to make social connections with individuals or groups in order to gain an advantage or earn a profit. Examples of these relationships are our places of employment, grocery and department stores, and even our housekeepers and baby-sitters. Like any business or professional person, everyone must learn to produce a good or provide a service that will earn money, credit, and securities.

In the for-profit world, the more valuable the good or service exchanged, the more of an advantage one may gain. People in almost every society work to make connections with both individuals and groups in order to exchange money, goods, or service for the things they need to advance their lives. These relationships are essential for building healthy lives.

The non-profit relationship provides people with a social link to individuals or groups, in order to give of him or herself in a charitable capacity. Non-profit relationships create opportunities for people to donate goods and volunteer services that would help others. Under no circumstances are the donated goods or voluntary services exchanged for a profit.

Examples of non-profit group relations are religious institutions, social or political organizations, and cultural centers. Individual charitable relations would be family members, friends, co-workers, and classmates. The non-profit relationship is charitable in nature and usually built on some moral, social, or personal sentiment. Non-profit relationships usually require some sort of tithe, pledge, or offering from its caretakers and members.

Although most people create fewer non-profit relationships than for-profit relationships, the non-profit relationships are in many ways more important. Non-profit relationships are personal and intimate in nature. For this reason, most non-profit relationships will continue to grow long after many for-profit relationships have ended.

People spend their entire lives building a wide variety of both for-profit and non-profit relationships. These relationships help people define themselves and connect with the world around them. These relationships also help people improve their understanding of the people in their society, as well as the institutions of socialization that help define their communities.

Building a relationship, whether for-profit or non-profit, is a sacred thing. Understanding the nature of a particular relationship is essential for the proper construction and management of that relationship. When a man and a woman build an intimate relationship, their union will have the same needs as any individual or group.

Just as a person or organization forms non-profit and for-profit relationships in order to grow, so will the union of a man and woman. It is essential that a man and his woman learn to build healthy relationships as a couple. It is also essential that the two of them build these joint relationships while keeping their personal for-profit and non-profit relationships intact.

A man and woman in an intimate relationship will build a number of relationships. These relationships will be created to help meet their needs both as a couple and as individuals. The nature of these relationships will be both for-profit and non-profit. Even though one of the goals of every couple is to develop valuable for-profit and non-profit relationships, the bond that unites them as man and woman will always be non profit. An intimate relationship is about the charity two people will share, and the voluntary services they will offer one another.

Although every man, woman, or couple will spend their entire lives building a number of different for-profit and non-profit relationships, the non-profit relationship is the only fellowship appropriate for lovers. When a woman reaches a stage in her life when it is best for her to connect intimately with her man, she will need to know how to plan, organize, coordinate, and create strategies for building healthy non-profit relationships.

Love is a charity and deep affection for the object of one's desire. It is a powerful emotion manifesting itself in deep affection, devotion, or sexual desire. A woman should know that to love a man is to commit to the charitable services she will need to provide for him. Love is about a person's readiness, willingness, and learned ability to responsibly serve another.

Check This Out!
Not Everyone Woman Deserves the Best!

The life of a human being is not simply a matter of survival, but a matter of healthy and successful growth and development. The advancements of man and woman are rooted in their successful use of tools, material, and other valuable resources. Men and women are expected to perform responsibly throughout their lives. People's performance may be graded on different levels and fall with in range from excellent to failure.

The range of performance from good to bad may be graded like this:
1. **Excellence (High above standard)**
2. **Good (Above standard)**
3. **Fair (Average performance)**
4. **Poor (Inadequate service and goods of low quality)**
5. **Failure**

According to the dictionary, the meaning of the word, "want" is to lack, to desire or to crave. The meaning of the word deserve refers to one's merit or value. The word deserve means to earn the right to or be worthy of a just reward.

In American society, people often confuse the things they want with the things they rightfully deserve. These are the people who often confuse the success of others with their own or blame their failures on the success of someone else. It is a common belief among many American females that every woman deserves the best.

For reasons no one can seem to explain, females all over the country are setting incredible standards for their lives in an intimate relationship and the lives of any potential suitors. Women, like these, have big romantic ideas about what constitutes a good man, and they live in the illusion that wanting the best is the same as deserving it. These females are requiring men to make great sacrifices and considerable investments in relationships that offer very little in return.

Consider This......

In the Olympic Games runners from all over the world compete in a number of events. In the 400m Run both men and women compete for the gold, silver or bronze medal. The gold medal goes to the fastest runner in the competition. The silver and bronze are awarded to the runner who comes in second and third.

The people competing for an Olympic medal are highly trained people who invest a lot of time and money competing in many races. The men and women who make it to the finals have qualified on a number of levels in order to compete for the gold. The people who are given the honor of running in the Olympic game represent the best runners of different countries, collective cultures, and global regions.

These people represent the best of the best, but they do not receive a medal for their want or desire to have the best. Despite the fact that every runner has sacrificed to stay competitive, worked hard, and invested a lot of time and money, only the top three runners will earn the right to stand in the winner's circle. Only the star athlete will earn the best.

Every female does not make the sacrifices necessary to be the best. Most of them fall far from it. The best is something one earns through education, extensive learning, proper discipline, and a commitment to perfection. A woman must learn that no one inherently deserves the best. She should know that being the best is the only way to have the best, and no one should receive an awarded or gift for that which they have not rightfully earned.

Making of a Black Woman

The African Woman

African women in the Americas must learn to value the important roles and responsibilities that every woman has to her Creator, her Man, and her family. These women must acquire a systematic form of development that provides them with the knowledge, wisdom, and understanding necessary to function as a true high speed woman. The African women in the Americas must learn to elect their potential suitor the way ambitious men and women choose their home, church, school, and government authority.

Relationships for adolescent or young women are part of a quest for spiritual enlightenment and self-actualization. When a true woman receives a gentleman caller, she is like a student who has committed herself to the profession and craft that will give her the means by which to build her life. Such women should only make themselves available to men who are institutions of life.

Examples of an institution of life are:
- Universities that provide academic and professional training.
- Religious organizations that are dedicated to supernatural, spiritual, and moral studies.
- Hospitals or clinics that provide medical care for aiding in the procreation of, providing therapy for the preservation of, and the restoration of human life.
- An elected government that manages a society and provides the structure and function needed to facilitate the safety and security of its citizens.

The Daily Meditation for all Young Women...

When adolescent girls begin thinking about the important decisions they will make regarding their future, they must learn to think with the mind of a woman. Life for a child is a world of great exploration and discovery. A child's first inclination is to smell it, touch it, and taste it. The life of a child is all about curiosity and experimentation. The common question in the mind of an exploring child is, "why not?"

Adolescent and young women must learn that the motivations of a mature adult are not the same as a child. As a woman, life is a number of forever changing roles and responsibilities. The lives of adults are a series of questions to be answered, problems that need to be solved, unwelcome challenges, and a never ending accumulation of debt.

In the life of a mature woman, there is no "why not?" For responsible men and women, the primary question is "why?" Young women must learn that the only real concern for an adult making real life decisions is how those decisions will impact their lives. They need to know their choices connection to their past, present, and future lives.

Every life decision an adolescent and young woman makes should:
- Contribute to her becoming a more whole human being.
- Make her a better woman.
- Help her learn to be more defined in her personality and character.

"One of the worse things the average female will do in her life is adolescent dating or adolescent courting."

The Black Woman
Adolescent girls choose their companions the way they would a source of recreation or entertainment. Relationships for young people during this stage in life are like a weekend vacation or a night on the town. When adolescent girls hook-up with a new boyfriend, it is like making plans for dinner and a movie. They are looking for a companion who has the qualities of a popular film and the charm and comfort of their favorite restaurant.

Popular films are:
- Interesting with many attractive features
- Filled with comedy, romance, drama, mystery, etc.
- Conveniently scheduled, economical, and does not require a lot of time.

Favorite restaurants offer:
- Hosts, waiters, and chefs that cater to the needs of their patrons.
- A wide variety of favorite foods, drinks, and dessert.
- A fun, welcoming, and entertaining atmosphere.
- A guarantee or assurance of satisfaction with all goods and services provided.

The Depreciating Value of Sex
Adolescent boys and girls place a premium on sex and their first sexual experiences. For both males and females, sexual intercourse is regarded as a way of asserting themselves as young adults. Males consider their first sexual conquests a right of passage and the experience is used as a ritual in male bonding. Females often see their first sexual experience as the first step towards being a woman. Many girls make the mistake of thinking that the sexual experience itself will redefine their lives, and bridge the gap between them and the mature women of their world.

In high school, boys use their parent's money, house, and car to gain the attention and win the approval of the girls with whom they want to have sex. The attention girls receive from boys and the respect the attention will earn them among their peers will go a long way towards influencing their decision to have sex.

Girls who are willing to compromise themselves are made to feel that they are the center of the world and deserving of the gifts and attention they receive in exchange for sex. Adolescent girls learn quickly that having sex with a boy commands great respect and admiration among her peers. They also learn that the power of their sexuality may increase their ability to manipulate and control their boyfriends.

The emotional and sexual influence a girl has over her boyfriend becomes a major benefit for most girls. The sexual power adolescent girls learn to wheel often becomes a major motivation to not only continue having sex, but it inspires them to explore the many ways to perform better sexually. The ability to sexually manipulate boys often gives adolescent girls a false sense of security.

When adolescent boys become protective, begin catering to, and even idolizing young girls, their behavior will commonly be mistaken for real love. Whether it is by natural desire, or simply one's ability to persuade the other, one's power to make the other bend to his or her will becomes the basis of their relationship.

As girls learn to relax their inhibitions and give sex more freely, custom dictates that the gifts they share increase in both value and number. Between the gifts, the sexual horseplay, and the admiration of their peers, many young people lose themselves to their adolescent relationships. At a time in their lives when they should be learning the importance of knowing themselves as individuals, most of them will allow themselves to be defined by their romantic relationships and the prestige of being a power or popular couple.

The prestige of a pseudo-intimate relationships coupled with an emotional roller-coaster of romantic feelings fueled by the supernatural powers of human sexuality will create an illusion of love that may prove very destructive over time. Adolescent boys, who learn to earn a girls approval through gifts and personal service, confuse the roles of a man and woman with the roles of a "sugar daddy" and his stable of whores.

Young girls, who learn to equate sexual relationships with money, gifts, and services, are often unaware that their relationships have become for-profit. These girls learn to define their companions by the things they may give them. They also learn to evaluate the quality of their relationships by the gifts and privileges that relationship may bring.

Many of these adolescent girls do not learn until much later in life that they have become whores. They often spend years trading in sexual favors before they reach a stage in their lives when they want more from the men in their lives and their pseudo-intimate relationships. It is not until then, that many of them discover that they have become "career girlfriends", and have no clue of how a better relationship is achieved.

Those who are made aware of their behavior and its potential harm to their lives often rationalize their behavior saying that it is no different than any other woman in society. These adolescent girls confuse the drama of their favorite television program and the behavior of their peers with the lives of responsible women. Many of these girls are easily misled by females, who are just as ignorant to womanhood as they are.

"Every young woman should know the importance of giving themselves time to blossom before making themselves available for an intimate relationship."

Mixing Apples and Oranges

For an adolescent, life is more an aspiration than anything. Young people live in the comfort and security that their parents provide and make decisions within a scope that their guardians ultimately control. Young people are made to think that they are making important decisions and taking on major responsibilities when most of the decisions have already been made and set in motion by those who are responsible for them. For this reason, teenagers often confuse their romantic ideas about themselves and their lives with the lives of the people on which they depend.

A girl is permitted to take on a part-time job and make a little extra money. She works hard, collects her paycheck, and saves her money responsibly. When her bank account grows to a size considerable for a teen, she begins to entertain thoughts of independence. She is aware of all the hard work she has performed, and the great many hours she has sacrificed to work and earn her money, but she has lost sight of the fact that her job and bank account only exists because her parents permit them to exist.

Young people will frequently forget that in a family they are a small part of a big thing. Adolescent boys and girls approaching young adulthood often lose sight of the well oiled parenting machine that pays the greater bills, and maintains the primary structure and function of their lives. Many teenagers struggle with the understanding that their lives and illusions of independence are nothing more than a reflection of the lives their parents have created.

During this stage, teenagers are torn between their desire to live free from their parents and their greater need to depend on them. In relationships that some teenagers may confuse as intimate, young people date and establish courtships that they share with their parents. Even though these boys and girls will regard themselves a couple, their parents are ultimately responsible for providing them with transportation, money, and a place to hang.

Most young people have the privilege of enjoying the pleasures and comforts of a boyfriend/girlfriend relationship, but few of them know anything about the greater responsibilities that make such mature relationships possible. In high school, a girl will go to the home of her boyfriend. In a single afternoon, the two of them will nibble on snack foods, have a pizza delivered, watch a little pay-per-view on cable television, rent a movie, borrow the car, and a number of other things that will not cost either one of them a dime. This is the signature of adolescent relationships.

"For most adolescent, what they learn about manhood, womanhood, relationships, and love will out live its usefulness by the age of 18."

Post High School Relationship

As girls advance to the golden stages of their sexual power, many of them have already traded their virginity and innocence for the acceptance of a grade school boy, a high school fling, and the admiration of their peers. After high school, the relationships between adolescent boys and girls change considerably. If the average teen couple does not find themselves abruptly separated by college or the military, the new challenges that come with young adulthood begins to put a major strain on their adolescent misconceptions about love and intimate relationships.

Relationships that evolve around the exchange of gifts for passion and sex will likely suffer a devastating blow. The high school boys, who have always depended on their mother's car and their father's money to entertain their companions and maintain their relationships, are all on their own. These boys no longer have their parents holding their hands.

At the ripe age of 18 and 19 years, their parents are cutting the apron string. These newly adult boys are expected to find jobs, work, and pay their own bills. They are expected to carry their own weight and take responsibility for their own lives. Some of them will move out of their parent's home and get an apartment. Many of them will want to attend college or some kind of vocational school. Regardless of their plans, the cost and their responsibilities are theirs.

Mature girls, who have grown a custom to dating boys with what seemed to be a limitless flow of cash, are suddenly limited to boys with nothing more than their good humor. For many girls, the days of having someone pick them up in a nice car, going to their favorite restaurant, and then exploring some upscale places for entertainment are all but over. Many are not likely to experience another classy night on the town for several years. Most of the girls, who want to maintain their adolescent courtships, will have to change their entire attitude and standards for dating adult boys.

When young people are spending their parent's money, there are no limits to the things they want. When those same young people have to rely on their own money, only the most conservative forms of recreation and entertainment are acceptable. Young adult girls often wonder why their relationships change so much after high school. Many girls, who have boyfriends that they have dated since high school, wonder why their companions choose to spend less time with them and more time with their friends.

Most girls do not understand what it means for a boy to lose the financial support he knew in grade school. Girls, who have never really been financially responsible for themselves, have a difficult time relating to the challenges of providing for someone else. A boy, who has a full-time job and a number of immediate financial responsibilities, has a limited cash flow for going out and having a good time.

Few young people have the education or skills to acquire professional or highly skilled jobs. Most of them do not earn the kind of money they knew living off of their parents. Most of them do not earn enough money to wine and dine on any basis. This is especially true for boys that have their own car, rent an apartment, or take classes at the local college. The money it takes to provide for them and build a possible future is more than most of them can afford even with the support of their parents.

After the average 18 or 22 year old pays their debts, there are probably only a few bucks left in their money jar. In high school, if a boy gives a girl his last $20, he often has the option of going straight his parents and asking them for additional money. As a young adult living on his own, if he gives his girlfriend his last $20, it is literally his last $20. The financial safety net that used to catch him when he misspent money or gave money away is gone.

After the average adult boy cashes his check and pay all of his bills, he may not have but $50 leftover. If he takes a girlfriend out on a date, and treats her to dinner and a movie, his entire bank account is shot until the next pay day.

A simple night on the town:
- The average meal at a simple restaurant will cost $10-$12.50 with a drink. For a boy and a girl, that is about $25 bucks with gratuity.
- A simple movie night will cost around $8 a piece ($16 for two.)
- Throw in a couple of small sodas at $3 a pop, and that is another $6.
- The average night out for dinner and a movie is about $47, and that did not include possible parking fees, gas in the car, or anything like that.

When that same boy goes out with his friends, he will split the cost of gas for the car ($5 a piece), split the cost of a twelve pack ($3.50 a piece), and end the night with a quick stop at Rudy's Fried Chicken for a two piece basket with fries ($3-4 per person). His entire evening might cost him $12 or $13.

If he takes a girl out to dinner and a movie, it will blow his entire bank roll in a single evening. An adult boy does not have enough money to entertain a girl the way he did with his parent's support. These boys elect to spend time with their friends because it does not cost as much. The same fifty dollars he would spend on a single evening will last a few weeks hanging with his boys.

Black girls dating older men…..

Many adult girls with vast experience in adolescent dating begin pursuing older men during their later years in college. After a few years of trying to adjust to the crippling changes that came with dating post high school boys, many of them will develop a hunger for a relationship with someone mature. They will begin to look for men who are already established in their profession and financially mobile. These college girls are usually ripe and aware, and focusing their attention on mature men that are likely to provide them with a deeper sense of intimacy.

In the later years of college many adult girls have begun to accumulate debt of their own, and are beginning to feel the overwhelming stress of working and going to school. For some college girls, meeting a mature man with a passion for young women and the means to provide for them is very much a dream come true. Even those girls, who never thought they would ever marry or live depended on a man, find themselves open to the possibilities of finding comfort and security in a mature man.

When these ambitious girls go out to meet such mature men, they are basically imitating the manner of women. Many adult girls approach men with the idea that a cute face and a lovely figure will get them where they want to be with almost any man. These college girls believe the things they have learned from mature women and their years in adolescent courtships, will be enough for their pursuit of real men.

When a college girl meets a man and the two of them begin getting know each other, everything is relatively simple and unfolds in away that most might expect. The two of them exchange pleasantries, and agree to go on a date. He picks her up at her college dorm, and they have dinner, and maybe a little dancing. At the end of the evening, if she is so inclined she will return to his place for a night cap.

The two of them share a night of passion and romance, and just like that the relationship is off to what seems to be a good start. Over the next few days the relationship is bliss and the whole thing is adding up to one of the best experiences of her young life. For the next few weeks, she spends most of her time with him at his place. There is so much warmth and trust between them that there are days and nights when she is left alone at his place to relax and enjoy herself.

When they first met his biggest concerns were, do we have anything in common, are our personalities compatible, and can I trust her to respect me and my things. After they had gotten to know each other, he welcomed her into his life. At that point his greatest concerns were, and can I trust her not to take anything from me without permission or violate my privacy. He is also wondering whether or not she will clean up after herself, and will she leave everything the way she finds it.

In the first few weeks they spent together, she borrowed his car and practically lived in his home. While she visited his home, she turned up the air conditioner and burned unnecessary lights with no consideration for the electric bill. She watched pay per-view movies and made what she considered a few long distant calls.

She cooked food for herself and only on occasion did she wash the dishes or clean up after herself. The girl prepared regular meals eating as much as she pleased, but rarely considered his lunch or dinner. When the college girl was permitted to entertain her friends at his place, they enjoyed plenty of beer and wine. They were also permitted to consume all of the food they could eat.

As a girl, who only knew the simple relationships of a high school adolescent, she never considered the time and energy that adults spent creating a comfortable home. She never considered the many sacrifices adults have to make in order to maintain their lives.

There were a few times that he permitted her to use his car and each time she kept the car much longer than she said she would, and always brought the car back dirty with the gas tank on empty. Even though he was in the practice of cleaning his home before going to work, he would often return home to find his house a mess.

In the little time they knew each other, she turned what could have been a very lovely relationship into a major regret. The college girl turned his place into a pigs sty. Everything he attempted to share with her was greatly exploited. She violated his personal space and his privacy going in things that were none of her business. His relationship with her was constantly demanding more, but giving very little in return.

She permitted her friends to treat his home like a zoo. In the few weeks that she was in his home, she ran up the cable bill, the telephone bill, the grocery bill, and did major damage to the content of his liquor cabinet. Even the time she spent in his car added stress on his financial budget. The time they spent together end up being a big waste of money and resources. In a very short period of time, the college girl had overstayed her welcome.

The next thing she knows, everything begins to change. All of a sudden, she finds him growing impatient with her. He is beginning to feel crowded and sometimes irritated with her being around. There is still some comfort between them, but it is definitely not what it used to be. She knows he care for her, she just cannot understand the sudden changes in his attitude.

She is still invited over to visit, but not as often. They still go out and return to his home for a night of passion, but afterwards he drives her back to campus. After a couple of weeks, he no longer allows her to use his car, stay at his place when he is not home, or permit her to bring her friends to his place to visit.

The adult girl is trying to adjust to the changes in her relatively new relationship, but becomes more and more frustrated with the distance that is growing between. She knows there is something wrong, and wants very much to fix the problem, but she does not know where to begin. Her friends tell her that there must be another woman.

They insist that she is no longer welcome to stay in his home because he is seeing another woman. Her girlfriend also explains that she can no longer use his car, because he does not want anyone to see her behind the wheel. Their frustration grows and eventually gets the best of them and one or both of them end the relationship.

Girls, who have grown to think that their primary role in a relationship is sexual intercourse, will have a difficult time understanding a woman's role in the fulfillment of a man. These girls will entertain that men are too needy, to controlling, or to demanding, when the reality is something considerably different. Many of them never learn the hierarchy of human needs and they have no knowledge or skills for providing for others.

Such girls will insist that they have done everything a woman could do for a man, and that the man just did not appreciate them. The reality is that these girls never learned to be women. They never learned a woman's place in the life of a mature man. Such girls grow up learning more about being whores, than being women. These girls learn to approach relationships as spoiled, selfish, overgrown children who have no intention on serving a true purpose.

A man, who is carefully building his life, has many responsibilities. He has to maintain his daily life, pay off past debts, and invest in his future. A man with a life has to maintain a responsible budget, keep his credit strong, and take good care of everything he owns. Every woman should know that her primary role in the life of a man is one of aid and support.

When a man has a good paying job, it does not mean that there is money to burn. Whether two people are having a friendly get together, or building a lasting love affair, a woman should be sensitive and attentive to her gentleman caller. A young woman has to be mindful of her companion's life and his many responsibilities. Every young woman should learn to be a proper helpmeet. She must learn to never be a burden. Any girl that does not learn to be a good and proper helpmeet will likely limit herself to the life of a "career girlfriend".

Closing.......

In situations like these, young college girls are confusing the life of a man with the life of an adolescent boy. With a high school boy who places a premium on sex, the role of a sexual partner defines the relationship. Mature men only put a premium on sexual intercourse if the woman is a virgin. In a relationship with a woman who is already sexually active, sex is a way for a man and woman to comfort and pleasure one another.

In the adult world, everyone has sex. It is not something that will win a girl points, popularity, or high praise. It is simple pleasure that when accompanied with other forms of affection reinforces feelings of intimacy. A woman has to know how to contribute to the life of a man and how to be a positive motivating force in his life. A woman does not just hang around. She cooks, cleans, and learns different ways to support and satisfy him.

In the mind of a girl, she will spend time at her boyfriend's house and he will pick her up in his car. It is not until she gets much older that she will realize that her admiration of her high school companion was mostly fluff. She will most likely be a mature adult when she realizes that her young boyfriend was wearing his parent's expensive clothes, that he was spending his mother's hard earned money, and driving his father's fine automobile.

A young woman will have real life responsibilities of her own when it is made clear that she spent years praising a teenage boy for his father's success and his mother's accomplishments.

Many women are almost 40 years of age when they say the words:

- "Man, I really thought I was in love with that fool."
- "Girl, I actually thought I wanted have that little boy's babies!"
- "It is hard to believe that he and I used to discuss getting older, and buying a home and getting married."

Hopefully, such women will one day look back on the time they spent with their high school sweetheart and smile when remembering all the things they shared. If they are fortunate and did not make some of the foolish mistakes that many adolescent girls do, some of them might be able to laugh to themselves when saying the word, "Isn't it is something what a young girl will do when she thinks she's in love!"

Check This Out!
The Truth in Our Word……

Angry and Bitter Females with Little or No Sexual Discretion who Trade in Sexual Favors for Goods and/or Services!

I often get dirty looks when I use words like "Bitches" or "Whores". People would put up a fuss so much that I decided to limit the use of these words altogether. I decided that it was easier to use the much longer definition of these words in daily conversations, instead of using the words themselves.

The definition of a word is based on its meaning through past use and the mechanics of the word itself. Each word has its own definition. Words and their definition are facts, and have no politics.

People often think that their personal feelings about a particular word and its use should change the significance of that word. They think that if they are uncomfortable with the use of a particular word, then that word and its definition should no longer be used in any context. Some people would even go as far as to argue that such words should be taken out of the dictionary altogether.

I am often approached by people who want to discuss relationships and all of the challenges and drama that seem to accompany them. I am at times surprised at the number of people who do not understand that their past romantic or sexual experiences affect their relationships. Average men tend to think of sex as a simple exchange of pleasure that symbolizes a woman's genuine desire to know them.

These worldly women tend to see their bodies as a type of gift card that through sexual intercourse builds cash value. Many of them believe that sharing a night of sexual pleasure with a man should build a financial account. They believe that a little "Horizontal Hokie-Pokie" could be used at a later date for the purchase of some good or services.

I meet women who have never learned the difference between non-profit and for-profit relationships. Many young women consider dating to be like getting a good job, and an intimate courtship as a major career move. They often see intimate relationships as a for-profit investment that is only supposed to increase in its dollar value as time passes.

Mature women tend to see relationships a little different. These women often see dating as a part-time job with few benefits, but a regular pay check. Many of these worldly older women see courtships as a kind of supplemental insurance or retirement plan. For mature women of the world, many of them are not really looking for anything grand, just something secure that they can lean on when necessary.

For reasons I have yet to understand, many women have a difficult time distinguishing one type of relationship from the other. These women seem to have trouble understanding that the behavior, values, and attitude for one type of relationship are completely wrong for the other. It is as if the whole idea of intimacy is a free-for-all and many want to pretend that the responsibilities that come with love and relationships are arbitrary and only apply to everyone else.

Women should learn the importance of being true to them, and those who love them. These women should understand that a woman never engages a man for an intimate relationship in order to gain an advantage. Parents should make sure that the women in their lives know that only a female of low account gets involved with a man to receive compensation for her affection. Such a female is not a woman, she is a whore.

In addition, prostitution is not strictly the short comings of weak women. There are plenty of men in our society who share the perversion. If a man pursues a woman with the intention of exploiting a woman for money or favor, he too is no man. When a man uses intimacy to take advantage of a woman, he is nothing more than a "He-bitch" or a "Man-whore".

People have said that the use of words like hussy, whore, and bitch are disrespectful to women. I strongly disagree. The proper use of such words, do what words in language are meant to do. They set perimeters that give the things in our lives an accurate measure, identity, description, and explanation. These words are meant to help us put a proper label on the people, places, things and ideas that shape our lives.

When we refuse the proper use of these words, or pretend that they have no merit, we undermine the morally responsible work of good women. We show disrespect to the righteous and ethical women that hold steadfast to a higher truth. It is my humble opinion that people who dismiss the use of these words only wish to turn a blind eye to the lascivious behavior of wicked people who challenge our civic and religious virtues.

The 7 Degrees of a Woman's Sexual Power

The degrees of a woman's sexual power are something every adolescent and young adult woman should know. Understanding the sexual changes every woman will experience, knowing their impact on her intimate and casual relationships and understanding the overall affect her depreciating sexual power will have on her life is very important. It is a delicate, but very important subject that should not be overlooked. This subject matter, like most discussed in this book, require an open mind and a great deal of patience.

The depreciating sexual power of a woman is broken down into seven stages. These stages are Platinum, Gold, Silver, Bronze, Pre-menopausal, Menopausal, and Post-menopausal. A woman's sexual power is a very fine balance of her physical, mental, emotional, and spiritual state of being. At different stages of a woman's growth and development, there are biological changes that will affect her state of being.

As a woman's endocrine, reproductive, digestive systems change she will experience great changes in her sexual power. At times, she will feel sexier in some ways than she will in others. In her youth, a young woman may find it very difficult for a man to emphasize his attraction to the sexual power of her mind, because of the overwhelming sexual power of her body and its physical beauty. This, of course, will be most common during a woman's golden stage.

The constant changes in a woman's sexual growth may make her more sexually powerful in some ways and not so appealing in others. When a mature woman begins experiencing the emotional and physical changes of pre-menopause or menopause, she may often overestimate the value of her physical beauty while underestimating the sexual power of her intelligence and intuition. A woman's mystique is a very important part of her sexuality. Unfortunately, many women are not taught the mystique of a woman. It is often taken for granted during a woman's youth and only learned by few women much later in life (See the Making of a Moor Woman, Volume II, Book 1 and 2).

The sexual power of a woman deals primarily with hormonal changes and her metabolic rate, physical conditioning, and her overall physique (body weight and proportion). It is also a woman's ability to make a baby, the quality of her pregnancy and birth, as well as her ability to recuperate after birth. When it comes to the sexual power of a woman, her attitude, sex appeal, and her emotional availability are very important.

The seven degrees of sexual power begin with that period of life when women wheel considerable sexual power, and gradually lowers to the period when a woman's power reaches its weakest point, and eventually retires. The purpose of this section is to help men better understand the changing attitudes, emotions, and manner of women as they descend from the highest level of sexual power to the lowest.

As a woman's sexual power descends from one level to another, there is an overlapping cusp where the decline of her power may very from one woman to another. Each stage is primarily five years in length with an additional two years marking the natural transition to the next lower stage. All blossoming women grow and develop the same, but the rate of their growth may very.

Heredity, diet and nutrition, education, and lifestyle may have a big affect on a woman's sexual power. Women who are voluptuous will appear to advance quickly while women who are petite or very thin may appear to develop slower. Women who are pleasing to the eyes or have very delicate features may look more youthful, while women who have more bold or distinguishing features may pass for much older women.

Women who are athletic and eat responsibly tend to stay youthful and strong. They will maintain a high level of energy and superior health. However, young women should be advised that extensive physical training may have a negative affect on their sexual development. Young women in high impact sports or competitions that require great physical strain may create a hormonal imbalance and bring about changes in their menstrual cycles.

A woman, who has a poor diet, and develops unhealthy habits like smoking will age quickly. If a woman does not stay physically active and get the proper amount of exercise, she will suffer a loss of energy, grow weak, and develop poor muscle tone. As we discussed in the first book, the health of a woman's endocrine, reproductive and digestive system can have a huge impact on her health and sexual development.

*Caution: Women who pursue careers that are stressful and time consuming may have difficulty maintaining their sexual power. Stress and poor diets contribute a great deal to the poor health in professional women. Educational and professional goals often conflict with those years best meant for making babies. Women should choose their career goals carefully if they want to maximize their time as a mother.

Careers that require many years of sacrifice may hinder a woman's ability to properly build a healthy family. Excessive stress and strain, on a woman's mind and body, may have a negative impact on her health. A woman's overall health and well-being, attitude, and state of mind will make all the difference in the world in her efforts to maintain her sexual power.

Platinum Stage/ "Ring of Honor" (10 years and Up)

With the onset of puberty and the start of menstruation, women enter the Ring of Honor. The Ring represents a sacred hoop between women past, present, and future. It is about the special gift of childbirth and the unique responsibilities all women have in procreation. The important role every woman plays in the cycle of life links her heavily to the spirit of life and Our Creator.

The Ring of Honor is a shared innocence and virtue that serves as enrichment to the human spirit. As responsible men and women, we have the important role of protecting and serving the woman and her virtue. (See the Section, "The Preservation of Innocence").

A woman is born a virgin maiden. Parents are responsible for the preservation of her innocence as she prepares for the role of being a man's woman and making his babies. When she is ready for the role of belonging to a man and making his babies, a woman chooses to pledge her life to the man who is ready, willing, and able to preserve her innocence and virtue. She embraces the life and the love of that man who will make her a Chaste Woman. (See the Book, "The Union of a Moor Man and Woman").

Golden Stage (17-23 years)/ Grand Opening

The Golden Stage represents those years when a woman's sexual power is at its peak. If a woman's overall feminine beauty and sexuality was a commodity on an exchange, the golden stage would be most valuable. The ages 17 through 23, are a prime period in a woman's life. Women at this stage are most fertile, ripe and ready to make babies. These women are highly disciplined and athletic. It is during this time that they are likely to reach their peak in performance.

Most of these women will peak in beauty. During adolescence, young women are often awkward in their appearance. As young women, they are taking shape and blossoming into more full figured women. If their bodies are healthy and strong, their hormonal tides are balanced and flowing healthy and strong. Their skin is smooth and their hair shines with the beauty of youth.

The golden stage is the period, when young women pursue careers that require a great deal of beauty to succeed. During this period, they are likely to become professional models, dancers, popular actresses, and professional sales persons. These young women have the ripe firm beauty and intelligence of a woman, with the freshness and innocence of youth.

The golden stages also represent the years of academic and/or vocational advancement. It is the period in life when a young woman sets her mark on what she wants to do with her life. At this stage in life, the possibilities of a woman's future are practically endless. A woman's pursuit of happiness, self-reliance, and personal growth will lay the foundation for her life. This will have a major impact on her ability to express herself sexually.

A young woman, in this period of life, will advance socially and begin to play more important roles in her community, culture, and religion. They begin to see the greater purpose of their politics, faith and ethnicity. The power that comes with this new level of awareness will give young women a deeper connection with the women before them and their sexual power.

This special stage is a time for young women to pursue love and deeply intimate relationships. During this period, young women will build their relationship resumes, and share road trips in pursuit of the best male prospects for making love and babies. This is the ideal time for a woman to begin her orientation for the responsibilities that come with being a man's helpmeet.

The sexual power of women at this stage is at a remarkable level. Every man from eight years old to eighty wants to hug them, kiss them, and love on them. A young woman's raw beauty, youthful innocence, and femininity are among her most valuable assets. Even those young women who might be considered "not so pretty" become radiant and beautiful with these attractive characteristics.

The raw sexual power and eager virginity of young women are almost enough to get them anything they want. These women may find it difficult to enter a room without turning heads, or standing on a bus stop without grabbing the attention of every man or boy passing in the street. The beauty of these young women can be captivating. In our society such beautiful women are often immortalized in photographs, paintings and films.

Women who greatly misunderstand their responsibilities to themselves may find it easy to compromise themselves for the gifts and favors their sexual power may bring. Some of these young women will make the mistake of pursuing intimate relationships for-profit. Other women will explore careers in exotic dancing, pornography, and prostitution in effort to exploit the beautiful power bestowed to them.

Physical Changes/Expectations
- Menstrual cycles are regular and easily gauged
- Bright-eyed and bushy tailed
- Energetic
- Comfortable and Healthy Sleep Patterns
- Ripe and Sexually aware
- Healthy Bladder
- Increase in Muscle tone
- Skin is tight and smooth
- Breast are perky and firm

Other Symptoms (estrogen related)
- Great Balance and Coordination
- Self-Control and Healthy Weight Gain
- High Metabolism
- Strong and Healthy Digestion
- Good Body Structure with Strong Teeth and Bones

Emotional Changes/Expectations
- Feeling more attractive
- Feels more feminine
- Increased interest in sex
- Care-free and high spirited
- High self-esteem
- Open and motivated.
- Feeling of total control
- Increasing self-reliance
- Healthy long-term and short-term memory
- A deep desire to be needed or useful
- A deep desire to explore feeling of love
- Romantic notions or daydreams (a mechanism of motivation)
- Wanting to be more involved and well connected

Biological Changes/Expectations
- Hormonal changes are steady and predictable
- Ovarian egg reserve is in its highest percentages
- Between 18 and 20 years, a woman's body (pelvic region) is fully developed to carry the stress and strain of childbirth.

Caution: Young women, who have been birthed and raised to be true women, should be cautious of older females who may attempt to deter them from making sound decisions regarding the love and intimacy of responsible mature men. As women decline to the lowest levels of their sexual power, those who have not secured a healthy relationship with a good man will find themselves in direct competition with younger, strong and healthier women.

In our society, many women choose to take marriage, sex, love, and their youth for granted. There are women who spend the most important developmental years of their lives in pursuit of careers, money, fine jewelry, and other superficial things. By the time they wake up from their foolish ways, many of them have grown old, bitter, and self-centered. Most of them have grown incapable of true love and commitment. It is not uncommon for women in the bronze and pre-menopausal stages of life to feel threatened by the power of younger, sexier women.

Do not be deterred by the selfish and often destructive behavior of older "cougar" women. A woman must learn to make tough decisions and do what is best for her and her future. Everyone has to choose their path in life, and those who choose foolishly have to take responsibility for their own lives.

Silver Stage (24-30yr)/ Advancing Business

In the silver stages of a woman's sexual power, young women advance to a level of womanhood that requires more stress and strain than the years before. At this stage in life, many women are either advancing to a more complicated level of education or they are completing their education and beginning their professional careers. Many of them have grown to levels of self-reliance and have begun to establish a life for themselves.

During this period, women at the age of twenty-five will begin to see a change in their metabolism. With this change, many women will find it difficult to lose unwanted pounds and stay in shape. They will begin to see more flesh in their face and waist, and they feel a difference in the way they carry their weight. Young women who are voluptuous may find themselves heavier in their hips, buttocks, and thighs. For young women who are thin, this will be a time when they will take on a shape that is more delightful and womanly.

As women approach 30 years of age, they will see an increase of creases in their face and larger folds in the flesh of their bodies. Their will also be the first signs of gray hair. At this stage, many women will visibly carry the stress and strain of their world in their physical appearance. There will be less tolerance for the insignificant things that take up their time, space and energy. They will develop a greater appreciation for their leisure time, and want to get more out of their personal lives.

As women fall into the cusp of the silver and bronze stages in life, even those young women who would be considered especially attractive will notice a difference in the quality of their sexual power. They will have great confidence in their ability to express themselves sexually, but will begin to see that there are noticeable differences in the attention they receive from the men in their lives. These women will begin to notice a difference in the way they attract men of different ages, as well as the quality of the relationships they create.

During the silver age of a woman's sexual power, most women will begin taking their relationships with men and women more serious. They will learn to be more exclusive in their friendships, and their romantic pursuits. The sexual power of these young women will be greatly affected by their social and cultural status. It will also be greatly affected by their changing attitudes toward religion and their connection to a higher power.

By age 30, most women would have settled on certain ideas about their educational and academic careers. They would have come to terms with the limitations of their abilities and are making the necessary adjustments to their long and short-term goals. If they have not found a man to make and raise babies, many of them will begin considering single parenting.

Physical Changes/Expectations
- Regular menstrual cycles
- Decrease in youthful glow
- Visible signs of stress and strain in facial features
- No Vaginal dryness
- Gain of fatty tissue and increase muscle tone
- Body curves are more full
- Visible signs of stress and strain in posture
- Skin is full with a more fleshy appearance
- First signs of creases in skin and stress lines
- Breast firm and more full
- Skin is full in appearance and smooth
- Appearance of gray hairs

Other Symptoms (estrogen related)
- Healthy balance and coordination
- Healthy weight gain and baby fat
- Changes in metabolism at 25 years
- Changes in digestion and diet (increased need for vitamin supplements)
- Changes in energy level
- Less tolerant of noise, and irritations. (increased need for stress management)

Emotional Changes/Expectations
- Growing concerns with being physical attractive
- Feels more feminine with increased concerns with acceptance
- Increased interest in sex with stronger emotional ties
- Increase in anxiety, stress, and tension
- High self-esteem and confidence
- Increased interest in stable relationships
- Self-reliant and Defined as an individual
- Highly organized and focused (On top of the world)
- Increasing self-reliance
- Strong healthy memory
- Feeling needed, useful and destined for greater success
- Feeling Loved and Appreciated with increased interest in meaningful relationships
- Romantic notions or daydreams (a mechanism of inspiration)

- Motivated for leadership and roles of authority

Biological Changes/Expectations
- At 30 years of age a woman's ovarian egg reserve has already produced 90% of its capacity.
- Metabolism has changed resulting in increased body fat. (Around 25 years of age.)

Bronze Stage (31-37yr)/ Securities, Long-term Investments and Partnerships

The bronze stage of a woman's sexual power is a time for major change. Women are approaching the middle of their lives and much of their world is quickly becoming finite. Their careers, social and financial status, and their limitations are beginning to give shape to their lives.

At 30 years, women have produced the majority of their ovarian egg reserve, and are quickly approaching a danger zone for reproduction. The changes in their bodies are becoming more visible. The gray in their hair is spreading and their wrinkles and stress lines are more pronounced. The stresses of daily living have left the mark of pain in her face. The physical and emotional changes of this period in a woman's life will have a big impact on how she feels about herself and her sexuality.

As early as 33 years of age, some women will begin experiencing early symptoms of pre-menopause. At 35 years of age, women enter the "mid-life malaise" and "mid-life slump". This is a period when changes in a woman's reproduction, hormones, and endocrine system are really taking their toll.

During this period more women are attempting to have children. If they have had children and are in good health, then women may find the stress and strain of making babies in the bronze stage comfortable. Their experiences with childbirth will go a long way. However, in this stage of her sexual and reproductive development women need to be concerned with factor other than physical strength and ability. Women need to be very concern with the hormonal changes of their mid-life development.

Women who have not given birth may find it very difficult between 31 and 37 years. These women often have trouble getting pregnant, carrying their baby a full and healthy term, and giving birth. Many of these women also find it difficult to recuperate physical after childbirth. Middle aged women may develop all kinds of problems with their health after childbirth. Women need to take special precautions when making babies at this late stage in life.

Physical Symptoms of the Bronze Age
- May be slight changes in menstrual cycles
- Occasional Insomnia and consequent tiredness
- Vaginal dryness
- Bladder changes
- Increase of fatty tissue and decreased muscle tone
- Slight changes in skin and increase in gray hair
- Breast changes

Other Symptoms (estrogen related)
- Weight gain
- Bloating
- Increased need for vitamin supplements
- Increased need for Calcium and Iron

The Emotional Side of the Bronze Age
- Increased concern in her physical appearance
- Increased concerns with femininity
- Changing attitude toward sex
- Anxiety and tension
- Medium self-esteem
- Occasional depression
- Occasionally touchiness and over-reactive
- Growing concerns with self-control
- Decreasing self-reliance
- Decrease in memory
- Feeling needed and useful, but at times over-taxed
- Feeling loved, but at time over-whelmed
- Romantic notions or daydreams (at time a motivation and others an escape mechanism)
- Increase need for alone time.

Biological Changes/Expectations
- Major changes in metabolism
- At 35 years of age, the likelihood of woman giving birth to babies with birth defects increases considerably.
- At 33 years of age, many women are already experiencing symptoms of pre-menopause.

Mid-Life Malaise
Malaise is the sensation of discomfort that women experience through mid-life. During this period, a woman may feel uneasy, slow and droopy. The malaise will begin at 34 to 36 years of age.

A Mid-life Slump
These are a few points that may give you a little insight into the emotional changes that a woman will experience in middle age. The mid-life slump takes place in the early stage of peri-menopause.

These are the most prevalent symptoms of the mid-life slump:
- Drops in energy level
- Decreased interest in sex
- Morbid or sadness (unusual feelings of sorrow)
- Loss of interest in hobbies or favorite activities

- Depression
- Doldrums (feelings of doom or future destruction)
- Touchiness and over-reactive
- Crying spells
- Increasing dependency
- Memory lapses
- Feeling unneeded or useless
- Feeling unloved
- Wanting to escape or get away
- Recapitulation (a review of past decision that bring about regret or worry for past deeds)
- Introspection "Woe is me!" (self-examination)

Pre-menopausal Stage (38-44yr)/ Liquidation Sales

During the pre-menopausal stage of a woman's sexual development, women begin experiencing major changes in their mood, appetite, sleep, and manner. At this stage, it is not uncommon for women to lose interest in having sex. However, it is important that a man not confuse a woman's lack of sex drive with a woman desire for love and affection.

If a woman says she does not want to have sex, it does not mean she does not want to be intimate. Due to the physical and hormonal changes in her body, many women will enjoy sexual "horse play" even if they do not care to be sexually penetrated. Massage therapy, reflexology, acupressure, shiatsu, and other similar approaches to self healing may be useful in caring for women at this stage in life.

At this point in a woman's life, she is feeling her age. The stress and strain of life at time may feel overwhelming. Women in the later part of the silver stage and women in the bronze stage of a woman's sexual power will depend on the love and support of their men more than ever before. When it comes to a woman's decline during these periods, the loving support of their significant other will make all the difference in the world.

Those women who enter the bronze stage without the needed love and support may have a very difficult time. These women may go through a period of jealousy and envy towards women who are enjoying the fruit of the gold and silver stages of power. Some of these women may have a great deal of resentment towards those women who have a loving man and/or family support.

Physical Symptoms of Pre-menopause
- Erratic menstrual cycles
- Occasional hot flashes and flushes
- Insomnia and consequent tiredness
- Occasional Vaginal dryness
- Slight Bladder changes
- Periods of Dry skin
- Slight Breast changes
- Unusual skin sensations

The Emotional Side of Pre-menopause
- Feeling less attractive
- Feels less feminine
- Decreased interest in sex
- Anxiety and tension
- Touchiness and over-reactive
- Crazy days (feeling out of control)
- Increasing dependence
- Feeling less needed or less useful
- Feeling unappreciated and out of place
- Romantic notions or daydreams (an escape mechanism)

Biological Changes/Expectations
- Slow metabolism
- Biological clock for reproduction is gearing down cycles
- At 40 years of age, a woman's ovarian egg reserve is down to 2% to 3%.

Menopausal Stage (45-55yr)/ Going Out of Business Sale

During the menopausal stage of a woman's sexual development, women continue experiencing major changes in their mood, appetite, sleep, and manner. At this stage, women may require a lot of personal space and continue to lose interest in having sex. Even though women at this stage will better enjoy their "me" time, there will still be a deep desire to strengthen their relationship with family and friends. The acceptance of those she love and respect will be a very important asset during this period.

Physical Symptoms of Menopause
6. Erratic menstrual cycles
7. Hot flashes and flushes
8. Insomnia and consequent tiredness
9. Vaginal dryness
10. Bladder changes
11. Loss of fatty tissue and decreased muscle tone
12. Dry skin
13. Breast changes
14. Unusual skin sensations

Other Symptoms (estrogen related)
15. Dizziness
16. Weight gain
17. Bloating
18. Gastrointestinal disturbances such as diarrhea and constipation
19. Calcium deficiency

The Emotional Side of Menopause

- Feeling less attractive
- Feels less feminine
- Decreased interest in sex
- Anxiety and tension
- Low self-esteem
- Depression
- Touchiness and over-reactive
- Crazy days (feeling out of control)
- Increasing dependency
- Memory lapses
- Feeling unneeded or useless
- Feeling unloved
- Romantic notions or daydreams (an escape mechanism)
- Wanting to escape or get away

Biological Changes
- Very slow metabolism
- Ovarian egg reserve on empty
- Biological Clock has complete its cycles
- Hormonal imbalances and decrease activity in endocrine system

Post-menopausal Stage (56 and Up)/ Sorry we're Closed-Happy Retirement!
　　　　Women at the stage in life often experience a rebirth in sexual desire. Their appetite for sex and companionship will take on new meaning as these women redefine their place in the world. These women have a desire to make deeper romantic connections and desire more from intimate relationships. At this stage in woman's sexual power, women will return to a pre-pubescent size and their sexual organ will provide the men in their lives with a richer and more fulfilling sexual encounter.

Physical Changes/Expectations
- Increased glow of maturity
- Vaginal size is almost pre-pubescent
- loss of fatty tissue and decrease muscle tone
- Visible signs of lowered stress and strain in posture

Other Symptoms (with hormonal balance)
- Healthy balance and coordination
- Healthy weight gain
- Changes in metabolism
- Changes in digestion and diet (increased need for vitamin supplements)
- Changes in energy level

Emotional Changes/Expectations
- Feels more feminine

- High self-esteem and confidence
- Increased interest in career and hobbies
- Highly organized and focused
- Increasing self-reliance
- Feeling needed and useful
- Increased interest in meaningful relationships
- Romantic notions or daydreams (a mechanism of inspiration)
- Motivated for leadership and roles of authority

These are some of the things a woman can expect during this liberating stage in her life:

8. There is a rise in her energy level.
9. A woman's general health is good.
10. There is an increase in sexual enjoyment
11. There will be more freedom and self-reliance.
12. They will have new desire for learning and socialization.
13. She will have a greater capacity to learn and grow.
14. There will be a greater capacity for love and sharing.

Section 2: Young Adulthood (8)

The 4 Archetypes of Woman

The four archetypes of women is a theory in human personality. It deals with the natural thought forms common to all human beings. Archetypes give rise to certain typical ideas, images and myths. These archetypes play a special role in shaping how a woman sees her place in the lives of others. The four archetypes are pleasure, recreational (or entertainment), utilitarian (or functional), and institutional.

Each archetype represents a progressing level of discipline and awareness. The advancing levels are meant to demonstrate the hierarchy of a woman's commitment to the Institution of Woman. Most women share qualities from all four archetypes with one type dominant. No archetype is inherently good or bad.

Pleasure Woman

A pleasure woman can be best characterized by her desire and ability to please those around her. This type of woman has a deep desire to be a special comfort and convenience to her family and friends. She is a comfort food for his family, a cocktail to her friends, a kind word to a stranger, and a source of intimate pleasure and comfort for her man.

When pleasure women engage a man, it is their desire to become as important to him as the simple pleasures or the harmless vice that he depend on to make through his daily routine. She wants to be the ice cold beer he reaches for the minute he gets home from a hard days work, or that spoonful of his favorite ice cream just before bed. A woman, who is in a growing relationship, is often made jealous of her man's little pleasures.

In intimate relationships, pleasure women are most compatible with pleasure men and are likely candidates for pleasure relationships. Pleasure women learn to better pleasure their companions. Their commitment to being the best pleasure they can be will define their role in the lives of their companions. In the beginning, pleasure women learn to explore the many pleasures of a man.

Pleasure Woman + Pleasure Man = Pleasure Relationship

Overtime, they learn to make use of tools and resources that enable them to provide for their companions in a variety of ways. As their ability to give pleasure and comfort becomes more diverse, these women advance to levels that teach them to be a more recreational in nature. At the peak of their development, they become recreational type of women.

Recreational Woman

A recreational woman can be best characterized by her ability to be a recreation and a source of entertainment for herself and the people in her life. She plays the host to her family, a comedian to her friends, a tour guide to strangers, and an amusement park for her man. These archetype women are use to being the center of attention and enjoy the power, authority, and responsibility that come with being a host.

When recreational women build relationships with men, it is their desire to become the primary source of recreation and entertainment. These women want to be that rodeo show or sporting event that seems to capture every man's attention. Men who enjoy sports and sporting events often find themselves involved with women who feel the need to compete with ball games on television, or their regular weekend round of golf.

These men are surprised when women disrupt football game or catch them just as they are leaving out the front door, to give them a "honey-do list". Many men have a hard time understanding why certain women choose the absolute worse time to sit and visit with them, or bring up a discussion that is a matter of great importance.

It is the goal of a recreational woman to become a man's favorite sport. She wants to be that special source of entertainment that a man plans to give several hours concentration. These women want to be that particular sporting event on which a man will bet his hard earned money. A recreational woman wants to be the Bowl Game that a man will invite his entire group of friends over to his house to see.

Recreational Woman + Recreational Man = Recreational Relationships

In relationship, recreational women are most compatible with recreational men, and will likely create recreational relationships. Recreational women are driven to learn how to be more entertaining, and over time they will become more artistic and skillful in their ability to entertain and serve their men. At the peak of their learning, they become more utilitarian in nature. These recreational women advance to the level of functional type women.

Utilitarian or Functional Woman

Utilitarian or functional women can be best characterized by their ability to artistically and skillfully serve those who love them. A functional woman is her sister's keeper, a true support to her friends, a helping hand to strangers, and a good and faithful servant to her man. These women live to serve in a capacity that is healthy and meaningful.

When utilitarian women get involved with men, their primary goals is to serve a man in a wide variety of ways that are all necessary. This archetype woman has no desire to limit herself to the life of a recreational or pleasure woman. She wants everything she does to have special meaning and serve a greater purpose.

When someone is experiencing car troubles or they have plumbing problems at home, they seek the aid of a highly trained professional. People who can provide a special and much needed service will always be in high demand. A simple pleasure people sometimes do without, and many recreations only work when it is convenient, but the necessary services provided by skilled craftsman take priority.

The functional women want to play the important role of a maid-servant, personal assistant, a nurse, or therapist. They want men to look to them as a master of useful skills and an artist. These highly developed women want be appreciated for their expertise in caring for their companion. The functional woman does not want to be a mere want or desire. She wants to be someone her man needs.

Functional Woman + Functional Man = Functional Relationships

Utilitarian women are most compatible with utilitarian men, and at times institutional men to a lesser degree. Such women are likely to create functional relationships and serve men in a utilitarian capacity.

Women who commit to building healthy functional relationships will learn to better serve their companion in a variety of ways. These women learn to address the needs of their men in ways that women of pleasure and recreational relationship may not. Utilitarian women and their relationships are driven by the fulfillment of needs and serving greater purpose.

As these women learn to better serve their men, they will broaden their scope on relationships and improve their plan of care. As functional women learn to serve their men in a more complete and comprehensive capacities, they will become a more institutional in nature. These utilitarian women will advance to levels similar to that of institutional archetype women.

Institutional Woman

An institutional woman can be best characterized by her ability to function as an authority on the virtues of life. The institutional woman embodies the power and authority of the basic organizations of socialization. She is a sacred temple to those seeking spiritual guidance, a school for those seeking knowledge, a hospital for those with health concerns, and a home to the man she loves and the children they create.

In our society, there are many institutions of life. There are schools for education, cultural centers that teach ethnicity, religious temples that teach some natural or supernatural doctrine. There are also community organizations, government authorities, and for-profit corporations that organize, manage, and provide goods and services necessary for survival. An institutional man or woman represents that wealth of knowledge, skills, talent, and training that makes such entities possible.

Institutional women are very rare. The Institutional woman primarily exists in ethnic groups that are spiritual in nature, passive, humble, and peaceful. In history this archetype would be found in societies that embrace the matriarch system. Institutional women represent royalty. This archetype is made up of the many philosophers and philanthropist that give backbone and roots to a society.

Institutional Woman + Institutional Man = Institutional Relationship

Institutional women require institutional men. Their stability and advancement depend on the guidance, structure, and security only institutional men can provide. Behind the relatively few institutional women there are in the world, there is a very powerful and loving institutional man. Institutional men and women naturally make institutional relationships.

Only institutional relationships, when properly designed and built, may be ordained sacred unions. In the tradition of the faithful followers of any lord or prophet, women who are like disciples to their institutional man, will learn to function on the highest levels of womanhood. These women will master those disciplines and inhibitions necessary for a true woman, and learn to rule and manage their world with the authority of a queen.

Note: When the institutional relationship is properly planned, organized, and coordinated, a man and woman will present their relationship to His Majesty on High. Once that relationship is ordained, it will be deemed sacred. Institutional men and women are not common in all cultures. Such a union represents the conceptual basis of the biblical union.

The union of a true man and woman is the primary union of all mankind. This sacred union is made up of the two primary institutions of the human family. Only the most spiritual and non-civilized ethnic groups have such men and women. (See the Union of a Moor Man and Woman Volume I and II.)

American Fashion: An Experiment in Human Sexuality

Fashion is about particular styles. When people most commonly use the word fashion, they are usually referring to the forever changing styles of clothing. Clothing styles and fashions that are passed down from one generation to the other is considered a custom, but those fashions that quickly come and go are called a fad.

Before the Middle Ages, only rich and powerful people concerned themselves with fashion. What we regard as fashion in our society began in northern Europe and Italy in the late Middle Ages. At that time, a system of social classes was created, and people were divided into groups classified by their occupation, wealth, and ancestry. Clothing was used to help identify people to a particular social class. People in those societies competed for social status, and fashion was one means by which they competed.

People follow fashion in order to connect with a person or group with whom they recognize as celebrity. In the past, fashions traditionally started with upper classes aristocrats, and trickle down to the more common people in a society. In our society today, fashion trends begin with athletes, musicians, actresses, and singers.

Fashion is a form of nonverbal communication that allows people to express their values, interests, and identities. For example, students in high school may wear sagging pants, gangster styles, and "gang-banger" apparel as a way of rejecting the rule set by adults, and connecting with a particular sect of the Hip-Hop culture. These fashions probably appealed to young people because so many adults disapproved of them.

Fashion is also important for those who want to make themselves look more attractive. When standards of beauty change, major changes in fashion always follow For example, when dancers of the performing art set a popular standard of good looks, people began to wear leg warmer and exposing leotards under their clothing.

As standards of femininity and masculinity change, those fashions considered appropriate for men and women change. In the 1900's, European and American women rarely wore pants, and their skirts and dresses almost always extended to their ankles. However, by the 1920's, women were less modest about their standards of dress and began wearing short skirts and trousers.

Although political events rarely cause fashions to change, sometimes political movements fuel fashion changes that have already begun. In the 1960's, during the sexual revolution, women's fashion grew more lascivious and provocative. The more society complained about women's fashion being inappropriate, the greater efforts women made to express their sexuality through fashion.

Around the 1950's, the fashion industry teamed up with psychologists, sociologists, and experts in human sexuality for a very special purpose. They wanted to know what it would take to turn the most plain, unattractive woman into the object of every man's sexual desire. Through their research, they learned how to design and engineer women's clothing to mock the most beautiful and sexy women in the world.

These scientists and fashion experts came up with a wide variety of ways to tailor a woman's body through fashion to titillate and tease men into high levels of sexual arousal. The push-up bras that make a woman's breast stick-out, the bras with a little jelly pack insert, and the special made bra that is equipped with a little pocket made for a small disc designed to make a woman's nipples appear hard and erect. Many of these undergarments were made to make a woman look nude. Underwear like these were designed to make a woman's body appear plump and ripe for love.

Almost every woman in America has at one point used or thought of using some type of clothing designed to sexually manipulate men. Many women, both young and mature, have different items in their closet designed with this purpose. One of the most important things women of our society will learn about their fashion is the nonverbal message it communicates, and the impact their clothing have been scientifically engineered to have on men.

This type of research was intended to explore human sexuality and exploit the natural inclinations of women, and natural desires of their men. These specially engineered clothing were made to give a false sense of confidence to women of low account, and empower them in their efforts to unnaturally seduce a man.

Bras   Bras are made to sculpture and accentuate a woman's breasts and upper body. Bras are made to give a woman's breasts a wide variety of shapes and forms. Some bras have little jelly pads that are designed to cup the breast, make it look fuller, and give it a more natural feel. There are bras designed to make a woman look pert and firm.

There are also bras made to squeeze the breast, cup the breast, and even jiggle the breasts. Many of these bras are engineered to lift a woman's breasts and they are meant to create cleavage. There are a wide variety of bras made for every type of woman and most of them have been engineered to titillate and tease men.

Panties   Women's panties have been engineered in a wide variety of ways of accentuating their figures, and to create a more sexually attractive woman. Women's panties have been made to cut a woman off at the base of her butt cheeks to accentuate her bottom. French-cut panties are made to catch the woman in the crotch and cut diagonally across her butt-cheeks. This type of panties was designed to accentuate the bottom of females who have no rear-end, or hips. The thong or bikini panties are engineered to make a woman look as if she is not wearing any panties.

Body sculpturing undergarments   These are undergarment that are designed and engineered to cup, lift, squeeze, shift, and tuck a wide variety of parts on a woman's body. This special made underwear is made to give an oddly shaped woman the support she needs to look more pert, firm, and curvaceous. It is how many women, who are insecure about the image and figure, create the sculptured figure that will best titillate and tease the object of their desire.

Pants or slacks   Women's pants are often designed to fit tightly and catch the contours of her figure. The pockets on certain pants are made to create the illusion of a broader backside. Some types of pants are made to catch a woman in the crotch of her pants, and creating a pocket to display and accentuate the size of her vagina. Other types of slacks and pants are engineered to catch a woman in the crack of her backside in order to accentuate her contours and cup her butt cheeks.

High-heel shoes   In addition to adding a few inches in height to short women, high-heels shoes were engineered to tighten a woman's calves, and arch her lower back. The arch in a woman's lower back makes her behind stick out, and make her toddle like a duck.

Make-up Make-up began to be used to give a woman a more exotic appearance. It was made to accentuate her facial feature. Red and similar shades of lip-stick were primarily meant to make the lips on woman's face resemble the folds of the labium minor (or vaginal folds).

Food for Thought…..
Sexuality in Fashion and New Concern with Allegations of Sexual Harassment!

Sexual harassment consists of deliberate and unwelcome sexual advances, unwanted requests for sexual favors, and certain other offensive behavior of sexual nature. It is a crime that may be committed by men or women in a variety of roles. There are two types of work-related harassment. One is offering a favor, raise, promotion or job in exchange for sex. The other is when a person creates a hostile or sexually charged environment.

There are many situations in our society when the clothing that scientists and fashion experts have created for women has created or contributed to a sexual charged environment. People in schools, places of employment, and even church, have felt the irritation of women who wear certain in appropriate fashions. Both men and boys have experienced the disgust of "stank" females who think that it is fashionable to wear clothing that "puts their business in the street".

As odd as it may sound, the people complaining about sexually hostile environment are not always men. There are many women who take issue with inappropriate women's fashion. The women who have suffered embarrassment by those who publicly flaunt themselves are often professional people who are more insulted by such behavior than many men.

It is important that young women understand the power and authority of their sexuality. It is equally important that they learn the responsibilities that come with such power. Women must learn to know the difference between the good and proper use of their sexual power, and the foul and abusive use of that power. Non-verbal communication makes up the majority of our daily communication.

If women are communicating something of a sexual nature, it is imperative that these women understand the messages they are sending, and how those messages are being received. Young women, who are new and inexperienced, may not always understand what their wardrobe is communicating about them and their intentions. These women will also need to know what they are receiving in terms of a desired feedback from the men they encounter.

The 4 M's of a Man

By the time women reach young womanhood, and enter the Golden Age of their sexual power, they should begin developing their relationship resumes. At age 17, those young women who have been taught how to build healthy relationships, and have been properly prepared to engage men in intimate relationships should begin receiving gentlemen callers. Following the rule of the "Five to Seven Year Gap," many of these young women will begin make themselves emotionally and physically available to quality young men 22 to 24 years of age.

The time these young women spend exploring and studying the lives of responsible young men will help them lay the foundation they need for building healthy relationships. These experiences will also help young women learn to properly serve as a good helpmeet to men. Most young women will only need 3 to 4 years experience learning to serve and protect their men.

By the ages 19 or 20, the average young woman should have acquired enough knowledge and experience to begin her pursuit of a mature relationship that is marital in nature. At this point many young women will begin setting their sights for men 27 years and up. In order for young women to properly choose companionship in older men, there are a few things they need to know.

There are four qualities or characteristics that every man should have before pursuing an intimate relationship with a woman. The first two are manhood and maturity. Every man should understand the dimensions of a man's life, and every man should understand the important stages of human development. The last two things are money, and a responsible means by which to build, secure and provide for his life.

Manhood represents the different stages of a man's life. It pertains to those things in life that are uniquely man. A man must have a very good understanding of the different stages of life. As a people grow-up, each stage of life presents a variety of challenges. A man must understand what is expected of him, prepare himself for any and all challenges, and know his limitations. He should know his role, responsibilities, and place in the world at each given stage of life.

Maturity is the power and capacity to comprehend and function. It represents the different stages of one's growth and development. Maturity deals with a man's place in his own heart, mind, body, and soul. It deals with his individual personality and the content of his character. If manhood deals with a man's level of self-awareness and selfless service, than his maturity would be more the level of his honor and loyalty to that awareness and service.

Money is a medium for buying goods and services, and an important sustainable resource that serves as the life blood of modern society. Every man needs liquid capital for the daily investments he makes in building his life. A man must know that money is not about how much he makes, but how much he keeps. There is no substitute for responsible budgeting, short-term and long-term investing, "Nest Egg" savings, and maintaining good credit.

Means is the education, tools, and materials needed to perform a particular task. It is the ability to produce security, wealth, and resources. A person's means is about his or her ability to take control of their lives and do for him or her when no one else can. No matter how much money a man has, he has to secure a means by which to build, invest, and secure his life.

Some people live in the illusion that inheriting wealth excuses them from the responsibility of securing a means by which to live. That is totally wrong. Acquiring an education, vocation, or developing a talent is not just about money. It is about self-reliance, self-esteem, and defining one's self as an individual. It is about a man or woman creating a meaningful place in the greater community and serving a purpose.

No matter how much money a man has, he has to learn how to be his own man. The most important characteristics in men have nothing to do with money or wealth. A man's confidence in his beliefs, values, and philosophy cannot be bought or sold. His disciplines and inhibitions are learned through meeting the many challenges of building a responsible life.

A Meditation for Young Women….

"If a man does not have the manhood, maturity, money and means to take care of what may come out of a woman, he has **no** business sticking nothing in her!"

Here are a few things every woman should know about intimacy:

Intimacy is defined as those things most private or personal to us. An intimate person is one who is closely associated, related, or very familiar. Intimacy represents that which is fundamental to our lives. Intimacy is about our willingness to give of ourselves, and share our personal lives.

In order for a man to establish intimacy, he must be in touch with himself and have a life of his own. He must first learn to define himself for himself. Then, he must create a place of his own that will give him the autonomy he will need for personal growth and development.

Giving of Ourselves

In order for a man to achieve intimacy, he must know and understand himself. He must learn to define himself without the influences of others. Before adulthood, the average male defines himself by the lives of his parent or guardian. The people who raised him define everything or almost everything he knows in terms of a religion, culture, and way of life.

As an adult, he will leave the home of his parent or guardian and make a place for himself. Away from his immediate family, he will learn to rename and redefine himself according to the new standards he sets for himself. Once he has successfully re-established his life in away that best suites him, he will be ready to introduce his newly defined self to the world.

Sharing Our Lives

Getting a place of his own is essential for any man learning to redefine himself. Breaking away from the world he knew as a child and creating a place where he can facilitate his personal growth is the second most important step he will make in defining his life. Only in an environment of his own can a man effectively plan, organize, and coordinate his life. Once a man has prepared a place for himself and learned to properly manage his life, he will be ready to begin learning how to share that life with others.

The "Help Meet"

The more a young woman learns to care for herself, the better she will learn to care for another. People have many needs. There are human needs, personal, needs, and sexual needs. The most basic of the three are the human needs. When a woman begins her preparation for the roles and responsibilities of loving a man, she wants to start with the basic needs and gradually advance to the more complicated needs. For young women starting out, Maslow's Hierarchy of Needs is a fair model and would make good starting point.

- Basic Physiological Needs
- Safety and Security
- Belonging
- Self-Esteem
- Self-Actualization

Young women preparing for the role of belonging to a man and making his babies should begin with the basic needs of all human beings. All people need food, clothing, and shelter, so start with learning how to cook balanced meals that are as good to taste as they are healthy. Women should practice clipping coupons and shopping for groceries.

They should also learn the proper way to set the table, or prep and garnish food. Women should learn how to sew, laundry, and properly care for dry-cleaning. They should learn how to care for different fabrics, fur and skins. It would also be good for women to learn how to get out stubborn stain and how to properly distinguish odors.

As far as a man's need for shelter, young women should learn how to straighten, organize, clean, and sanitize a home. They should also look into interior/exterior decorating, gardening and landscape, arts and crafts, and other areas that might be useful in creating a healthy and peaceful environment for their men. Everything a woman learns about caring for a man is an asset to earning his favor and winning his heart.

Road Trip

Young women who have made responsible decisions and have gained the necessary experience in dating may be prepared to engage mature men by the age of 20. Between their education, maturity, and dating experiences, the average young woman should be ready to begin her pursuit of both newly established men, as well as those men who are more accomplished. Before young women begin taking steps to receive potential life partners, there are a few things they should remember:

- Young men graduate from high school at 18 years of age.
- Many young men will likely finish their Bachelors Degree at 22 years of age.
- Many men who attend graduate school will likely finish their Masters Degree around the age of 24, and their Doctorate around age 28 or 29.
- A man who attends law school, pharmacy school, or some other professional program, they may graduate around 26 or 27 years of age.
- A man, who attends medical school or a similar professional program, will likely complete his training as early as age 26.

The average man will need time after graduation to, relocate, find a job, and make himself at home. Regardless of his profession, most men will not have a solid footing until their 28th to 32nd year, and sometimes later. Women should not be surprised if they find that most men are reluctant to getting deeply involved right after college. A responsible man will want to get his ducks in a row before making any major changes in his life or making any major commitment.

Young women who want to build their lives with successful men should invest in their future wisely. Few highly educated men want to limit themselves to women with little or no education. Successful men need to know that the fortune they build, the children they make, and the prestige they establish will be properly protected and served. These men want to invest their love as responsibly as they do their education and money.

At 20 years of age, the professional lives of most young women are more potential than actual. As far as their careers are concerned, much of what they are will be based on their future professional goals. The personal lives of women will be based on their life's preparation in womanhood. These young women will have to be well established in one, while actively building the other.

These young women must be committed to completing their education or vocational training, and dedicated to building successful lives. Young women with a well developed relationship resume should be able to communicate and demonstrate their ability to perform the duties of a woman, while working hard to earn a place in their professional arena.

Young women should plan road trips to visit graduate and professional schools. They should go during graduation week or other special events. These young women should visit these institutions to interact with professional men as they celebrate their career advancements. These events are also good for meeting and mixing with future graduates, as well as other member of that particular profession.

When planning a road trip, there are a few things young women should remember:

- Only travel in groups of two or three.
- Be prepared to spend as much time as possible meeting as many professional men and women as possible.
- Remember that road trips are not meant for making over night love connections.
- The idea of a road trip is meant for those who want to build solid associations and acquaintances with people in professional, academic, and high class social circles.
- Network with women who work in professions that enable them to interact with groups, attend social functions, and do business with professional men.
- Women who are courting professional men may be distant at first, but once they marry their significant other they will want their husband's friends and co-workers married too. Married women rarely want their successful husband hanging out with successful single men, so they will be working over time to introduce good women to their husband's friends.
- Young women should always use caution when meeting men through other women. They must make sure they only network with women who are ethical, positive and confident.
- All talented young women should try and interact with other respectable professional women who are not threatened by the youth, ambition, or beauty of younger women.

There are around 102 historically Black colleges, and another 16 predominately Black colleges in the United States. Many of these institutions have graduate program and professional schools. Some of the graduate programs and professional schools are Mehary Medical School, Mehary Dental School, Dr. Charles Drew Medical School, Thurgood Marshall Law School, Dillard University School of Nursing, and Xavier University School of Pharmacy.

An important part of higher education is the social, religious, and cultural educational organizations that exist on college campuses. There are several Greek and non-Greek fraternities and sororities. These organizations and many other are a great source for professional and social networking. Young women who join social, professional, and cultural organizations will be in the best position to meet such men.

Love and Intimacy

Loving Relationships

There will be times when the notion of love will be very confusing for your daughter. Knowing the different kinds of love will help her better understand. Every person will one day know the experience of loving a sibling, a friend, and even a more special companion. The better a woman understands the different forms of love; the more successful she will be in dealing with her feelings and emotions, as well as the feelings and emotions of others.

The Two Dimensions of Love

Love is a deep affection or liking for someone or something. It is a powerful emotion felt for another person manifesting itself in deep affection, devotion, or sexual desire. Love is charity. Love is both rational and irrational function. Our rational love is regulated by our ability to think and feel. In making decisions, we are guided by thoughts, or we may give deep consideration to emotional factors and value sound judgment. People who experience rational love usually regard it as "loving someone".

- When love is rational and logical, we make decisions on the basis of facts.
- When love is based on feelings, we are made sensitive to our surroundings, we behave tactfully, and we have a balanced sense of values.

Our irrational love is based on perceptions either through sensation or through intuition. People who experience irrational love usually regard it as "being in-love".

- Love through sensation is about surface perceptions which rarely make use of one's imagination or requires any deeper understanding.
- The intuitive love seeks to find meaning beyond the obvious facts, and will attempt to predict and invent a possible future.

Whenever we experience love both functions will play a role in giving shape to our feelings and emotions, but one of them will usually dominant. A healthy love is one that balances the rational with the irrational functions of our heart, mind, body, and soul.

The Different Types of Love

Love is a combination of physical attraction and genuine feelings. The six types of love will have an impact on the heart, mind, body, soul, and personality/character. When a woman feels intimate love for another person she will feel empowered and centered. Love will be both exciting and sobering at the same time.

By definition, romance is a fanciful or fictitious idea. It is not practical and strictly visionary. Romance was a 19th century cultural movement characterized by the freedom of spirit and form, and is based upon fairy tales.

Romantic love by definition is an impractical, but powerful emotion felt for another person manifesting itself in deep affection, devotion, or sexual desire. It is an imaginary connection based on a fairy tale.

Romance is a combination of feelings, physical attraction, and fantasy. When a woman feels a romantic love for another person, she will often feel vulnerable, desperate, and confused. Romantic love is an infatuation that is often mistaken for a more fulfilling type of love. When young women develop strong feelings of attraction and admiration for someone for the very first time, if she has not been given proper instruction she will likely think her romantic love is more than it really is.

In a romantic relationship her feelings will grow quickly and they will seem explosive and passionate. One sign of a romantic love is the exaggeration of another person's abilities or importance. Another sign of a romantic love is a when person focuses on a particular characteristic like someone's eyes, or the car he or she may drive.

Romantic love cannot be put on a time table or gauged in its growth. It has no clear beginning or ending. Romantic love always needs props and a setting. Little things like flowers and candy, or the warm glow of a fireplace is essential for romantic love.

In contrast to romantic love, the more genuine types of love are based on attraction and acceptance of the whole person. Where a relationship of romantic love is motivated by the pleasure and pain a woman may know with her significant other, a true or real love would be motivated by her responsibilities to him. Loving feelings that are not considered fanciful or fictitious may be best described as revolutionary.

Revolutionary feelings are steady and offer security, but fanciful feelings are limited and may end as quickly as they begin. The overwhelming feelings of romantic love with its meaningless gifts and superficial gesture can blind a woman to the reality that her love is inadequate. Over time, pain and disappointment are sure to follow.

Overly possessive or jealous behavior is common for people engaged in a romantic love. When a woman is involved with someone and she is limited to fairy tale images of what a companion and a relationship should be, she will often make unrealistic demands of her partner's time and personal space. Jealousy sometimes indicates that a woman is insecure and unsure about her place in a relationship. A mature person embracing an unromantic love is not easily threatened in a relationship. Such a woman would know her place, understand her responsibilities, and be ready, willing and able to perform her duties.

Real is something existing as or in fact. It is actual and genuine. Realism is a tendency to face facts and be practical. It is a portrayal of people and things as they really are. Real love is a practical and powerful emotion felt for another person manifesting itself in deep affection, practical devotion, or unromantic sexual desire. Real love is based on a portrayal of people and things as they really are.

Truth is an established fact or principle. True is defined as faithful and loyal. It is conforming to moral standard. Truth is righteous and lawful. A true love is a powerful emotion felt for another person manifesting itself in deep affection rooted in faith. It is a devotion based on principles, morals and responsible sexual conduct. A true love is good, righteous, and conforms to the highest standards.

A spiritual love is a powerful emotion felt for another person manifesting itself in a deep and soulful affection, a supernatural devotion, or soulful and sexual desire. A spiritual love is rooted in the life, will and faith of all living beings, and a shared collective unconscious.

Natural is that which is of or arising from nature. It is innate and not acquired. Naturalism is the action or thought based on natural desires. It is faithful adherence to nature. A natural love is a powerful emotion felt for another person manifesting itself in deep affection, innate (inborn) devotion, or inherent sexual desire. When two compatible personalities engage each other and there is a mutual unspoken agreement to share their lives, an inherent bond is created between them.

A nurturing love feeds or nourishes. It is meant to train, rear, or foster someone. A nurtured love is a powerful emotion felt for another person manifesting itself in deep affection, learned devotion, or fostered sexual desires. A nurtured love is one we only know through nourishing relationships where the role of one person does not exist without the role of the other. In these unique relationships, both individuals look to each other for validation. (Nurse/patient, teacher/student, master/apprentice, mentor/protege)

* A special note: When two people are involved in a loving relationship, it should be understood that they may feel different types of love at the same time. The different types of love two people share will reflect the depth of their intimacy and commitment.

Facts and Fictions about Love

Romantic love is often accompanied with myth or legend that we have absorbed from the world around us. These myths persist because they often give comfort to those who do not know what to expect from a loving experience. Myths offer an escape for those who struggle with the nature structure, function, and responsibilities of a loving relationship. When people are faced with what seems to be an impossible situation, they often turn to legends and other forms of wishful thinking to cope.

Fact and Fiction: "Finding a Perfect Love."

A fairy tale like Cinderella is a good example of the romantic myth of a "perfect partner." This myth carries the belief that one day your daughter will find that special someone, the one person destined for her and only her. This romantic love is supposed to begin with a magical experience that she will never for get. That she will fall in love and from that moment on, her life will be filled with joy and happiness.

Fantastic ideas of finding perfection in the people we meet fall directly in line with the concept of romantic love. Romance is all about the magic of two people falling in love. In the beginning, a person will look at the object of their desires as flawless and the feelings they share as ideal. It is the belief that two people can magically complete one another. Romantic people often think that the only thing you need in life is to be with that one special person.

When your daughter experiences romantic love, she will feel a rush of excitement. After that first rush, she will begin to have other feelings. Some of those feelings will be positive and others negative. The positive feelings will support her romantic ideas. The negative feelings will make her feel that she has been misled. If your daughter discovers that her companion is not very smart or that he has a bad temper, she may begin to question whether he is worth her time. She may also wonder if the two of them were wrong about each other in the first place.

Your daughter should know that finding imperfections in a person does not have to be grounds for no longer seeing each other. She should know that being misled by the myth of the "perfect partner" does not mean her relationship is doomed. When two people find mutual differences, they should be viewed as healthy challenges necessary in building mature relationships.

Your daughter must learn to handle negative feelings and work towards finding solutions to problems in her relationships. She should know that even in the best relationships people experience irritation and anger. Learning to bring the good in her relationship in balance with the bad is essential and can help to strengthen loving relationships.

Fact and Fiction: "The One True Love."

The myth of a romantic love that is "true" states that "true romance" is not "infatuation" or "affection." Even if your daughter entertains the myth, she may have a difficult time distinguishing between "true romance" and other feelings she will experience. For many people, only after the romantic feelings have passed can they look back and debate whether their feelings were real.

Some people think that all loving feelings that people have are real. They believe that love is just love-neither true nor false. That is non-sense. "True romance" is nothing more than romantic love, and romantic love by definition is a fiction. Love is never simply love. The idea that "true romantic love" only occurs one time in life is a joke. Your daughter should know that "true love" is not "romantic love," and that love is not a rare find. There will always be a great many opportunities for love.

Fact or Fiction: "The Same Old Love."

Feelings and emotions are gauges used to measure the state of the human heart, mind, body, and soul. Love is the highest degree of self-awareness. It is the motivation of all self-actualization and spiritual enlightenment. When people speak of "romantic love" they experience while falling in love, they often talk about the strong feelings that fuel the beginning of their relationship.

The myth of a "love that never changes" is based on the beliefs that the intense romantic feeling they share will never die. Romantic love by definition is fanciful and made from fairy tales. A romantic fantasy by its very nature is fragile. With just a little stress or pain, a so-called beautiful and romantic experience can feel like a nightmare.

Love is among the strongest and most enduring of all emotions. Teach your daughter to always expect changes with life and love. It is the nature of human emotions to change with the conditions and circumstances of life. Anxiety, stress, and other life experiences can take their toll on romantic feelings, but true loving feelings will never disappear.

How two people feel about themselves and their significant other may affect different aspects of their relationship, but it should not affect the loving feelings they have towards one another. Feelings of love are always changing, but the most vital relationships include periods when feelings of love go from hot to cold. Regardless of the many ups and downs, the love two people share should continue to grow stronger. Your daughter should know that the longer two people responsibly work at their intimate relationship, the deeper their love should grow.

Fact or Fiction: "You Make Love Happen."

Your daughter should know that she is the basis of her love. People sometimes make the mistake of thinking that they owe their love to the person they care for. That is never true. Loving someone is about connecting with the best of what is inside of you. When something about our companion opens our eyes to the beauty inside ourselves, the experience connects us with our potential self.

Fact or Fiction: "Love Conquers All!"

"If you really love someone, you would do what they expect of you," is what you may hear from people involved in a romantic relationship. Some people believe the myth that merely loving each other more will solve all of their relationship problems. Having deep feelings for a person does not mean that conflicts will be easily resolved. Love does not fix problems.

People who believe the myth that love conquers all are likely to be upset about even the smallest problems. They may begin to question their love or the love of their companion when problems are not easily solved. Your daughter should know that understanding the nature of relationships, problem prevention, and problem solving will enable her to protect and properly serve her relationship. Love will only stimulate a couple to think, discuss, and care for their relationship.

Loving Relationships

A woman falling in love with someone who is in love with her is simply the beginning of what will be one of the greatest gifts of her life. Love is always joyful and rewarding, even when the relationship is painful and demanding. Falling for a romantic love is very easy to do; however, building an unromantic love affair requires a great deal of learning, preparation, and work.

In a healthy love affair, the people involved are committed to recognizing inequality in the relationship. Inequality means that the ideas and feelings of everyone involved are important, but not necessarily a determinant when making decisions that will affect their relationship. A relationship is a team effort. On any team, each player has his or her position. Each position has a job description and specific responsibilities. Everyone on a team has to trust the ability and talent of their teammates and each teammate must be committed to excellence and trustworthy.

On a football team, the quarterback does not have time to worry about the decisions the defensive linemen are making. He has to trust his fellow athletes. In a healthy relationship, everyone must know their place, and be well aware of each others strengths and weaknesses. With this understanding, there is mutual respect and a balance of power.

The person who is most knowledgeable of a particular subject is expected to make the wisest and most prudent decision he or she can make for the good of their team. People must learn that every couple selects the arrangement that works for the both of them. If both of them take responsibility for their relationship in their own way, they are able to focus on their individual roles.

Instead of trying to learn every odd and end of their relationship, they can specialize in their field of play. People in a relationship must learn to work together while respecting each others boundaries. Each person must take responsibility for their decisions, and be open to the opinions and criticisms of his or her companion.

Practical Tips for keeping good relationships healthy:
- Slow it down. Relationship need time to grow.
- Maintain your own interests and friendship. Do not let your love life take up all of your time.
- Communicate both positive and negative feelings. No one can read minds.
- Share. Do not try and dominate the relationship.
- Compromise as often as possible.
- Celebrate the little things and simply acknowledge the big things.
- Be open to trying new and positive things.

People in loving relationships must learn to function as one unit and learn how to share common thoughts and feelings. They must learn to do this while maintaining their own individuality. It is important that partners have separate interests, activities, and friends. Partners must learn to balance out the time they spend together with the time they spend apart.

The Knight and his Lady Love

Romantic love is often confusing and full of contradictions. Just when you think everything is going well, something that seems very simple will make everything complicated. The same things that gave you pleasure in your relationships, begin to give you great pain. Have you ever wonder where the myths and customs of romantic love originated?

Historians believe that the concept of romantic love began in the Arab world. The code of honor and the formal manner that guided an Arabian knight was called chivalry. It involved a spiritual quest, service to a greater cause, and protecting the honor of a true woman (or lady).

Stories of the Arab culture often told of a knight's adoration of a beautiful woman. Typically, the knight would have an idealized image of his love interest, and love her from afar. The worship of a woman was known as courtly love. If an Arabian knight was in love with a lady and she was from a different social class, they would not be permitted to marry. Thus, the courtly love he and his ladylove shared involved longing and pain.

In old tales, a knight shows his ability to serve and protect his ladylove. He rescues his "damsel in distress" from evil men who wish to do her harm. Modern day versions of such rescue story are still popular today. Old westerns, stories of medieval knights, and even cartoons like Popeye are all examples of men saving the life or protecting the honor of a love interest.

When the Arabian knight was not snatching his lady from the jaws of death, he would have sword fights to show bravery. He would also impress her by performing feats of strength. In return, the object of his desire would reward him with gifts and small tokens of affection. If a knight is preparing to go off to war, or compete in some sporting tournament, his lady love would give him a veil or handkerchief. These tokens in modern day romantic relationships have changed. They may include jewelry, lingerie, or small trinkets of sentiment, but the feelings have not changed.

The love that the knight and his lady shared only existed from a distance, so their illusions about each other stayed intact. People today, often view their companion in romantic terms and create expectations that no one can live up to. Understanding the difference between romantic and unromantic love, means being able to create a healthy relationship based on principles and not romantic fairy tales.

A Parallel: Academics/ Profession/ Dating

As young women take their first steps in life after high school, they need to know the importance of balancing out their lives. Women need to understand that as they advance in their academics and profession, they must also advance in their personal lives. Many young women focus so much attention on their college education and profession that they take their personal live for granted. Every woman should learn to balance out their lives and allow them to grow one step at a time. Each level of her academic, professional, and intimate relationship development should advance simultaneously.

Before the age of 16

Education   These years make up the majority years of grade school learning. Education was primarily academic with no clear picture of how the information or the experience would shape our lives.

Profession/Job   Professions at this stage in life are a dream at best. Most young people have a difficult time grasping the responsibilities of a full-time job, let alone a career. Relatively, few young people at these ages have jobs.

Dating   Dating consist primarily of holding hands, kissing, and flirting. Dates are usually group outings and heavily supervised. The title girlfriend is important but poorly understood. Most of what adolescent women are doing at this stage is imitating the senior girls of their social group and their favorite celebrity.

17 to 19 years of age

Education   These are the later years of high school and the first years of college. Education at this stage begins to take better shape. At this age, most adolescents are seeing a possible future doing something they respect and enjoy. Young people quickly grow familiar with their academic strength and weaknesses. They begin to narrow down their choices and interests towards choosing a profession or career.

If they have a history in sports, arts or crafts, this is the stage in their development when they are likely to advance in skill levels and separate themselves from the competition. At 18 and 19 years of age, many young people begin taking basic college classes. Many of them will choose major and minor studies long before they are sure of what they want to do with their lives.

Professional/Job   Jobs start out primarily part-time, but begin advancing quickly towards full-time employment. For most young people, choosing a particular profession is more of an aspiration than an actual plan. They have some ideas about what they would like to do with their lives, but the reality of earning the needed credential, acquiring the necessary training, gaining the experience, and the knowledge needed to skillfully market their abilities is out of their reach. At this age, many young people begin working part-time jobs for extra money and personal expenses.

Dating   Young adults who have been prepared for this stage in life are very particular about their relationships. For responsible young people, choosing their relationships is like choosing a college and profession. They are focused on their future and all of the responsibilities that await them. These young people want to make the most of every experience and learn as much as they can about building healthy relationships.

Dating at these ages is very difficult for most young people. Adolescent misconceptions, romantic myths, and a Walt Disney World version of love, will lead many of them in to very destructive sophomoric relationships. Most of them will make careless decisions that will lead them to major errors in judgment.

For misguided young people, boyfriend/girlfriend relationships begin as early as junior high school. Many of them will reach their later years of high school with all of the wrong ideas about relationships. By age 19, much of what the average adolescent will learn about relationships will be useless. Many young people will enter middle adulthood before they know the destructive impact their youthful indiscretions have had on their lives.

20 to 23 years of age

Education   These years typically represent the later years of undergraduate school. By age 20, many students have narrowed down their professional interests, and have gotten over any romantic ideas they had about certain high profile jobs. This is a stage when their educational and professional goals merge in many ways. In the last years of their undergraduate studies, students are expected to participate in volunteer work programs, and seek-out professional internships.

Professional/Job   During these years, many young people are working full-time jobs and shouldering most of their life's responsibilities. Many of these students are working to pay bills, but they are always looking for an opportunity to work in their field of study. At this stage in their academic career, most students are looking for jobs that are paid or unpaid internships. These young adults are seeking positions that will give them the type of experience and training needed for their professional or academic resumes.

Dating   Intimate relationships at this stage in life are like an internship. They are meant to prepare young people for the role and responsibilities of an intimate relationship. Like an internship, these relationships should throw them directly into the job of being a homemaker and provider. The job duties should be specific and they should be graded on a professional level. The only relationships young people pursue at this stage in life should be marital in nature and worthy of their relationship resume.

24 and Up

Education   By this age most will have advanced to the graduate level of their education and hopefully working in their field. On the graduate level, student studies are specific and specialized.

Professional/Job   Most people are working in their professional fields and investing in a graduate level of education. At this stage, young adults are setting up their retirement, insurance package, and investment portfolios. Their goal is to pay off long standing debts, and buy a home.

Dating   Building a relationship at this stage is like building a new house or business.

The Relationship Resume

Food for Thought.....
* The Importance of Developing a Solid Relationship Resume.

Between 10 and 16 years of age, your daughter should be learning the up hill road of being a woman. She should be receiving instruction on the proper care of a woman's heart, mind, body, and soul. When she is not in school focusing on the three R's, or in church learning to bridge the gap between our reality and the supernatural, she should be learning the social, cultural, religious, and militant roles and responsibilities of being a woman.

Your daughter should be spending quality time with only the most responsible men and women. The people you and your woman choose to share your daughter's life training should be those who are recognized authorities in your immediate families, and those who represent the pillars of your community. Each years of your daughter's life and every stage of her development should only be studied and explored and with the aid of competent men and women in her world.

During her adolescent years, your daughter will be inclined to open her self up to new experiences. This can be a very dangerous time for her. Be very mindful of the company she keeps. Make sure both you and your woman know the people in her life and the nature of their relationship. Do not under estimate the influence others may have on your daughter.

"It really does take a Tribe to raise a child."

As a young woman, your daughter should be engaging men to learn about mature relationships. Between ages 17 to age 20, she should be learning to make use of everything she has been taught about building healthy relationships. She should have learned how to analyze, synthesis, and evaluate the personal life of her companion. Your daughter should have acquired an in depth understanding of the hierarchy of needs, as well as the unique role of a nurturer.

By the time she is 21 years of age, your daughter's experience with young men should have served as a useful tool for exploring intimate relationships. At this stage, she should have the knowledge needed to engage any mature man. She should know enough to carefully read her gentlemen callers and clearly see the possibilities of a healthy and responsible connection. With this level of awareness, your daughter is ready to begin developing her relationship resume.

Like a professional or academic resume, your daughter's relationship resume should be straight to the point. It should not leave room for question or doubt regarding your daughter's personal mission. The purpose of a relationship resume is to outline specific goals and objectives. It is meant to outline a person's relationship training, experience, credentials, and skills.

Remember, your daughter's resume has to do two things. First, it has to sell her as a learned woman capable of working successfully in the best interest of her man and his life. Second, it has to sell her as an institution of life and a faithful servant who is prepared for the role of a supporter and homemaker. She has to sell her self as both a student and a teacher.

Although your daughter will probably never give an actual piece of paper to a potential suitor, it would not hurt for her to write her personal information down and see what it looks like on paper. It would also be a good idea to discuss the details of her resume with you and your woman, and practice the delivery of her presentation.

<u>Step-By-Step Resume</u>

Introduction

Teach your daughter to always give her full name if she is interested in a man, and only offer her last name with a formal title (Ms, Mrs., or Miss.) to those who she has no interest. Meet every newcomer with a full and formal introduction, but be less casual with those who she has no interest. Never use another person's name. Do not give out fake telephone numbers.

If she is not interested in a man, she should say so. When she does decide to give out her telephone number, it should be a direct line. It is important that her potential mate be able to contact her with ease. Giving out telephone numbers that are not a direct line may communicate unnecessary complications. It may give her potential suitor the impression that she is involved with someone else, or simply too busy for dating.

When your daughter is interacting with a potential suitor, she should be careful about maintaining a particular degree of communication. It is important that formal conversations and informal conversations be kept separate and neat. Never give out your work number. Keep your work life and personal life completely separate.

Objective

When your daughter meets a potential suitor, she should know that learning what he needs in a relationship and what he has planned for his life is essential to her finding a possible place in his world. She should inquire about any long-term and short-term plans he has for his personal and professional life. Making that initial connection and leaving with a good impression is essential.

A man that has it "going on" will meet many women. Those who take interest in him will be propositioning him in every way possible. Their goal is to give him a clear image of how they can contribute to his life.

"If your daughter does not make the Job Title clear, she may find herself playing a role in his life that does not suit her. She may even find herself pushed aside all together."

When he meets your daughter and they speak for the first time, she must be able to clearly communicate what she wants in a relationship. She must be able to give him a clear understanding of what she has to offer him, while also explaining what she expects in return. Teach your daughter to be straight forward in her communication. Your daughter should feel free to explain what she wants in full detail.

She should use specific titles and their definitions when discussing the roles that she will play. If your daughter is concerned with originality, she should find ways to communicate creatively. Your daughter will have no way of knowing how the man of her choice will screen the women he meets.

A responsible man is under a lot of pressures when choosing a companion. He will never have the time to explore every woman he meets. That is why it is so important that your daughter learn to clearly identify the role she is to play in his life. She should learn to communicate word-for-word that which a mature man would describe as an ideal woman.

Remember, your daughter should briefly mention any long-term or permanent goals, and focus most of her attention on those immediate and short-term goals. A man wants to know that he has a woman that is ready, willing, and able to be all he needs her to be.

Summary of Skills

One of the most important things your daughter needs to learn about communicating her personal skills is "keywords." These keywords can be skills, years of experience, character traits, church and school, tools, weapons, or just things that she knows a man finds important. Any man that is real about his life and future will want to know your daughter's qualifications. Advise your daughter to discuss her skills and be precise.

Have your daughter select her skills from a list of skill words and consider every skill she has. It is important for your daughter to learn how to think like "her male suitor" as she chooses her skill words. She should ask herself which of her skills will be wanted for the relationship he requires - and focus only on those skill words that are required for the relationship. She should also make sure that those things required of her are things she can and really wants to do.

Relationship Highlights

This is where your daughter discusses her relationship history. She should know that it is traditional for people to start with his/her present or most recent relationship, and go backwards. Most men will only be interested in what she is doing now, or what she was doing in her last relationship - anything else would be considered ancient history. For this reason, your daughter should give her current or most recent relationship priority.

When your daughter discusses her responsibilities in her relationships, she should arrange them in the order of their importance. Accomplishments are always a good way to punch up your daughter's resume. She should know that any accomplishment that she considers important is good. It does not have to be something for which she received a letter or award.

Only discuss the positive things in your past relationships. No one wants to sit through a conversation that is depressing or foul. If your daughter is ever asked to discuss something of a negative nature, she should speak briefly, try and put a positive spin on it, and be as tactful as possible. Putting the men in her past down is tacky and will reflect badly on both her judge of character and her relationship experiences.

Accomplishments that are tied to money, education, and children tend to make the best impressions. When a woman can show a man that she is good at making money, saving money, or wisely spending money, it demonstrates great discipline. Teach your daughter to never lie or misrepresent anything in her resume, but be careful not reveal things that could be interpreted in a negative way if she can help it!

Your daughter should never put anything of a sexual nature on her resume. Anything of a deeply personal nature should be kept confident. If her suitor initiates dialog of a sexual nature, she should always be discreet. Remember, if a man sees that your daughter is willing to betray the confidence of the men in her past, he will know that his personal business is no safer than theirs.

One of the most important things your daughter will learn to share when discussing her relationship resume will be the way dating will be measured. Teach your daughter that when she meets a potential suitor and begins going out with him the time they actually spend together is the time they have spent dating. She should never mix the time frame of knowing someone with the time she has actually visited with him.

If a woman meets a man and they go out on several dates over a period of two years, she should measure her time with him separate from the overall time they have known each other. Many young women make the mistake of looking at the overall time she and her gentleman caller have known each other, and overestimating the time they actually spent getting to know one another.

Example

Your daughter meets a guy. In a six-month period, they go out once a week (around 24 times). If their average date last only four hours, then they have visited for about 96 hours. The time they have known each other may be six months, but the time they have actually spent getting to know each other is only 4 days. Your daughter should be advised that four days is not enough time to get to know a male suitor. (*Check out Food for Thought in the Next Session!*)

"Your daughter should know that although the quantity of time she spends with her male suitor is important, the quality of that time is even more important. It is important that she take her time!"

Job Descriptions

When your daughter discusses the many roles she has played in the lives of those she love, she should make a list of job descriptions. Give your daughter a list of traditional jobs and help her study their detailed descriptions. Have her explore job categories like bookkeeping, food service or chef, nursing, paramedics, self-employed, and teaching or counseling.

Your daughter should take four or five descriptions and arrange them in her resume. She should focus on the relevance of each description and their order of importance. She should be taught to avoid being too technical when discussing her specific duties. The most important duties should always be emphasized in her presentation.

Education/Training

Education is more than just academics. When your daughter discusses her education and training, she should be as detail with her religious, military, and vocational disciplines as she is her academic and cultural experiences. Make sure that your daughter understands that in the eyes of a man, her home, spiritual, and family training should be as descriptive and detailed as her academic training.

Teaching your daughter the importance of education in regards to getting a good job is one thing, helping her understand its importance in matters of her personal life is another. One of the most important things your daughter will learn from you and your woman about education is how it will apply in everyday life. Your daughter's ability to successfully communicate her ability to use her education in building her personal life is essential.

A responsible man will need to know that your daughter is resourceful in caring for him and his children. When a man is looking for a woman to mother his children, he is not just looking at what she can do with him as a couple. He is thinking about the mother his wife will have to be if anything ever happens to him. Your daughter should know that being a disciplined and resourceful woman is very important to any responsible man.

Certificates

In this area, your daughter has a chance to discuss those certifications that might be useful for the relationship she wants. If she is a gourmet chef, then she can not only prepare great meals for her husband and children, but she can also teach her children how to cook for themselves. That will enable them to not only cook for themselves, but one day find employment if necessary. Cooking is a very useful talent for any woman.

There are many areas that your daughter might consider exploring. She should consider pursuing some certification in health care, teaching, counseling, clothing design, etc. Anything your daughter can learn that will help her provide for aging parents, children, handle emergencies, or survive natural disasters will be "a feather in her cap".

Memberships

In this area, your daughter will discuss memberships relevant to the type of relationship she wants. Religious and cultural memberships and social organizations like college sororities should be discussed. These social institutions have a lot to do with who your daughter is and how she will live her life. Your daughter should make sure that her companion understands the importance of these institutions and the future role they may play in their lives together.

In her initial meeting, your daughter should emphasize those things that make her a unique candidate for the intimate relationship her suitor requires. Be sure to remind her that the use of skill words and traits are still very important. Have your daughter look at the sample strengths and discuss them.

Sample Strengths

If your daughter has a difficult time finding good things to say about herself, have her look at these samples. These are just a few ideas. Encourage her to make whatever changes necessary to come up with something original.

1. An intimate love affair reflecting hard work, attention to detail, and the ability to meet exact specifications as well as expense, quality, and time objectives.
2. Positive and enthusiastic, able to communicate with companion on all levels and direct those in their service in a manner insuring maximum efficiency.
3. High motivational level, excellence of leadership technique, and personal attention to detail supplemented by the ability to influence and stimulate those in her charge.
4. Ability to create and present an excellent image of her relationship and family, and to coordinate and communicate well with extended family members and friends at all levels while efficiently meeting their objectives.
5. Expert organizer and energetic, aggressive communicator with proven ability to accomplish the most detailed, and sensitive activity while remaining within our prescribed policy.
6. Have been successful in performing assignments because of the following attributes: qualified by thorough, practical knowledge and considerable experience in developing new relationship and parenting techniques, initiating and formulating new parenting and relationship concepts, cognizance of potential threats and the ability to analyze community needs and to focus specifically on those needs.
7. Capable of initial program development and handling liaison with government agencies, community sources, as well as cultural, religious and private organizations.
8. Creative and energetic, capable of the sustained effort necessary to see relationship and family projects through from conception to completion.

Tips for Your Relationship Search

In most cases, I do not recommend that your daughter try and meet men on blind dates or through casual friends. Only those who are close to your daughter can give information that is true to her character and personality. Someone who does not really know your daughter may give negative information - such as a desire to share something intimate and personal when what she really wants is something simple and casual.

When your daughter desires to meet someone new, she should not go to large parties, clubs, or popular hangouts. She should instead pay a little visit to the community gym, church or cultural functions, recreation centers, barbershops, and sports bars. She should go where men casually hangout. A place where there are few pressures to impress each other, and everybody is more relaxed.

Every woman who wants to meet a guy will go to a singles bar or night club, so there is a lot of competition. The music is usually too loud and limits conversation, the lighting is usually poor, and the women are almost always scantily dressed. It is not in your daughter best interest to try and meet a man in a place where everyone knows that the women are competing for attention.

"Your daughter should know that when it comes to meeting someone special, it is not who meets him first, but who makes the best impression."

The indirect approach to meeting and getting know a potential suitor is always the best way to go. If your daughter can, she should try and meet him through someone she knows and trusts. She could get to know little things about him from close friends, find out where he works, where he worships or maybe even attends school. By doing this, she can get some background on him and be best prepared for their first formal or informal meeting. **SHE SHOULD ALWAYS DO HER HOMEWORK!**

Tips for the First Date

Before I go into dating, I would like to go over some important things about the process of connecting with an accomplished suitor. Since every guy has his own policies, I will have to discuss this in a general way.

Men who are seriously looking for someone to love will usually call a woman to set their third or fourth date. When the two of them get together, he will probably take her to a social function where she will meet his family or close friends. When the two of them arrive to this social engagement, there will be people important to him asking her all kinds of questions.

Since your daughter has done her "homework," the only problem she might have is with questions regarding her relationship expectations. My advice to your daughter would be to stay "Open" or "Negotiable."

If you have the fortune or misfortune of hanging out with his family and visiting with the women in his life, they are likely to share your suitors history, the benefits of knowing him, and how wonderful it is to be apart of his life. While your daughter is visiting his family and discussing the life of her potential suitor, it is proper for her to ask whether or not he is looking to marry or has any special plans regarding a potential marriage partner.

When your daughter finally sits down with her potential suitor, there is some very important information she needs to consider. A responsible man needs to engage a woman who is best qualified for the role of his homemaker, his love, and the mother of his future children. He wants the best woman he can find, and the less he has to sacrifice to get her the better. Every man is prepared to make the necessary sacrifices to get the woman he needs, but there is always a limit.

Intimate relations are complicated and require a lot of hard work, so a man is going to want a woman with who he will enjoy working. When a responsible man is looking for a woman of his own, he is much more interested in what she is like during hard times, than any thing else. For this reason, your daughter should expect her first few dates to be fun and interesting, but have an underlying serious tone.

She should be instructed to open up and let her personality show. If she can, she should avoid answering questions with a simple "Yes" or "NO". These kinds of answers will not reveal her personality and character.

Rehearsing is good. Have your daughter sit down with friends and go over some of the sample dating questions on the next page. It may help her to write some of her answers down and read them aloud (reading her answers aloud is very important). It is always a good idea for your daughter to try and match skills that she has done in the past with the requirements of the relationship her potential suitor is seeking.

Samples of Dating Question

1. Why do you want the responsibility of being with someone like me?
2. What did you like the most about your present or last relationship?
3. Why do you want to leave your present or past relationship?
4. If you have no desire to leave your current relationship, what do you hope to gain from your part-time service to me? (Young college women)
5. Tell me about the role you played in your present or past relationship?
6. Tell me about a problem you had with your companion and how you solve it?
7. How long of a commitment can you make?
8. What type of environment do you like to live in?
9. Do you have any long term goals? (10-15 years)
10. Do you have any short term goals? (1-5 years)
11. Why were you out of a relationship for so long?
12. What are your five strengths and your five weaknesses?
13. How do you handle stress?
14. Why should I choose you for the role of being my woman?
15. Why should I choose you for the role of a homemaker?
16. Why should I choose you to make my babies?
17. Why would I want you to help me care for my extended family or aging parents?
18. Tell me a little about yourself?
19. What do you require of me?
20. Do you have any questions?
21. How do you feel about polygamous relationships where you share the role of being my woman with other responsible young women?

Here are some sample questions to help your daughter get started.

1. When would you like me to start taking responsibility for you and your life?
2. How would I best serve you?
3. If this is a new position, where is the person who had the job before me?
4. What would I be doing on an average day?
5. What is the most important part of my duties?
6. Will I be the only woman serving you in this capacity?

The initial date is the most important part of your relationship search, and first impressions are everything. There will be no time for your daughter to think, only to perform. Every question her potential suitor asks will be very important, and her ability to answer quickly with confidence shows how prepared she is for a mature relationship. The time your daughter spends studying, practicing, and rehearsing the answers to the sample dating questions will be wisely invested. She should keep in mind that the difference is not always <u>what</u> you say, but <u>how</u> you say it!

Your daughter should never say anything bad about her past companions. Her decisions to get to know, and date a man is a reflection on her. Her putting him down only makes her look foolish. It also makes it easy to picture her doing the same thing to him in the future. No one likes a person who complains all the time.

If a guy is looking at a few potential marriage partners, and each has the same skills and experience, and he like them equally, the candidate that does not put up a fuss, and requires the least amount of his time and money will be his likely choice.

When a gentleman caller has narrowed down his choice for his future woman, there will be "slim pickings". If your daughter is in pursuit of such a man and he does not have the means to provide for more than one woman, I suggest she say something like the following when a possible suitor asks her what she requires.

"I really like you, and I want you to share whatever you feel is appropriate with me until I have had a chance to show you how good I can be to you. If possible, I would like to serve you and have my performance reevaluated in a few months." This will go a long way to helping your daughter beat the competition. Every man loves a woman who is willing to give of herself.

If she really wants the object of her desire, she should get his physical address (not e-mail) and send him a "follow-up letter." This is an important tool in communication that many women forget about. The letter should be a personal, hand written, and very brief letter thanking her potential suitor for his time and courtesy. It should be written the same day as their date when possible.

Tips for Your Relationships

Just as you would have your daughter develop good study habits for school and good work ethics on her job, she should learn good relationship practices.

1. Always approach responsibilities before he does.
2. Never bring your man a problem without a possible solution. He brought you into his life to think, not to complain.
3. Help other young women and men meet potential marriage partners, because what goes around comes around.
4. Never play sick or pretend to be too busy to serve your man.
5. Treat him the way you want to be treated. There is nothing worse than an inadequate woman who wants to be treated like a queen, but does not feel it her responsibility to treat her man like a king.
6. Treat everyone, from young children to the elderly with respect, and do not ever be patronizing.
7. Never take credit for someone else's contributions to a man's life.
8. Avoid all relationship maintenance and trouble shooting on the weekends. Work longer hours serving your man during the week if you have to.
9. Always attend family parties and events.......... but do not over indulge (food and/ or alcohol)!
10. When it comes to relationship and family business write everything down; someone is sure to ask about it - usually your man.

11. Always have an answer to the question "What if my relationship ended tomorrow?" And always work to improve and up date your resume **(KEEP THAT RESUME FAT!).**
12. Intimate relationships are like everything else in the world. They are here today and gone tomorrow. There is no such thing as a lifetime commitment. Every relationship must be taken one day at a time.

    "True happiness is not liking what you want to do, but learning to love what you have to do."

Unknown

Intimate Relationship Development

Food for Thought.....
*** Teaching a Systematic Way of Building a Healthy Relationship.**

Where is this relationship going?

When I think back on the number of women I have had the privilege of knowing, I am surprised at the number of times I heard the words, "Where is this relationship going?" As a young man in high school, I found the question oddly perplexing. I never quite knew how I was supposed to answer it.

It was not until I got a few years older that I realized why that question rubbed me wrong. I learned that particular question was one I was never supposed to answer. A relationship is two or more people interacting with one another. In order for me to know where "we" are going, I would have to be the only one responsible for the course of our relationship.

The women I dated were attempting to give me the burden of knowing our future, instead of sharing in its planning. When your daughter begins receiving gentlemen callers, she should understand what a relationship is and how it is achieved. Understanding the different levels of a relationship will help your daughter keep the advancement of her relationship in perspective.

When your daughter starts a relationship with a man, she should be able to gauge the relationships growth with her companion. The following section is a general break down of relationships and their different levels of development. See if this helps your daughter put the various stages of relationship development in perspective.

The Seven Levels of Relationship Building

When most people begin a relationship, the biggest mistake they make is how they measure the time of their acquaintance. People who see their companions once a week, and meet for only for a few hours, often make the mistake of thinking that they have been in a month long relationship. This is not a healthy way to measure the time shared. Many young people make the mistake of over estimating the level of their relationship's development, by trying to measure it in "real time".

Clocks and calendars are no way to measure the time two people have invested in their relationship. People must learn to clock the hours invested in their relationship one hour at a time. If a couple spends six hours a day, one day a week together. In one month, they would have only known each other for a day. Six hours a day for four weeks is only twenty-four hours.

Relationships should be measured in "actual time". Actual time is the quality time two people spend working on the substance of their relationship. If we were to break down the process of building a relationship in terms of number grade and degrees, it would look something like this:

Level One (1st-3rd grade)
1st grade: *Initial Attraction*

2nd grade: *Initial Rapport* (sympathetic relationship); agreement, harmony

3rd grade: *Initial Affinity* (empathy relationship); intellectual or emotional identification with another

Note: The first meeting may be a formal or informal introduction.
- Formal Introduction
- Informal Introduction

Level Two (4th -6th grade)
4th grade: *General Associate*
These are people who attend or visit common school, community or general work place.

5th grade: *Casual or Familiar Associate*
These are people who are members of the same class, community activity or events, and co-work in same department.

6th grade: *Personal Associate*
These are key people who are study partner, co-workers on the same team, or co-volunteer who share the same project.

Level Three (7th – 9th grade)
7th grade: *General Acquaintance*
These are people who are familiar and share information of a general nature.

8th grade: *Casual or Familiar Acquaintance* (Fair)
These are people who are fairly familiar and carry on casual conversations about things of a common interest.

9th grade: *Personal Acquaintance* (Good)
There are people who are closely familiar and share thoughts and ideas of a personal nature.

Level Four (10th-12th grade)
10th grade: *General "Fair Weather" Friends*
These are people who know you and are fond of you. They are your casual support and your ally when things are fair and your life does not require much of them.

11th grade: *Casual "Good" Friends* (Dating Level I)
These are people who know you well and care about you. They are a good source of occasional support and your ally when conditions are less than favorable. These people will be there for you when life requires a little strain. They will help you figure out a

possible solution to your problems.

12th grade: *Personal* "Better" *Friends* (Dating Level II)
These are people who share a history with you and treat you like family. They are a good source of regular support and your ally when conditions are extreme and your life require a lot from them. They will help think of a solution and be there to help you carry-out the solution.

Intimate "Best" *Friends* (Dating Level III)
These are people who walk in your shoes and shoulder your weight. They are your primary source of support and a life or death companion in any given situation. These are people who welcome the challenges that come with loving and caring for you.

Note: Each level of dating should run for a term of no less than 7 days (or 168 relationship hours).

Level Five
This is an undergraduate or vocational school level of building relationships. This level of training is meant for those who want a firm foundation for building responsible intimate relationships.

Associates Degree: *General Courtship*
This is part one of a formal relationship created to facilitate the healthy growth and development of the intimate "best" friend relationship At this stage in a courtship, a couple establishes a formal curriculum that will lead them in their preparation for a more advanced relationship. Their focus is a general knowledge of the tools, materials and resources necessary for building a greater intimate relationship. This is a time for laying a solid foundation for your advancing relationship.

Bachelors Degree: *Advanced Courtship*
This is part two of a formal relationship created to be a school for the intimate "best" friend level of a relationship. At this stage in a courtship, a couple advances in their development and make modifications to their formal curriculum. This level of courtship focuses on an advanced knowledge of tool, material, and resources application. This is where a man and his woman sharpen their skills for building an intimate relationship.

Level Six
This is a graduate or professional school level of relationships that represents advanced training in intimate unions. This level is meant for those who want to be a master of relationships through specialized training.

Masters Degree: *Promise*
This is a special time in a relationship when a man gives a woman his assurance that they will one day advance to the next relationship level. It is an informal proposal. The promise marks the beginning of the pre-engagement stage of a relationship.

216

Pre-Engagement
This is a time for marital plans. Like the blue print and the schematics for building, marital plans should break down in the greatest detail what the institution will be all about.

Level Seven
This is the highest degree of development for intimate relationships. (It is an advanced degree of continuing training and should only be considered by those who are at the pinnacle of their relationship development. People advance to this level of intimacy in order to establish themselves as a philosopher of intimate relationships.)

Doctorate Candidate: *Proposal*
This is a formal proposal. This is an earnest offer to engage a woman in a marital fellowship. It represents the level of intimate love for men and women who wish to be philosophers of love and intimacy.

Doctorate Degree: *Marital Engagement*
This is the actual construction of the marital relationship.

Wedding or Ceremonial Pledge (Christening)
This is the graduation ceremony that celebrates the completion of their relationship preparation and development.

The Owner / Operator

Stage 1: The Operator

Life is all about the business of managing our growth and development as human beings. When mature people begin exploring the possibility of building a healthy relationship, their primary focus is the business of fulfilling needs. The business of non-profit relationships is similar to the business of non-profit organizations. One of the most valuable things a young woman will learn in her life is how to manage her personal and professional life with the same efficiency and professional skills of a traditional business.

As children our lives are both owned and operated by our parents. They provide us with food, clothing and shelter. Our parents teach us right from wrong. They encourage us to grow, explore the world, and be all that we can be. During those early stages of life we depend on our parents for everything. They are responsible for every aspect of our lives at birth, and continue to wheel a considerable amount of power in our live late into our adult years. They are the owner/operators of our life business.

It is not until the average person reaches his or her 13th year that things begin to change. It is usually around this age that parents begin shifting some of the power and authority of life to us. We begin making our own decisions (or being led to believe we are making our own decisions), with our parents guidance and support. We begin learning how to take care of ourselves, and how to assume some responsibility for those who care for us.

Between the ages 10 and 17, we begin learning to function as the operators of our lives. In our youth, we take baby steps toward self-reliance. By the age 17, we are making major life decisions practically on our own. We advance from being completely owned and operated by our parents to sharing many of our life's responsibilities.

With the title of operator, we are able to exercise a great deal of freedom. We are responsible for going to school and to church. We build friendships and visit distant relatives. We join organizations and participate in community activities. Not only do we exercise a great deal of freedom, but we do all of these things with very little supervision.

As operators, we have a great deal of power, but our parents still control the greater perimeters of our lives. Their ownership of our lives gives them "veto" powers over most of our decisions. At about 18 years of age, we begin our training for ownership. By the time most of us are 21 years old, we have succeeded to the level of owner/operator.

Stage 2: The Owner/Operator

Once we become the owner/operators of our lives, all of life's challenges are ours to overcome. We are responsible for every aspect of our lives. As owners we have to preserve the infrastructure of our lives. We have to acquire an education and/or vocational skill that will give us the means to provide for ourselves. We have to define ourselves as individuals, and govern our lives morally.

As operators, we have to maintain the basic operations of life. We have to keep a roof over our heads, buy food and clothing, and pay our own debts. We have to build healthy relationships that are necessary for building successful lives. We also have to make long term preparations like medical insurance, retirement, and emergency savings.

When we get to a stage in our lives when we want to give of ourselves in an intimate relationship, we begin looking for those special people who have the potential to make us whole. As mature people who are responsible owner/operators of our lives, we seek companions who are equally responsible owner/operators of their lives. When a man and woman come together to build a healthy relationship, they do so with the understanding that their needs are equally important. The man knows that he has to take full responsibility for his woman, and the woman knows that she has to make the same sacrifices for her man.

When the two of them come together, there is an exchange of power and authority. Each one will become the operator of the other's life, while maintaining full ownership of his or her own life. The man is the boss of his life's business, but he hires his woman to be the general manager and handle important operations. At the same time, the woman maintains ownership of her life while giving her man the authority to manage her everyday responsibilities.

Both of them are responsible for their own lives while taking on specific responsibility in the lives of one another. Building a healthy relationship depends on both of them understanding the role and responsibility they have to each other. They must be able to fully understand both of their individual goals and objectives, while being mindful of their goals and objectives as a couple.

When your daughter reaches 20 to 21 years of age, she should be able to sit in the company of any man as both a boss looking to hire a qualified employee, and a highly trained employee seeking gainful employment. Your daughter should understand that when she meets a man he must qualify as a good general manager for her life, and a quality owner providing a good place of employment.

As a boss, she should be able to talk to him about the preparations he has made to be a successful man, a dedicated companion, and a provider for her and her future children. These things are essential to his being a good general manager. As a woman seeking gainful employment, your daughter has to wisely choose the man she will faithfully serve.

A woman should know her potential suitor and his ability to trust and share. She should know that it would be almost impossible for anyone to work in an environment of distrust, fear and insecurity. If she is to build a healthy relationship with a man, she will need to know what she can expect from him as both a good and faithful servant, as well as a relationship facilitator.

Now that you have taught your daughter to wisely choose both a good employee and place of employment. You have to teach her what it means to be both a good employee and a good person for whom to work. She must learn to sharpen her interviewing skills so that she can effectively communicate her skill level as a potential marriage partner. Your daughter must be able to demonstrate her ability to serve and protect her man, while also displaying a talent for overseeing any executive duties.

Any responsible man looking for his life partner is going to be very careful in choosing his general manager. He will expect her to give detailed information about her preparation for womanhood, marriage, and motherhood. Help your daughter develop a strong "relationship resume" that will clearly outline her training and experience in helping a man build a responsible life.

You daughter must also learn how to present herself as a healthy facility for which to work. Like any institution of life, your daughter has to be specific regarding her resources, tools, and securities. As an institution of life, she must be able to communicate specific goals, objectives and a clear perspective on her duties.

She must be able to clearly define her purpose and the philosophy of her life. You must teach your daughter the importance of her knowing her duties as a boss, as well as her duties as a good employee. Remember, the rule of thumb is structure determines function.

Comprehensive Learning for Advancing Relationships

Many men in our society are deeply committed and even married to females who are less than women. They have engaged females young and old who have a very poor understanding of womanhood and little preparation for the roles they are to play in the life of a man. Most of these females were never taught by the women in their lives, and others simply chose to take their role and responsibilities lightly.

Females, who do not learn to be good women, develop poor life skills. As they grow older and try and build relationship, their inadequacies visibly cripple their ability to function. When such females try and build a relationship, they often fall short of their duties in serving a man. These females find it difficult to care for themselves and play a responsible role in the life of a man. The deeper the relationship, the more difficult it is for such females to function effectively.

As these females become homemakers or laborers in a two income family, they often struggle with the responsibilities that come with caring for themselves and those who care for them. When they become mothers, these inadequate females grow even more overwhelmed with the challenges of being a woman. If a female does not learn to master each level of a woman's development many will never function as an adequate wife or mother. There is no substitute for good old fashioned up bringing.

Grades of Advancement:

Single Woman (Caring for herself)
A single woman must learn how to care for herself. It is essential that young women learn the needs of their heart, mind, body, and soul. They should be well aware of their strengths and weaknesses, and how that knowledge must be applied in their daily lives. Women who learn how to create a healthy environment and how to properly care for themselves efficiently will not struggle when they are required to take on new responsibilities.

Woman in a Courtship (Building healthy relationships)
When women engage men to build intimate relationships, they are required to give of themselves and make the necessary sacrifices to be apart of her man's life. She has to learn how to take the same nurturing techniques she uses on herself and apply them to the life of her man. She will learn to cook, clean, and care for her man, and do so with proficiency. Her ability to efficiently provide for herself means being able to focus on her man.

Wife and Homemaker (Caring for a husband)
Before a woman becomes a wife and homemaker, she must be efficient in caring for herself and adequately protect and serve her man. Making a love connection with a man and building a marital relationship will require more hard work and sacrifice than anything in her life. If a woman is not efficient in caring for herself and being a proper confidant, she will find herself easily overwhelmed with the greater responsibilities of being a wife.

Mother (Creating a family)

When a woman wakes up in the morning, she should be able to multi-task her responsibilities to herself and her man. The duties of a confidant are considerably different from the role of a wife and homemaker. After a woman tends to revolving needs of her and her man, she can perform the duties of a wife while learning to be a mother.

As a woman advances in her ability to birth and care for a new baby, she will become more efficient in all aspects of her life as a woman in a loving relationship. There is no reason for any sober minded and able bodied woman to fail herself or her husband after making a baby. A woman learning to be proficient in her womanly duties as a good woman, better friend, wife, and homemaker is essential for being a successful mother.

Godmother (Supporting and managing the community institutions)

Women who learn to function proficiently as a woman and companion are capable of being and doing more for themselves and their families than average females of a lower standard. Where inadequate females are easily distracted and overwhelmed, stronger women who are better prepared for the life of a woman function with confidence and competence.

The responsibilities a woman has to herself and her family will often pull her away from her career and home. Many of the important challenges that will face a man, his woman, and their children will require the support and efforts of people outside the family unit. A woman's ability to function in her community and influence the institutions of socialization will go a long way towards helping her provide for her family.

Grandmother (Managing the extended family)

As an elder, many women will share the load of inventing the future of her grandchildren and community. A woman who has spent her life functioning proficiently and achieving great things will play an important role in the lives of her family, extended family, and community. Even though an elder woman may have retired from the business end of raising children and building a family, her wisdom and experiences are priceless treasure that will benefit their family for generations.

The only limits to the life and power of a good woman are those set by His Majesty on High. A woman should never be afraid to push herself and test the limits of our world, but she must be wise in her every decision and know her limitations as a woman, person, and human being.

Section 3: Middle Adulthood (5)

Pleasure and Pain VS Justice and Balance (Homeostasis)

I have heard scholars say that the primary motivation of all mankind is pleasure and pain. They argue that everyone is governed by a lust for pleasure and a fear of pain. It is believed that the determinant of these primary motivations is feelings and emotions.

Feeling and Emotions

Despite what your daughter might hear in school, feelings and emotions are not life determinants. They are, for the most part, human weather and climate. Just as certain conditions make up the weather on our planet earth, conditions and circumstances affect the way we feel. Feelings and emotions are a gauge, like the speedometer or gas hand on a car. The purpose of these gauges is to inform us of specific things that might be affecting our hearts, souls, bodies and/or minds.

These gauges help us to assess our position and readiness, but they are not meant to dictate our actions or control our lives. It is important that you teach your daughter that feelings and emotions are not determinants in making decision. She should know that a responsible young woman makes decisions on the basis of her knowledge, wisdom, and understanding of what is true and natural. She should know that a responsible life is a life built on principles in the pursuit of truth, and not happiness.

Truth

The primary motivation of all mankind is the need we have to maintain balance in every aspect of life. Our lives are governed by a need to maintain what is known as homeostasis (a state of equilibrium in which the internal environment of the body, and/or life remains relatively constant). The determinant of our primary motivations is the actualization of our human, personal, and sexual development.

Balance

Human Heart

The motivation of the human heart is the sense of fair play. Human beings do not have to be taught justice and fairness. Whether it is in the spirit of competition or something as simple as sharing a bowl of ice cream, children know when they are being treated fairly. Justice is all about balance and fairness. It is an essential part of our nature.

Human Mind

The human mind is motivated by a need for balance in both logic and sense.

Whether it is language and communication, or science and math, balance is the center of our mental and intellectual development. For every problem, there is a potential solution; for every cause, there is an effect; and for every question there is a possible answer. The stability and growth of our minds depend on the natural balance we work to maintain.

Human Body

In the human body, one side of the brain controls the opposite side of the body. In respiration, there is a relatively even exchange of air inhaled and exhaled from the lungs. In circulation, there are so many vessels pulling fluid away from the heart and so many vessels pushing fluid to the heart. We eat food for nourishment. The vitamins and minerals that we get from food provide our bodies with everything we need to maintain our metabolism. It is all about balance.

Human Soul

The energy of life flows up the front and down the back of our body. This flow can be deficient or excessive. Maintaining a healthy flow of energy depends largely on the balancing of the yin (cold; dark) and the yang (hot; light). Spiritual wellness is all about balance.

Note:
Our primary motivation is our need to maintain the natural balance of life.

Our primary determinant is our self-awareness and the actualization that comes with the natural balance of our life force.

Food For Thought.....
Learning to Avoid Hardships in a Relationship

Over the years, most of my best friends have been women. Having the privilege of befriending so many women has been one of the greatest pleasures of my life. When I look back on my high school and college years, I am often reminded of the different conversations we have had about life. One of the things we discussed more than anything was the joys and sorrows of womanhood.

Whenever we discussed their lives and the many challenges of being a woman, I was surprised at the number of women who found the challenges of being a young woman depressing. Many of these young women told me, with great disappointment that being a woman is hard. Most went on to say that for women life and relationships were also hard.

For years, I listened as young women expressed their many fears and uncertainties about the roles and greater responsibilities of being a woman, but I never gave it a lot of thought. I always wrote their pain and disgust off as being over-emotional or just assumed that they were venting their frustrations from the stress of school work or the behavior of some immature boyfriend.

It was not until college that I began to really listen and hear more than the words of their complaints. When I truly began listening, I realized that the young women in my life were not just ignorant or confused. I realized that their ignorance and confusion went far deeper than their feelings. I learned that their problems were rooted in their core belief and value systems. These young women had embraced ideas and images about life that was making it almost impossible for them to make heads or tails of what they were doing.

One after noon, back at Dillard University, I was visiting with my best friend Kimberly Williams (This is your only "Shout out" so enjoy it), and we were discussing men and women in relationships. She was telling me how difficult it was for a woman to function in a relationship. She was saying that men should do more to make relationships easy and less stressful on women.

I explain to my friend that womanhood, manhood, relationships, and life are like anything else in the world. They are, for the most part, only as hard as we make them. I explained that the many challenges we face in life are only hard to most people, because they were not better prepared to handle them. There will always be challenges and hardships, the key is to acknowledge that fact and accept it.

"To love is to labor; that which we love we will labor for, and that which we labor for we will love."

Job (Paraphrased biblical text)

I have always told the women in my life that everything is work. Love, relationships, money, and nice home all require work. Once people get that simple fact through their heads, they will find everything else relatively easy. Young women must learn that the problem with womanhood is not that it is hard; the problem is that too many young women have been led to believe that it is supposed to be easy. The quality of her womanhood is what an adolescent woman learns to makes of it.

These are a few simple things people should consider when trying to avoid complications in their lives.

- Doing things that are not meant to be. A midget playing professional basketball in the NBA. It's just not meant to be!
- Doing things that are wrong. Robbing and hustling people for money or favor. It is simply the wrong thing to do.
- Doing things when we are unprepared or unlearned. Taking a test in a subject we have not studied. You do not know what you are doing and are sure to fail.
- Doing things at the wrong place or time. Trying to build an intimate relationship with a new acquaintance. The relationship may have all the potential in the world, but if it is rushed to levels that two people are not prepared for, it will fail.
- Doing things for or with the wrong people. Working with people who do not share your values or ethics, may put you in a position to be exploited. Serving people who are immoral and irresponsible may compromise your honor and

integrity. Your agenda and the agenda of those you serve should always be honorable.

- The "X" factor. There are things in our world that we can not control, and unspeakable horrors that befall us that know one can explain or predict. When unpredictable things happen in life and we are helpless in our ability to defend our position in life, these would be considered X factor complications.

Check This Out!
Preparing Your Daughter for a Knight in Shining Armor

There are many important things a father will do to prepare his daughter for the unique responsibility of building a healthy relationship with a responsible man. A father has to set the right example for the women in his life and teach his daughter the proper purpose, mission, philosophy, core values, and belief systems necessary for a young woman in waiting. As young women begin receiving gentlemen callers, they must be mindful of that man's primary responsibilities to the Spirit of His Majesty.

In pagan cultures, the term soul-mate is commonly used to identify with people who believe that everyone has but one person to who he or she will fall in love. In such cultures, intimate relationships and the supernatural take on considerably different meanings than other spiritually faith based ethnic groups. In this topic, "soul-mate should be viewed as two people embracing the same spiritual disciplines.

Ephesians Chapter 6; Verses 10-20.

"10. Finally, my brethren, be strong in the Lord, and in the power of his might. 11. Put on the whole armor of God that you may be able to stand against the wiles of the devil. 12. For we wrestle not **against flesh and blood, but against principalities**, against powers, against the rulers of the darkness of this world, against spiritual wickedness in high places. 13. Wherefore take unto you **the whole armor of God** that you may be able to withstand in the evil day, and having done all, to stand. 14. Standing therefore, having your **loins girt about the truth**, and having on the **breastplate of righteousness**; 15. And your **feet shod with the preparation of the gospel of peace**; 16. Above all, taking **the shield of faith**, where with you shall be able to quench all the fiery darts of the wicked. 17. And take **the helmet of salvation**, and **the sword of the Spirit, which is the word of God**: 18. **Praying always with all power and supplication in the Spirit**, and **watching there unto with all perseverance and supplication for all the saints.** 19. And for me, that utterance may be given unto me, that I may **open my mouth boldly, to make known the mystery of the gospel**, 20. For which **I am an ambassador in bonds**: that therein I may speak boldly, as I ought to speak."

Ephesians Chapter 6; Verses 13-20.

13. Wherefore take unto you **the whole armor of God** that you may be able to withstand in the evil day, and having done all, to stand.

Armor is a form of cover used for battle. Throughout history armor was made from such material as animal skin, bronze, and steel. Since the Stone Age, armor has been modified to match advancing weapons. With the invention of firearm, the use of body armor declined. Individual armor became too heavy for a soldier to wear.

In early times, primitive people wore armor to weaken the blow from clubs and axes. The Romans wore helmets, cuirasses (short body armor), and greaves (leg armor). They also carried shields. The armor carried by Romans was made of bronze or steel, and it served to protect soldiers against arrows, spears, and swords.

14. Standing therefore, having your **loins girt about the truth**, and having on the **breastplate of righteousness**;

The loins consist of the hips and lower portion of the abdomen. The loin area is regarded as the region of strength. Loin guard and Tasses (skirt) are fastened around the waist of a soldier by a girt or belt. These armor parts were designed to protect the abdomen and give added support. The truth of Yahweh is meant to serve as protection and added support to a man's primary region of strength.

A breastplate, back, and shoulder-pieces are a parts of armor designed to protect the upper body. The breastplate protects the front of a soldier's upper body. The breast is the home of the heart, and it is regarded as the center of emotions. Righteousness must always serve as armor meant to protect the center of a man's emotions.

15. And your **feet shod with the preparation of the gospel of peace**;

Sollerets are armored shoes made for combat. Greaves are shin guards made to protect the leg. The feet represent the body's foundation and the potential for mobility. The life of a true man is always rooted in peace. When a soldier is performing the duties a responsible man, he should always be working in the pursuit of peace.

16. Above all, taking **the shield of faith**, wherewith you shall be able to quench all the fiery darts of the wicked.

A shield is a piece of armor that is worn on the forearm and used for protection against arrows, axes, and swords. A man's faith is his protection from the wickedness in the world.

17. And take **the helmet of salvation**, and **the sword of the Spirit, which is the word of God**:

The way of a warrior is to remove him from the field of battle and disregard his own death. By faith, a man's love and humility has secured his place with His Highness. Helmets are protective, rigid head covering for use in combat or sport. For a man who knows his own heart and soul, his spiritual salvation is secure.

A sword is a hand weapon used in battle. It is a long sharp-pointed blade set in hilt. For a righteous man, the word of Yahweh is the weapon of choice.

18. **Praying always with all power and supplication in the Spirit, and watching there unto with all perseverance and supplication for all the saints;**

Every man has the responsibility of praying faithfully with ability, authority and influence, but he must also never forget his limitations and be mindful of his every weakness. He must stay focused on the "uphill road" to righteousness despite the potential or occurring threats. A man serves Our Creator with humility for the good of the saints.

19. And for me, that utterance may be given unto me, that I may **open my mouth boldly, to make known the mystery of the gospel,**

A man prays for the words needed to communicate. He seeks inspiration through the wisdom of Our Creator, so that he may express himself openly and honestly about the many unknown and unexplained secrets of the gospel. A woman should be encouraging and open minded when listening to his message.

20. For which **I am an ambassador in bonds**: that therein I may speak boldly, as I ought to speak."

Every true man is a representative of good, truth and righteousness. It is his obligation to humble himself and boldly speak the gospel. A woman must learn to be supportive and provide the kind of positive feedback needed when discussing matters of religion, spirituality, and faith.

This topic is meant to help fathers give the women in the lives a heads up on the unique challenges they will face when trying to both share and contribute to the spiritual life of a man. In the book, The Making of a Moor Woman Volume II, and the Making of a Moor Man Volume II, the spiritual growth and development of women and men will be discussed in detail.

Every woman should know that no man will completely abandon his youthful passions, but through discipline and self-awareness will learn to live more, and more responsibly. A man's commitment to righteousness, genuine faith, sincere charity, and true love will be his motivation, and the bases of his life. He will be a man who knows his place and the importance of following the truth of Our Creator.

"True happiness is not liking what you want to do, but learning to love what you have to do."

Unknown

Finding Mr. Right

When I ask different young women what they want in a man, I am often surprised at the unusual answers they give. Some women will try and describe a physical description of their dream man, and others will go into a laundry list of things their dream man should own. Of all the unusual things I have heard, the thing I found most peculiar was the way many young women had arrived at their answers. I was surprised to hear that many of the ideas young women had about men, women, and relationships came not from going out and meeting people, but by reading books, watching television or simply day dreaming.

I learned that many young women build their entire image of a future love on their fantasies and what they wanted. These women actually sit at home and create their fantasy man from head to toe. Then, they go out into the world, and mix and mingle with people in hope of finding their dream man.

When these women meet potential suitors, they would immediately start looking for the qualities of their dream man. When the real people they interact with do not fit their fantasies, such women suffer great disappointment. Over time, these young women lose interest in meeting new people and begin to doubt if they will ever find someone who is right for them.

It had never dawned on me those young women, who meet and interact with people everyday, could put more energy into a romantic image of men, and relationships, than they do exploring the real thing. Young women must know the difference between, real men, true men, and dream men. They need to understand the measure of a man and how a real person differs from characters in a book or television show.

Dream Man

A dream man is a fantasy. Like romance, it is a fanciful fictitious idea that people create in their minds. Like a fairytale, the dream man has no beginning and no end. Dream men have no substance. There is no chemistry to their personality, and character.

Real Man

Real men are actual people. Real men are birthed, made, taught, and raised. They are the descendents of their parents and part of a family lineage. The personality and character of a real man is dictated by their place in the universal scope of human personalities. The lives of real men are defined by their culture, religion, and their place in society. There are a great many things that separate men from fictitious characters.

True Man

A true man, like a real man, is an actual person. Like a real man, true men are born and raised, have unique individual qualities and characteristics, and have genetic connections to people long past. However, true men differ from real men in their level of commitment to principles and virtues. The lives of true men are defined by their ethnicity, spirituality and faith, and their place in the service of a high purpose and power.

True men represent the apex of human development and enlightenment. When one speaks of a true man, he or she is usually referring to a prophet, ruler, scholar, or great warrior.

It is unhealthy for anyone to live their lives confusing fanciful ideas about people with the reality. A young woman must learn to socialize and interact with other people. These people should be from different age groups, different races, and varying cultures. Women must learn at an early age that people are something she must learn to engage individually.

They must learn how personality and character types vary, and what to expect from each personality type. Men must instruct the women in their lives not to sit and daydream about the possible good in men and the relationships they may create. Women should instead, go out, mix and mingle. A woman selects a companion from the people in her life, not an image in her head.

They must learn that choosing a man is not like designing their wedding gown, but more like shopping for a nice pair of work shoes. Each woman has to get out there, try on several pair, and choose the shoe that properly fits her feet. Like a good pair of shoes, she must select a man that will best serve her.

Young women who are crippled by their fantasies of men and relationships may not realize the extent of their confusion early in life. Where some young women may learn at 19 and 20 years of age that their ideas about men are crippling their ability to build healthy relationships, many others will not learn until later in life. Women, who lose themselves to professional careers, may not know that their inability to connect with a man is deeply rooted in the romantic ideas that they have entertained since their youth.

Young Women in the City

When young women finish college and enter their professional careers, many of them move away from home to get a place of their own. These young women move to places that are ideal for young women who are "footloose and feeling free". Young women, at this stage in life, often make themselves at home in places that cater to singles. They choose to live and frequently visit areas of town where bars, night clubs, and other popular social spots flourish. This is the life for young women in their mid to late 20's.

These young women also tend to pursue the company of men and women who share the desires for fun, excitement, and pleasure. Young women, who have not been taught to be women, often limit themselves to people on their level. If they are in a particular professional arena, or part of a secret society, they rarely venture outside of their immediate social circles. These women tend to distance themselves from men or women who want to marry or settle down. They do not consider themselves ready for any major commitments, and want to live a life with as few restraints as possible.

The things these young women value, outside of their professions, are usually superficial and short-term. Their desired lifestyle is one of forever changing fashions, fads and crazes. Such women define their world and the people in it by the most basic terms. If a man is educated, drives a nice car, and has a prestigious job, then he is a good man. The lives of these young women do not require much of them, so they do not require much of the people with whom they share it.

Most of these young women want adventure and romantic experiences more than anything else. The ideas common to many young women at this stage in life evolve around their desire to enjoy as much of their lives as possible. Many of them see middle age as a time for settling down, and they have a difficult time imagining what their lives are going to be as they mature.

Mature Women in the City

After a few years of living the life of a single, most women will quickly lose their appetite for fast times and late night partying. They will get tired of meeting the same kind of people and having the same conversations over and over. Many will not lose their interest in going out and having a good time. They will simply want to get more out of their evenings by spending their time with someone who cares for them.

These women will find themselves limiting their time to those people, places, and things that give them some fulfillment. The biggest challenge for many women who live the "Sex in the City" lifestyle is the major transition they must make in order to upgrade their lives to something more meaningful. As these women enter their 30's, they begin to concentrate on the possibilities of finding, dating, and falling in love with men who will spend the rest of their lives with them.

Unfortunately, most of these women will not have a clue how to go about pursuing men on that more mature level. Many of the women who have lived the single life for several years will wake up one morning and decide that they are ready for something new. They are going to decide that day to change their lives for the better. These women will commit to the thought of finding someone to share their live.

The problem for most of these women is that the only real changes they will make will be in their minds. These young women will decide to change their lives and find that special someone, but they will leave the same apartment, walk the same street, visit the same social circles, and frequent the same bars that attracted them in their youth. In their minds, the same places they frequented for the pleasures and adventures of the single life is going to offer them something that it never had before.

Young women of the world need to understand that when they want to make changes in their lives, they cannot just focus on their desires for more. They will have to do at middle age what they did after college. These women have to relocate, change social circles, spend time in places popular for established couples, and build friendships with people who share their relationship quest.

The people that a young woman knew when she was "footloose and feeling good" may have been great for the single life, but they are no use to a woman in need of change. Even those who might share a woman's desire to upgrade her life will not likely be any better prepared than she is for change. Women should not expect the people in their lives to change just because they have decided that they want more out of their lives.

Women should make an effort to spend time with women who are married or in long-term committed relationships. They should engage these women in conversation and learn to think and communicate like a woman who is responsible for someone other than herself. She must learn to spend time with other couples, dine alone, and interact with families and extended families of friends.

These women must learn to communicate in ideas common for couples and families. Her ability to function as part of a larger group will be important when trying to connect with a potential suitor and his family. After years of embracing the single life, many women may feel like a fish out of water. That is to be expected. Women should know that although things may feel uncomfortable at first, overtime the discomfort will fade.

Check This Out!
Cautions of Interracial Dating!

Sexism

Sexism is the unequal treatment of individuals based on sexual prejudice. Sexism exists for both men and women, but the traditions and laws of most societies place the greater weight of sexual discrimination on women. Attitudes towards sexism vary from one culture to the other. In Western societies, sexism is considered unjust, but in many Middle Eastern or Asian cultures sexism is considered natural and necessary.

Since the origin of sexism began with the physical differences between men and women, many women embrace the roles of a traditional woman without protest. Despite the changing ideas about sexual roles for men and women, unequal treatment continues. In families, some men still see the roles of cooking and cleaning as women's work. Even though many women work outside the home they are still considered to be the primary caregiver for their children.

In our society, women are often discouraged from pursuing a profession in mathematics, engineering, and science. There are many men who feel that a woman would not make the best police officer or soldier. Many of the prejudice ideas used to fuel sexual discrimination are believed by men who are married with young daughters of their own.

Ageism

The Gray Panthers is an organization that fights ageism. It was founded in 1970 and is based in Philadelphia. It has over 80 chapters throughout the United States, and about 70,000 members. The Gray Panthers are committed to ending age discrimination in the workplace and housing. They support the national health care service and programs created to increase the supply of fair affordable housing.

The Gray Panthers also work to end the negative portrayals of old people by the mass media. The organization produces a bimonthly newspaper called, The Network. Ageism is the unequal treatment of individuals based on their age. In our society, there are elderly people who are ignored, abused, and neglected. Many of these elderly people suffer at the hands of their own families.

Racism

Racism is the belief that people can be divided into groups based upon physical attributes. Racism is when members of some races are considered inferior to members of other races. Despite the differences between groups, there is no scientific evidence to support claims of superiority for these differences.

Racism is widespread and has caused major problems all over the world. Racism is form of prejudice. Many people consider their appearance to be normal, and may distrust people who look or behave differently. The more visible the differences, the greater the distrust and fear.

In the United States, racism has been directed mainly by European Americans towards non-white minorities groups. Such groups Americans, Hispanics, Africans, Asian, and others have suffered discrimination in housing, business, employment, government resources, and education.

People often think that dating someone of another race inherently makes them culturally literate and not a racist. If a Caucasian male and a Negro female met and began dating, it would be assumed that both of them were open to each others cultures and respectful of each others race. That is what many would think, but it is rarely true.

More often than not, there is a great deal of racial prejudice that they both try and humor or ignore. Racial prejudice comes in different forms. Many times when two people from different races and cultures come together, the weaker person allows him or herself to be suppressed by the other. In order to bridge the natural gaps that separate the two of them, a couple in an unhealthy relationship compromises the life, religion, and cultural traditions of one person in favor of the others.

The thought that anyone who provides care for the elderly would not harbor prejudices against the aged is absurd. A person does not have to alienate him or herself from the aged to be a bigot. The elderly are often abuse and neglect by experienced caregivers, as well as members of their own families.

Just as a man, who is overtly sexist, may marry a woman and raise a daughter, a racist man with poor values and destructive beliefs may marry a member of a different race. A person does not have to see his or her companion as an equal or respect their religion or ethnic group to date or marry.

Some people pretend not to notice racial differences. These people believe that not acknowledging a person's race and culture is a demonstration of respect and acceptance. These are people who pretend not to know that ignoring a person's culture and race is a form of prejudice. A healthy relationship is built on mutual respect, and there is nothing respectful about tearing someone away from their roots.

I once met a lovely Asian woman named, Lonyi. She was the daughter of a European American man and a Korean mother. Even though Lonyi was born in Korea and lived there for the first few years of her life, she never learned to speak Korean.

As a child, she was told that she would not be permitted to learn the language of her mother's native tongue because her father did not care for the Korean-American accent. She explained that for many White people in her community, foreigners who learn to speak American-English after first learning their native tongue often speak with an unpleasant accent.

According to Lonyi, the father felt that it was more important for her to learn how to blend in with their predominantly European American community, than for her to learn the language of her maternal grandparents. Her father had the highest respect for his family's culture and social circle, but had little respect for the culture of his wife and in-laws.

The Death of Relationship

These five stages in the acceptance of death have a lot in common with any major loss. Although reactions to great failure and major disappointments will vary in degrees, there are general guidelines for accepting the process of getting out of a failed love affair.

Stage 1: Denial. It is an attempt to avoid the truth or a conscious decision to not acknowledge the facts. They treat their failed relationship as if it is a temporary break. They behave as if it is all a big misunderstanding. These people will often feel isolated and helpless.

Stage 2: Anger. This is the why me stage? Anger and resentment is a natural reaction. People at this stage often vent their anger through envy towards those who have a healthy relationship. They may develop feelings of jealousy towards the object of their former companions new love interest. Their family and friends will offer love and support, but those who are angry may strike out at them. People suffering a failed relationship or abandonment may reject the love and affection of those close to them. Family and friends may see the person's attitude as ingratitude. As the people around them pull away, those who are suffering may feel isolated and rejected.

Stage 3: Bargaining. People begin to think that there is something they can do or say that will save their failed relationship. They will attempt any couples counseling, prayer, and make major promises to change their lives for the better. People, who are in abusive relationships, often feel that if they stay in the relationship and support their companion things will get better over time. They are like people who visit casinos and gamble their money away. They often feel that if they place just one more bet, they will finally win at Black Jack.

Stage 4: Depression. This is a time for people to grieve for all they have lost and everything that will be lost. This is commonly a time for silence and withdrawal. Their feelings are one of great loss. People at this stage should be encouraged to grieve.

When a woman meets a man and begins to develop deep feelings for him, she will often create a romantic image in her mind of what her life with him will one day be. In her mind's eye, she will construct the house of her dreams, the children she will birth, and the many successes they will share. Some of the images in her head will be based on real life experiences and real expectations, but many of them will be romantic images that lack substance and true meaning.

After their relationships end, women may carry a great deal of pain and disappointment. Many women may confuse the loss of the life they dreamed of building with the loss of the person they were dating. Their feelings of loss may lead them to think that they are missing their former companion when they are really grieving over the loss of the relationship and the life they had hoped to one day build.

Stage 5: Acceptance. This is a stage for facing the reality of their failed relationship.

Acceptance leaves a person feeling helpless. People are not happy or unhappy. They are at ease and ready to make proper preparation for the changes in their lives. People at this stage have, for the most part, dismissed any superstitions they may have had about a great miracle saving their doomed relationship. They have given up on any bargaining that might save their dream home. The period of depression and anger is over.

The primary emotion that operates throughout these five stages is hope. People hope for a solution to their relationship woes. When women learn that their relationship is failing, they are hopeful that it is all just a misunderstanding. In their anger, there is the hope that venting their frustrations will help them through their troubles. They bargain with the belief that there is something they might do to repair their failed relationships.

It is important that women learn to respect the natural process of breaking away from a failed relationship. If they learn how to end relationships properly, and understand the stages everyone must experience, they will make those transitions with confidence and security. Young women must learn that failure is a part of life, and that their healthy growth and development depends on their ability to handle failures responsibly.

Section 4: Late Adulthood (5)

The Root of Negative Thinking

In the minds of the women in our community, there is a great deal of negativity. Most of the negativity that people in our particular subculture know comes from foreign cultures and their influences on our society. It is also the result of the standard education we receive in the United States. Our public educational system teaches an approach to thinking and learning that falls in line with the Western tradition.

In school, when we are introduced to analytical thinking, the primary approach to learning is the scientific method. The scientific method is a problem solving approach to learning that is based on one's ability to isolate a problem, observe that problem, and form an educated guess on what is causing the problem. The next steps are to gather information about the problem, research and experiment with the factors of that problem, and draw a reasonable conclusion to the cause of that problem.

The six steps to the scientific method:
- State the Problem
- Observe
- Form Hypothesis
- Gather Data
- Experiment
- Draw Conclusion

The scientific method has been used for a long time and has proven to be a very effective learning tool. However, a problem solving method of thinking requires preexisting problem to be explored in order to be effective. People who are trying to learn how to improve their intimate relationships or how to enhance their role in the lives of their significant other have to find problems with their relationship in order to learn better.

The scientific method is a tool meant for solving problems and should not be our primary approach to learning. Solving problems are important, but not as important as problem prevention, the understanding and preservation of supernatural processes, or the healthy advancement of natural processes. People should not be taught that their learning begins with the destruction or failures of the world around them.

Problem solving begins with finding problems. Problems are all about things that are broken, bad, or thing that do not function properly. People who want to improve their lives or get more out of a commitment, or responsibility may not have a problem to solve. Their growth would depend more on their creativity, their particular taste and preference, or individual self-expression.

Those who learned to use the scientific method as a primary approach to learning live with a preoccupation with problems and negative thoughts. People in our culture are consciously bombarded with the troubles of our world. We read about crimes and political corruption in the newspaper, we share the struggles of all mankind in books and movies, and we hear about the many challenges that come with everyday life with our family, work associates, and friends.

The average person spends more time trying to understand the troubles of our society, than learning to appreciate our many successes. When people ask each other how are things going? If one of them answers negatively, there are usually probing questions about any problems he or she might mention. If someone gives a positive answer, there are rarely further inquiries about the good situations or pleasurable experiences he or she may have mentioned.

People who are taught to seek problems to solve for personal and intellectual growth often see the things in the world in a negative tone. Whether they are pessimists, or optimists, most people view the world under a cloud of negativity.

- The pessimists are given more fuel than they need to feed their fears of doom. There are plenty of television programs, and radio shows giving the community a first look at the many problems that seem to be consuming our society.
- The optimists are positive in their perspectives, but unfortunately their positive point of view too often fall to the bottom of the curve. These people take a hopeful view of a matter with a comparison to the worse case scenario. "The new boss isn't the nicest guy in the world, but at least he's no Adolf Hitler." Instead of comparing their new boss to someone good with a compliment, their optimism is based on their choosing a lesser of two evils.

How often have you been involved with a woman and heard one or more of these questions?
- Do you know what your problem is?
- Do you know what's wrong with this relationship?
- Do you know what is wrong with your friends?

Many young women build their entire relationships with men around the hopes of changing him to fit the romantic ideas in their heads. When many women enter relationships, they already have ideas of what they want and how they plan to get it. Women, who have the desire to improve their intimate relationships but do not know how, often begin exploring the possible failures or short comings of their relationship. When they cannot find anything wrong with their relationship, they begin to studying their companions.

Women often look for problems in their relationship, because they think solving a problem will make them feel closer to their significant other. They want to feel more useful and be more involved in their companion's life. Women, sometimes go to great lengths to find something wrong with their relationship or companion just to get some idea of what they can do to improve their relationship.

Self-fulfilling Prophecy

Women, who go to extreme measures to find problem in their relationships, may do more harm to their relationship than good. A self-fulfilling prophecy is when a person convinces him or herself of a potential failure, and then consciously and/or subconsciously makes decisions that insure that failure. Women, who are desperate to find problems with their companion or relationship, may make irrational decisions and find themselves creating problems they hope to solve.

When these women solve the problems they create, there is little or no fulfillment. Solving the problems they create rarely gives them the satisfaction they were seeking. If these women make the mistake of accidentally creating a problem they are unable to solve, they would have made their relationships worse than they were before.

There are two scientific perspectives on the relationship between nature and science. One is the belief that nature is unstable and destructive, and it is the purpose of science to bring nature into balance. This is the basic thinking behind Western science and it falls in line with allopathic thinking. The human body is sick, and science will make it better.

The second perspective is the belief that nature is whole and healthy, and it is the purpose of science to help maintain the balance in nature. This point of view is the basis of osteopathic or holistic thinking. The human body has the power to heal and maintain itself. The role of science is to help the human body maintain balance, and general well-being.

A negative woman who always seems to be looking for something wrong with her relationship or preoccupied with the possibilities of things falling apart is a good example of how negative thinking may impact our lives. Young women must learn the importance of intellectual health. Women must learn to break away from the negative thinking that plagues their minds.

Women must learn how to improve their lives and serve a greater purpose without being preoccupied with problems of the world. Learning to see the world through the eyes of a holistic healer and knowing that the world is naturally beautiful will go a long way towards correcting her unhealthy thinking. They must learn different methods of healthy learning and thinking. They must learn to see the world and the lives of people in the world in their proper perspective.

Our Agenda: Technology vs. Morality

Technology

In Western civilization, there is a common belief that the advancement of mankind and civilization is based on improving technology. It is believed that one can measure the advancement of a society and its people by the quality of their tools, and the professional skill level of their craftsman. The more technological the members of a society are the more developed and accomplished the societies are considered to be.

Throughout the world modern societies have ranked nations as first, second, or third world countries. The first world countries represent the most technologically advanced, while the second and third world are recognized as being relatively less. Technology and its use for many people is the measure of a culture, its members, and its overall quality of life.

Morality and Virtue

In other parts of the world, one's quality of life, the measure of a man, and the measure of a society's advancements are measured by morality and virtue. In societies that value morality above technology, people focus on enlightenment through a spiritual and faith based religions, self-actualization, and an ethnic based cultures that observes the time honored traditions of their family members long past. Individuals are valued more for their self-discipline and virtue, than their academic or professional achievements.

In a society that values morality and ethics above the proficient use of tools and weapons, the quality of life is measured by varying degrees of peace and harmony. Societies that embrace technology as the measure of a culture observe morality as simple rights and wrongs, or having to choosing the lesser of two evils. Members of morally advanced societies acknowledge that morality is the measure of mankind's individual virtue in terms of good, better, and best.

Historically societies with the greatest advancements in technology were motivated by one or more of the seven deadly sins. The motivations of these societies and the people who governed them were pride, envy, greed, gluttony, lust, sloth, and wrath. Most of these high-tech cultures were aggressive and very self-destructive. Many of the members of such cultures are warmongers, degenerate gamblers, mass murderers, con-artists, and serial killers.

Most of our societies owe their scientific and technological advancements to great leaders who suffered from major psychological abnormalities. Men and women, who were driven to rape, pillage, and plunder the world around them, while fueling their technological growth through murderous exploits.

Although their have been many advancements made to improve our quality of life, the majority of technological advancements in history have been used for more immoral reasons. It was through wars that weapons advanced for fighting, and tools of medicine advanced for medical treatment. When technology was not being used to build fortresses and secure national borders, it was used to exterminate and enslave other human beings.

As government leaders expanded their borders and work to gain greater control of natural resources, much of the scientific and technological advancement were made to mass produce goods and weapons. Societies that value money and political power above morality and human life have often misused science and technology. Technological advancements that should have fed the hungry or clothed the poor have instead been used for war.

One of the most fascinating things I have learned in my study of world history is the number of societies on the globe that have never fought a single war. Before the trans-Saharan slave trade and 500 years of European imperialism, there were a considerable number of African ethnic groups that had never fought a war. Many of these societies did not even have a word for war in their language.

I have often sat and wondered what it must have been like to live in a world where there were no wars, or even rumors of a potential war. I think about the nature of peace and harmony, and what it would mean to live in a world where peace is not just the absence of war, but a commitment to justice and a life of liberty. When people begin measuring the advancement of a culture not by the ability to change and control nature, but by their ability to humble themselves before nature, and commit to work with nature, we open ourselves to the possibilities of more positive change.

As we explore the teachings of the Lotus Sutra, the Holy Quran, and the Hebrew Bible, we find ourselves catapulted into a world defined by enlightened men and women who live for moral virtue. From the wisdom of the ancients, we have learned the higher meaning of love, mercy, and compassion. We have come to know man's place in the universe, and the role we all play in the life of His Majesty on High.

Moral excellence is the measure of a man and woman. It is the measure of the family they build, the cultures they create, and the societies they govern. There is nothing more important to the development of man and the evolution of mankind than our commitment to the wisdom of Our Creator, and the essence of His truth.

Consider this:
If the greatest power in the universe sat with you on your death bed and offered you an opportunity to choose the fate of your world, how would you answer these questions?

- Who would you choose to reincarnate to lead your immediate family? This person would be responsible for tending to your wife, and the raising of your children. He or she would also have the leadership role of commanding your extended family and friends.
- What person in history would best serve as the head of our institutions of socialization? (mass media, schools, churches, and peer groups)
- Who would you choose to shape our culture and lead our society into the future?

When I talk to African Americans who have been taught that an advanced society, and an advanced individual is determined by the use of technology, I am surprised at how most of them choose to answer these three questions. Even though many Blacks will quote the texts they read in high school when approached with the subject, most of their views about life and the world are the opposite of what they were taught.

People who were asked to give the names of a few people from history they would like to have care for their wife and children in their absence always chose religious philosophers, spiritual leaders, and human rights advocates. For all three questions, both African Americans and Black Americans selected people like the Hebrew Nazarene Jesus or Muhammad. They also selected people Martin Luther King, Malcolm X, and/or Marcus Garvey.

Of all the people in history men and women could have chosen as a leader, none of them selected Albert Einstein, Alexander Bell, Bill Gates, or Mr. Divinci. Not a single person chose a person in history that represents scientific or technological advancement. When those same people were asked why they selected moral leaders over technological leaders, everyone basically said the same thing. They all said that the clear choice for true leadership is a person of strong moral fiber and good moral character.

When I ask most people to describe the changes necessary to advance our society and improve our quality of life, I was not surprised to hear people speak of world peace, less crime, and the importance of healthier marriages. As much as most people enjoy the comforts and conveniences that come with living in a highly technical world, there are few people who would not trade most of our scientific and technological advancements for a healthier more moral society.

"Science without morality is like justice without mercy, what one provides has little value without the other."

Christopher McGee

The purpose of this topic is not to undermine the significant role that technology plays in our daily lives. It is meant to help people put science and technology in their proper perspective. Technology and science is very important to our lives, and should be taught and managed responsibly.

Our children should learn to value these necessary tools, but they should not learn to govern or define their lives around them. Our children need to know the true measure of a human being is not his or her use of tools and high-tech machines, but the quality and measure of his or her character and personality.

The five most important areas of study are diet and nutrition, health and medicine, law and government, finance and investments, and survival training and self-help. Yet, these are the academic areas in school taught the least. Our society needs an educational system that is designed to prepare the members of our subculture to function in the most healthy and efficient way possible. As African Americans, we must learn to put greater emphasis on morality and truth, while maintaining our advancement in technological skills.

The Illusion of an Independent Woman

Feminism

Feminism is the belief that women deserve the same political, social, and economical equality as men. It is also the basis of the political movement that works to gain such rights. That political movement was known as the women's liberation movement. Feminist beliefs have been around for a long time. Such views are necessary in societies with people who regard women inferior and less important than men.

In societies that consider men an opposite sex of women, feminism is a must. In cultures that recognize the conflict theory as a fundamental aspect of human interaction, feminism has grown in power and it has won a number of rights for women. Feminists may be men or women, and of any age or race.

There are 4 types of Feminists:

- The **Natural Feminists** are those women who embrace the natural women and have the highest respect for the majestic role a woman plays in procreation. These women know and respect the role that they are to play in the lives of loving men, and pride themselves on their ability to fulfill the needs of their family and extended families. The natural feminists recognize that the power and strength of a woman is different from a man, but in no way weaker than a man. The natural feminists understand that living in a world without double standards for men and women, means living in a society that would compromise who and what a woman was made to be. These are predominately women who were birthed to be wives and mothers.

- The **Privileged Feminists** are those who in the tradition of the American Blue Bloods have considerable resources. These women are from affluent families that have accumulated power, wealth, and prestige. The privileged feminists are upper class people who work to use the political power of feminism to help feather their own nest and build greater wealth for their families. These feminists pressure the middle and lower class feminist supporters to do the grunt work of the movement while they manipulate the system for their own ends. The privileged feminists want only to be the elite beneficiary members of the women's liberation movement. These are the ones who are not likely to make the greater sacrifices or ever get their hands dirty.

- The **Opportunist Feminists** are those who believe in the equality of men and women when the benefit of that equality provides women with the instant gratification they desire. However, these feminists will entertain inequality, if it provides them with the comfort and convenience they want. The opportunist feminists want the right to vote and they want to be equal in politics, but they do not want to be required to register for selective services or be called to fight on the front line. They only want to support the goals of the women's rights movement that give them what they want at a given time. These are the feminists who do not want to make any sacrifices large or small. They are the type of feminists who consider exotic dance clubs disrespectful to women if a man owns the business, but considers it a good business practice if that dance club is owned by a woman.

- The **Anti-Feminine Feminists** are those who believe the only strong women are those women who imitate men. They believe the femininity is inherently weak and that women should be more masculine in their manner. The anti-feminists frown on anything that glorifies femininity, like beauty pageants, cheerleading, or modeling. They do not care for any role that is considered proper for a woman and reject anything that is considered a female priority. These feminists also question the natural role of women as wives, mothers, and homemakers. Any woman that is not walking, talking, and thinking like a man is considered weak and inadequate. These women are sometimes considered butch and often assumed to be lesbian.

Independence
The word independent means to be free from the influence or control of others. Independence is self-governing and not depending on other for support.

Self-reliance
The word self-reliance is defined as one who depends on his or her ability, talent, and skill. Self-reliance is about the discipline and inhibition one needs to do for him or herself and function responsibly.

Autonomy is the act of an individual. A communal act is one that requires to or more people working together. Humans are social beings who rely on each other for healthy growth and stability. Creating a human being is a communal act that requires an intimate connection between two people.

In order for a human being to survive the first several years of his or her life, others must provide adequate service and protection. As infants and children, individuals depend on others to provide the basic essentials to life. After puberty, people depend on family and friends to help them understand themselves and see their place in their culture, religion, and society. As social beings, most of our development depends on our ability to connect and socialize with others. This is the nature of a human being.

Our self-concept depends on 4 combinations of different perspectives:
- People know things about themselves that others do not know.
- People know thing about themselves that others also know.
- People do not know everything about themselves. Sometimes people know things about a person that the person does not know.
- There are things that people do not know about themselves that others do not know either.

Independence is a concept of science, and is unnatural. It does not exist in divinity, the supernatural, nature, or the infer-natural. In our universes, everything is connected.

In our celestial sphere there is a link between all heavenly bodies. They turn and travel a course that is dictated by universal rules that govern our universe. On the planet earth, we all share an ecological system that maintains the balance and health of our planet.

Independence is something that is created in a laboratory within an experiment. Only in a controlled environment can scientists facilitate some degree of independence. Human beings are in no way independent. We are a needy, highly complex, highly advanced and motivated being that requires social interaction and physical touch to survive.

Imagine a boy who grows up in the country with his grandmother and no siblings. Imagine this boy had a basketball goal mounted in his grandmother's backyard and he played alone everyday from the age 5 to the ripe age 20. If he went off to college and tried out for the basketball team, what would be the pros and cons of his game?

Pros of his game:
- He may develop a near perfect shot (jump shot, free throw, etc).
- He may know how to bounce he ball between his legs and behind his back.
- He may be able to make a shot from anywhere on the court with relative ease.

Cons of his game:
- He may not know how to play ball with other, and know how to trust and depend on other teammates.
- He may not know how to be the athlete who teammates may depend.
- He may have a difficult time taking a shot against an opponent.
- He may have a difficult time dribbling the ball against an opponent.
- He may not know the ethics, roles, and responsibilities that come with competition.

There are many short coming that come with solitary living and the illusions of independence. Intimate relationships, marriages, and family are communal. All of the organizations that make up the institutions of socialization are communal. They are all highly organized groups that require teamwork, learning, and skills. These institutions are all about dependence.

Groups or teams are based on people who depend on each other to play their role and make their fair contribution. The basis of any healthy relationship is the ability to trust and depend on each other. People who entertain ideas of independence grow up spoiled, selfish, and unable to function as part of a team.

Females in our society often confuse the privilege of being with a loving man, with an opportunity to get what they want from him. The foolish females, who think that relationships are opportunities have the misconception that a good relationship are those that provide for them, and center on their happiness. Such females have no respect for men or relationships, and think that exploiting men is an acceptable way of life.

Single women should be taught to know the difference between independence and self reliance. They should remember the importance of keeping the politics of the world around them separate from the intimate and more personal world of the natural woman. Women must understand that a life dedicated to independence is a solitary life. The type of women who would limit themselves to such a self-absorbed way of life are not worthy of an intimate relationship.

The Minstrel Show of the New Millennium

The sacred roles of a man and woman are important to the advancement of the human family. The bond of man and woman make-up the basic building block of all human kind and it serves as the cornerstone of all religion, culture, and societies. The love and intimacy the two of them share represents the first organization, community, and institution. There are few things in our world more important than the healthy connection between a loving man and woman.

Many fathers are concerned about the practice of alternative lifestyles in the United States. Men are concerned that the women in their lives may be getting the wrong ideas about homosexuality and the less than positive impact it is having on the community. Both men and women in the United States are struggling with their moral responsibilities to themselves and their families, and their civic duties as United States citizens.

The Moors Society is a pro-heterosexual social circle dedicated to the health and well-being of the African families in the Americas. Homosexuality is recognized as an orientation that certain people choose to practice. It is viewed, no different than a person's choice of religion, profession, or politics.

In the Moors Society, females are taught to be women, human beings, and people of character with the highest standards. There are no accommodations made for females who compromise themselves or those who entertain them. By choosing a way of life that may limit their ability to function as true women, they cripple our advancement as a human family. The life and sacred role of woman is a fundamental part of human development and essential to the healthy growth and well-being of the human family.

Women should not be taught to entertain the life or fashion of homosexuality. Women should not only be concerned with homosexuals, but they should also be cautious of those males or females of low account who find delight in such an abomination. Men and women must hold their role and responsibilities to the nuclear family and its place in human development on the highest level. There is no substitute for the love and intimate relations between a man and woman.

It should be understood that only people who are inadequate entertain such behavior. Men, who are damaged, unprepared, or fearful of their roles as men make excuses for that orientation. Women, who have not been taught to be true and natural, find homosexuality fashionable. Only people who have little or no sexual discretion find such behavior acceptable.

Homosexuality should be recognized as a slap in the face to a true man and woman. Such males and females are the opposite of men and women. The lifestyles of homosexuals are in complete opposition to the sacred union of man and woman. Responsible people live for the sacred love between man and woman and the children they create.

The lives of a man and woman are defined by needs, responsibilities, and principles for the preservation of life and love. People who embrace alternative lifestyles have no respect for manhood, womanhood, human sexuality and/or gender. They do not hold the survival of the human family in high regards. They instead, elect to undermine the tremendous impact natural men and women have in shaping the future of our societies.

Inadequate women entertain the lives and behavior of homosexuals, because they lack self-respect and dignity. These women lack respect for womanhood and everything His Highness made in woman. The more young women learn about being a woman and the sacred institution of womanhood, the less time they will spend entertaining assorted perversions.

The confusion that inadequate women know is similar to the confusion many Black Americans have known from being nigger-slaves in the Americas. Black Americans, who are products of slavery and racial segregation, have lost themselves to the high crimes of American culture. As slaves before the civil war, Blacks were stripped of culture, religion, and identity.

As slaves in a segregated United States, the black African was given derogatory information about the continent of Africa and its residents. Many were taught that they were less intelligent, less industrious, and less capable of functioning as a European American. Blacks were also taught that their hair, dark skin, and distinguished facial and body features were ugly.

Due to racial prejudice and discrimination, many Black men and women grew up with a deeply rooted self-hatred that haunts them today. These men and women learned to hate themselves and be distrustful of each other. The curse of American culture was that Black people were to hate themselves and accept a defeated life of poverty, depression, and pain.

Consider Race….

Minstrel Shows were the first unique European American form of show business. Minstrel shows began during slavery around the 1840's and reached their peak of popularity during the days of the United States westward expansion around 1870. Most minstrel shows were performed by Caucasians who blackened their faces to imitate Black Americans.

Al Jolson was one of the popular Minstrel show actors who had a great talent for this unsophisticated form of entertainment. Minstrel shows were designed to entertain people through the degradation of Blacks in America. These shows were meant to reinforce the negative images of Blacks, while perpetuating White supremacy.

- The **social stigmas**, like the general attitude that Negroes were incapable of functioning on the intellectual levels of a Caucasian. The purpose of the Black American was defined by European Americans and their political, cultural, and social agendas. The social stigmas regarding Blacks as intellectually deficient, emotionally unstable, and as wild as animals, helped fuel the prejudice of the Caucasian community.

- There were **cultural stereotypes** about Blacks that served as ammunition for their racial bigotry. The ideas of Blacks being only a fifth of a human being, and that Africans were born of a different specie of animal than Europeans, were just some of the beliefs Caucasians entertained in order to appease their conscience.

- There are several **religious superstitions** that Caucasians used in effort to justify the crimes committed against the Africans in the United States. One of these irrational beliefs was that the Hebrews spoke of in the King James Bible were Caucasians, who had earned the approval of Yahweh, and the Negroes represented the wicked descendants of Noah. Religious superstitions like these and others helped Caucasians entertain and rationalize their abuse of Black Americans.

People like Jolson in black face would turn social stigmas, cultural stereotypes, and different religious superstitions about the American Negro into fun and games. Such savages found dark pleasure in taking the African that Our Creator made whole and human, and reducing them to nothing more than a sketch or character. Africans were made to be objects without substance, purpose or meaning.

The physical appearance of minstrel show performers in costumes:
- They would cover their entire face with black paint, with white paint around their mouths to make their lips grotesque in size.
- These performers would use black wigs that resembled mop heads, or they would dye their hair black and use a hair jell that would make their hair stand bushy and stiff.

The behavior of minstrel show performers:
- Performers would speak in what was regarded as Black dialect, with the use of slang and broken English.
- They would shuffle their feet when they walk, and bounce around as if hyperactive when strutting across stage.
- The performers would buck their eyes and stick out their lips and buttocks, while dancing around on stage.

Black Americans, who have no self-respect and harbor deep resentment for the color of his skin, find minstrel shows and playing "the dozens" entertaining. Due to their self-hatred and lack of dignity, these people get dark pleasure from seeing other Blacks insulted and emasculated. This is a good example of how a lack of identity, self-awareness, and feelings of self-hatred may lead people to think that even the most destructive behavior is acceptable.

As Black Americans learn to be African Americans, and learn about their history and cultural heritage, they better identify with themselves and other Africans. These men and women come to know the true measure, description, and identity of who they are. Africans that make the sacred connection with their true selves, learn that there are no limits to their abilities to grow and function.

As men and women became aware of the 800 or more ethnic groups, the over 400 spoken non-European languages, and the 3,000 perspectives on the practice of African Tradition, they learn that there is great diversity to their true beauty. These black Africans in the United States have begun to make a greater connection to their race, faith, and ethnicity. The more Negroes learn to love and respect themselves, the less patience they have for those who want to insult and degrade them. Black people will learn to no longer entertain the mockery of themselves or their people.

Now, Consider Sexuality.............
　　　　As Black Americans learn the truth about their race and the collective African cultures, they learn the role they have played since the earliest settlements of mankind. With a deep connection to their African heritage, Blacks will compare their collective cultures with the cultures of other human families. They will learn the true measure of African strength and beauty.
　　　　Black men and women entertain homosexuality are no different than the nigger-slaves who find dark pleasure in minstrel show. Young girls, who have not learned to genuinely appreciate the true and natural beauty of woman, tolerate the lewd and mocking behavior of homosexuals.
　　　　When these young women understand the impossible challenges of their grandmothers, the necessary daily sacrifices of their mothers, and the important preparation of their future daughters, they will no that the destructive behavior of homosexuals are not a little thing. As young women learn the pride, courage, and honor that has gone into the past 3.5 million years of womanhood, young women will understand the insult and inherent dangers of entertaining such sexual deviants.
　　　　With greater self-awareness, Black women will rebel against the negative images that homosexuality reinforce. Women will no longer entertain the social stigmas, and cultural stereotypes about woman that homosexuals embrace. They will no longer entertain males batting their eyes, flipping and bouncing, and acting a fool. These women will no longer find delight in boys calling themselves, "girlfriend" or "honey child!"
　　　　These young women will learn to see that non-sense for what it is, and they will call that individual out. They will remind him that he is not feminine, and that a woman's femininity is not some superficial thing. These women will let that confused individual know that all the twisting in the world will not substitute the natural curves of an African Queen. Those who respect woman and hold her sacred place in the human family in high regard will remind such males that no matter how wide they spread their legs what they have will never ever produce human life.

　　　　The physical appearance and behavior of those who participate in the homosexual minstrel show:

Males
- Males are wearing the hair in styles that are traditionally for females. There hair is worn feminine with highlights and colors that are gentle and pretty.
- Males wear make-up to accentuate their features and soften their appearance. Their goals are to look less masculine while trying to look more feminine.
- Many males who choose what is regarded as an alternative sexuality wear women's clothing. They wear everything from women's underwear to straight leg or skinny jeans.

249

- Some of them speak in queer tones, lifting their voices several octaves to sound soprano, and even imitating certain speech impediments. They talk in slurred speech or with a lisp.
- When many of them walk, it is with a pronounced swag, swish, or twist that is unnatural to their body's anatomy and physiology.
- Many homosexual males and females are seeking the aide of unscrupulous scientists who misuse medical science to butcher and exploit the diseased minds of certain males. They receive hormonal injections, have foreskin clipped, tucked or removed, and even go through very dangerous operations to alter the natural state of their bodies.

Females
- Females are wearing close cropped hairstyles in effort to imitate men.
- Many of these females refuse to wear make-up or women's jewelry, choosing instead to wear large medallions and big gold chains.
- These females dress butch, wear sports bras to hide their femininity, and walk around sticking their chests-out in a masculine demeanor.
- Many of these females speak in rough tones, lowering their voices several octaves to sound baritone or bass. Some of them attempt to use the more masculine forms of slang when holding conversations.
- When many of them walk, it is with a pronounced toddle like a rooster spoiling for a fight. They try with great effort to walk as masculine as men.

The flaming homosexual is an example of a modern day minstrel show, an Al Jolson in drag. It should be understood that not all homosexuals perform in public. Many of them are smart enough to know that their behavior is vulgar and choose to put on their performances in the company of those who share their interests, or in the privacy of their own homes.

The primary focus of this topic, are those homosexuals who walk around with their candles lit in public, or those who believe in camping it up. The focus is own the Little Richard types, or the stereotypes popular in Urban plays. When males and females behave this way, they show nothing but disrespect to the true man and woman. A man must teach his daughter to have the utmost respect for her and the amazing women who paved a way for future women.

Something to Know..............

African Tradition

In spiritual faith based ethnic groups, it is understood that man and woman are two parts of the same whole. It takes a man and a woman to procreate and make a whole person. In these societies, men and women were made for one another. The nature of their spiritual connection represents the basis of human sexuality, and the continuing cycle of life. Spiritually based societies recognize the supernatural connection between man and woman, and consider the roles and responsibilities of man and woman sacred.

These cultures share an understanding that the nature of man and woman is to meet, engage, and advance through life together. Because they have the utmost respect for the sacred union of a man and woman, they are inclined to see more men take responsibility for more than one wife. In such societies, it is common for men to have a number of wives and raise a number of families.

Man and Woman make a whole human being, and as a whole person they create their offspring. A man is masculine being and a companion to women. They are the protector and the provider for their families. A woman is feminine and created to be the womb of a man.

A woman was made to belong to her man. She is his lover, life partner, and makes his babies. There is nothing more sacred than the love between a man and the woman he is doing it to. In order to honor the sacred love between men and women, we will need to recognize the importance of men, who are capable of taking responsibility for more than one woman, to build more than one family.

The opposite of a man is a homosexual male who does not make the sacred connection to a woman or commit to the role of protector and provider. The gay is an effeminate who is crippled by his lust for sexual gratification. The opposite of a woman is a lesbian who does not recognize the natural role a woman plays in the life of a man. The homosexual female is out of touch with womanhood and the supernatural role she was created to play as the womb of man.

Paganism

In pagan cultures, a man and woman are considered opposites. These cultures believe that conflict is an essential part of a relationship and necessary for growth. Men and women in such societies are taught to perceive conflicts in relationships as an opportunity to assert their will onto their companions.

It is the nature of these relationships that men and women learn to compete with each other. In such relationships, two people square-off on one another and one person either suppresses the other for power or the two of them work to negotiate a fair distribution of power. The only real peace two people are likely to find in such a relationship would be reached through temporary treaties that the two of them mutually respect.

In pagan culture, gays and lesbians have a very deeply rooted history. Before Europeans expanded their influence and began absorbing the religious beliefs of African and Middle Eastern religions, most of the cultures of Europe were wide open to sexual experimentation and alternative lifestyles. With the roots of the United States of America being so firmly planted in the European tradition, the widespread tolerance of homosexuality should be expected.

The Nature of Our Infidelity

It is common in our society for people to define their success in life by their professions. In grade school, we begin the practice of defining ourselves and our peers by their talent or skill, and the role they play in their immediate social circles. From the athletes and cheer leaders to the different artists and craftsmen, those who are academic inclined or share special interests are quickly cataloged, tagged, and easily referenced by the social group to which they are assigned.

When people in our society advance to college their social circles or peer groups become more formal. People on the college level are expected to enter the educational environment with an understanding of whom they are and where they belong. At this stage in their academic careers, people are supposed to know what their goals are, and what those goals will require of them. They are expected to build relationships with students who share their professional and academic interests and begin learning how to professionally network with others.

In our society, people learn to see education as the only responsible way to build their lives. Students are often discouraged from looking into traditional labor jobs or low skilled vocational training programs. People are basically taught that anything less than a college degree or college level certification is beneath any person of substance. It is not uncommon for a professional people to share the belief that people are nothing without a college education.

If you were to ask an average group of college student to discuss their lives, most of them would discuss the people they hope to one day be through the use of their education. Few students learn to see themselves or a possible future outside of their professional goals. Most of them are more in tune with their career goals than anything else in their lives.

When a person's identity evolves around their job, business or professional title, they often characterize their entire lives in that tradition. People often look at their lives in corporate America as a model by which to live their lives. They begin to see their lives as a spouse, parent, extended family member, and even community member in the same light as their place in corporate America.

The Corporate American Marriage

Many married couples in America see the life of a spouse and parent as a full-time job. Men and women, who also have professional jobs, consider their roles and responsibilities to their families as a second job to the one that pays the bills. For people who define their lives around their profession, marital and family roles take on a very unique perspective.

Consider This.....

People attend college or some type of vocational school and invest a lot of time and money. They make these sacrifices in preparation of building successful careers. After they complete their education and receive their credential, people enter the job market with the hope of earning the job of their dreams and reaping the many benefits of their professional goals.

People in our society learn to see dating and courtships as preparation for marital type relationships. For many people, the relationship they share with a potential lover or marriage partner can be compared to the time people spent in school preparing for their careers. People invest a lot of time and energy learning what it means to care for someone in a mature, responsible relationship.

In high school, people begin dating and learning the little odds and ends of a proper courtship. By the time they get into college, most people feel confident in their ability to function in an intimate relationship. It is then, that people begin pursuing deep, long-term romantic relationships. Most people feel that their years of experiences in dating will be rewarded by meeting that special person and building a healthy, lasting love affair.

People select a potential suitor the same way they choose their profession. They choose on the basis of their needs, short and long-term goals, and natural appeal and ability. Men and women choose both their companion and career for pride, honor, security, and confidence. They hope that their job and their relationship grow healthy and strong, giving way to great success and prosperity.

After their college or vocational training, many people have a difficult time finding that dream job or a job that represents an opportunity to advance in their given career or profession. **People who are unable to find a good job out of college often take jobs just to pay their bills**. Although these jobs are unfulfilling on a personal level, they provide a person with everything they need to continue moving their lives forward.

In the beginning, most people consider these jobs temporary. They are usually meant to be used as a stepping stone to something better. Sometimes, the stepping stone people see as a temporary job becomes an opportunity. Other times, that great opportunity never comes, and people often find themselves settling for position in a field that does not interest or fulfill them.

As young adults, men and women begin to pursue relationships that are more nurturing, supportive, and fulfilling. For many, finding a companion who possesses all of the qualities one may be searching for is very difficult. Despite their best efforts, many people find it almost impossible to find a suitable mate.

Even though most people know what they want in a companion, they often settle for someone less. These individual elect to date people who provide a simple relationship that meets certain basic needs. They build such cookie-cut relationships to past the time, keep them in tune with what they really want, and give themselves much needed companionship. Few people will advance in life and meet their ideal mate, but some will discover great potential in one of their temporary relationships. For these people, the opportunity they had come to know will evolve into a rare, but greatly appreciated privilege.

Unfortunately, most people will tolerate their meaningless relationships until they dig a hole for themselves that make their temporary relationships necessary or create a false sense of comfort and security with their temporary companion. These are individuals who will use a lot of romantic non-sense and religious superstitions in a desperate attempt to modify their relationships into something that looks meaningful. This is the nature of the corporate relationship search.

One of the most important things people learn about changing jobs is that **one never leaves a first job before securing the second**. When money is needed to function on a daily basis, one can not afford to be without a paycheck. Finding a job and/or keeping a job in a forever changing economy can be a major challenge.

People who have not made the love connection they dream will pursue short-term, temporary relationships in order to meet their basic needs for companionship. These relationships, by design, are not meant to be more than a quick fix to satisfying their immediate needs. People in these relationships are committed to keeping their relationship resume up to date and they work to verify that their applications are always on file with those who might be considered the objects of their desire.

Men and women work hard to keep their options open, because when those dream jobs come available they want to be free to pursue any and every opportunity. Sometime opportunity knock at inconvenient times, and people have to make quick changes to their lives. These changes are often made at the drop of a hat, and may leave the temporary job inconvenienced.

Corporate relationships require both men and women to keep their options open. When someone in a relationship gets an opportunity to go after their soul-mate and build his or her dream relationship, there is always a chance that the companion of the temporary relationship will suffer some inconvenience. If a person goes in for an interview, orientation, or is made an offer, the temporary relationship will likely be given notice. On the other hand, if the time invested reveals that the potential relationship has no real future, then the applicant will plan to continue their employment with his or her temporary relationship.

The roles and responsibilities that women have in intimate relationships create special challenges. As a help meet, women are a lot like lawyers. Whether they are earning $25,000 a year or $250,000 a year, their work hours and sacrifices are pretty much the same.

The emotional investments most females make for the roles of the woman require a great deal of time and energy. It is the nature of women and the nature of intimate relationships that dictate a woman serve only one man. Their transition from one man to another, even on a temporary basis, usually represents an extreme change. For this reason, women will rarely arrange for interviews with a new man or breakup from a temporary companion until they have found a potential relationship of much greater value.

Because of the nature of intimate relationships and the role men are expected to play, some men may elect to receive the comfort of two or more inadequate women if it means that collectively their efforts will satisfy him. Men are likely to breakup with a companion after they have secured a relationship that is of greater value than their temporary one. However, if men are in a relationship that does not meet their needs, they may opt to start an additional relationship to supplement the substandard one. In other words, a man may work to relationships at the same time if the primary relationship does not adequately provide.

Advancing in intimate relationships is like advancements in careers:

- Poor jobs or relationships are avoided.
- Fair jobs and relationships are taken as needed on a temporary basis.
- Good jobs and relationships put people closer to what they want and/or deserve, but may require a second job while working at low paying entrance level positions. (Sometime, in early relationships, it may take a person a while to open up and give of themselves.)
- Excellent jobs and relationships are fulfilling in most everyway and satisfy a wide range of needs.

When men and women pursue professional jobs, they are primarily looking for **full-time employment, with designated work days, and preferred work hours**. They hope to have designated or preferred time-off. While on the clock, most people want to focus as much attention as necessary on their job and its duties. At the end of the work day, most people hope to free themselves from their job and all of its responsibilities. They want to break away and not think about work until their next work day.

In corporate relationships, people want to build relationships that enable them to be a part of something special, but they do not want to have to lose themselves in the process. People want to be in a whole relationship that will provide for both parties. Men and women want to work and contribute to their relationships and care for their children, but they also want a healthy amount of "Me" time.

It should be understood that everyone needs to serve their companion and their children. It should also be understood that everyone needs their designated time-off. Men and women need to be able to give their undivided attention to their families, and do whatever is required for them. They also need a chance to break away from their duties. Most of them need the freedom to find a place that is not family related and forget about the many demands their families.

On their **days-off**, people rarely want to see their work place, work oriented materials, or anyone from their place of employment. They want to focus on non-work related matters and their personal pleasures. Many of these people live what maybe described as double or triple lives with as many as three different identities. Such people have an employee personality for the work place, their "home life" personality they share with family, and the "single life" personality shared with close friends and the general public.

Although these three personalities maybe similar in many ways, they are not meant to stand together. The "game face" most wear on the job is totally different from the attitude and state of mind they know with their families, and the person people reveal to their friends at a night club or bar is considerably different than anything co-workers and family members might see everyday.

For some men and women, the very thought of bumping into people from their work place on their day-off is a source of great irritation. The anxiety people have at the thought of running into a co-worker away from the workplace can be so great that some people may get in the habit of spending their time-off on the opposite sides of town. They may even put off doing things that might mean having to interact with people they only have professional relations.

When men and women get a day or a few hours away from their families, they rarely want to see their families, hear about any family related matters, or speak to anyone in their families. They want to focus on non-family related issues and their personal or private pleasures. Whether they are playing a round of golf or just doing a little shopping, few people want to have their companion or their children sitting at their feet.

For many people, trying to break away from their families is a source of great friction. People often feel rejected when they are told that their companion needs space or time away from them. Most of the time, men and women find it difficult to spend their personal time with their significant other. Both men and women tend to feel as if they are always on deck when they are with their companion.

Men are not always able to break away from the role of the protector, and women find it difficult not to serve their man. People who try and share their personal time with their companion have a difficult time not discussing family related issues. The stress and strain of their traditional jobs and the job of being parent and spouse makes it difficult for some individuals to find the time and space for adequate rest and relaxation.

Problems like these may get so bad that people will find themselves seeking out members of either sex to share their personal or vacation time. People begin finding comfort in the company of casual associates, casual acquaintances, and even strangers. Spending time with people who are not acquainted or associated with their families or jobs, and even good friends become a common practice. For many people in corporate relationships, building casual relationships with people foreign to their personal world becomes the norm.

A Special Note: When men or women find themselves in the arms of someone other than their significant other, it is often the result of spare time shared with people who respect their need to sometimes be work and family free. Men and women often find themselves having an affair with other married people, because they share the same need for both individual space and companionship.

"People having sex with individuals outside of their intimate relationships are symptomatic of much larger issues."

Some people may argue that benefits and privileges are the bedrock of a real profession, **everyone wants the big paycheck**. With the exception of individual fulfillment on the job, the most important thing to most people is their salaries. Professions are highly competitive and there is only room for a few at the top. For this reason, most people make great preparation for their careers.

Most professionals spend several years in college for their degree and after college many professional jobs require continuing education courses. Updating licenses, re-certifying for special skills, advanced research are just some of the preparations professional people have to make. Many work hard to the best at their jobs and establish themselves as an authority in their field.

The compensation for all of their hard work is a major marker for measuring people's success. People work for regular pay, bonuses, raises, and even professional and advancement. For most professionals, compensation for their hard work goes a long way towards defining the purpose of their daily sacrifices.

In relationships, people expect adequate compensation for the time, energy, and hard work they invest. The basis of any relationship is the purpose one person serves to the other. Intimate relationships get their vary meaning from the shared goals and objectives people have for building a healthy fellowship.

One of the most important things people will do in their relationships is develop a menu of goods and services that may be offered to their companion in order to properly compensate them for a relationship properly served. How men or women reward their significant other goes a long way towards expressing the importance of their companionship.

Caution: Risk VS. Reward

The United States is all about capitalism and free enterprise. People invest money to make great profits, and the best investments are those that pay handsomely with very little loss. In American society, people work for a living. They make considerable sacrifices to earn as much money as humanly possible. People work to earn as much money as they can, as fast as they can, while working as little as possible.

People, who define themselves and their life's successes along the lines of a professional career, often think that relationships should yield great rewards with as little work as possible. They may even pride themselves on their ability to gain all of relationships rewards without giving anything in return. Men and women should take the necessary precautions to ensure that their potential suitor is motivated by the role and responsibilities of a relationship and not its benefits.

Bonuses and special accommodations are important gratuities offered to people who give over and beyond their normal responsibilities. These special rewards represent high praises and thanks for being one of the most valuable members to a professional work team. Companies give out such gifts to acknowledge the defining moments in a persons career.

Defining moments in relationships require proper acknowledgment and a just reward. In addition to the daily or regular menu, there should be a special list of gifts and awards for a companion who has went over and beyond their call of duty. No payment or bonus has to be expensive or necessarily large in size, it only has to be given from the heart with genuine love and appreciation.

Vacation Time and personal days are two of the benefits people use in measuring the prestige of their position and their importance to their employer. The time people are paid to take for their personal pleasure or comfort is generally recognized as a special benefit only given to key members of a work team. These are benefits used to compensate employees who work long hours and sacrifice a lot of personal or family time. Everyone needs time from work, whether time from their job or time from their companion and family.

When people go on vacation, they often visit the islands or other far away places. People sleep in fine hotels, rent cars, and eat at nice restaurants. People do not sleep in fine hotels because they have a problem with their beds at home. Men and women do not travel to exotic places because they do not enjoy the city in which they live.

Vacations are not about problems at home or on the job. Vacations are about shaking up one's routine. They are about doing something exciting, fun, and different. People go on vacations when they are in need of a refreshing change. It is often assumed that people who have affairs do not love their spouses. That is far from the truth. Most people love their companions and their families, and want very much to stay married.

The time people spend with a new and different companion is often nothing more than a little vacation. It is a simple opportunity for them to explore something fun and new. Many people in American culture have affairs and most of them are short lived adding up to nothing more than a simple change in a cramped daily routine.

During certain times of the year, people may need to earn a little extra money for something special they need and they do not want to burden their companion with the debt. When these people have a good companion who is working hard and doing their best to care for them, they do not want to over tax them with an issue that could be easily resolved through the services of an intimate friend.

These people elect to take on a part-time or temporary relationship so that they do not have to burden their significant other with a selfish pleasures or needs. These relationships, by their very nature, are meant as stress relief and comfort. They are a quick fix, and are usually short lived. Like any part-time job, they rarely interfere with the full-time duties of the primary corporate relationship.

Retirement and long term financial securities are also important benefits of a professional job. In addition to what people put in social security, they work in their given professions and invest money in retirement plans. Retirement is primarily designed to provide for people after they get too old to work for themselves. Retirement packages usually pay 25 cents or more for every dollar an employee invests in their retirement accounts. In 25 years or more, an employee may accumulate anywhere from tens of thousands to millions of dollars in retirement.

The retirement stage of a corporate relationship may be the most challenging time for most couples. Retirement is a time when people feel they deserve to be rewarded for many years of sacrifices, hard work, compromises, and investments. People typically recognize retirement as a time when they receive all the benefits and privileges for past work. It is considered a time when people no longer have to work to reap the benefits of their relationships.

Because people consider the compensation and benefits of a long-term relationship as "paid for", many people begin to treat their intimate relationship as if it is something they used to do. Some treat their significant other as if their role and responsibilities of the relationship are for the most part over. Both men and women begin treating their companion as if their duties are a burden and a nuisance.

People who live in the illusion that relationships enter a stage of retirement need to re-evaluate the nature of their corporate relationships. Every year couples who have been together for 25 years or more are ending. These failing relationships are in no small part the fault of unhealthy thinking and poor perspectives on relationships.

One important aspect of corporate relationships is the responsibilities people have in redefining their relationship after all or most of their major relationship goals have been met. People, who spend 25 years or more working with their companion to build homes, raise children, complete their education, and build successful careers, often find themselves lost in a relationship that no longer seem to have any purpose. These people have to learn how to get to know themselves and each other all over again, and find new goals and objectives for their corporate relationship.

A Perspective on Infidelity

Fidelity is a faithful devotion to duties and a commitment to accuracy in reproduction. When a man and woman come together to build an intimate relationship, each one of them have responsibilities to him or herself, to his or her companion, and to the fellowship itself. Fidelity in a relationship is about a man and woman's commitment to the duties of being a companion.

Infidelity is simply defined as being unfaithful or disloyal. Someone who is faithful would be described as conscientious, respectable, and responsible. A faithful relationship is one built on trust and reliance. Only when both a man and his woman are ready, willing, and able to adequately serve each other, can an intimate relationship be regarded as one of equal fidelity.

In our society, misguided feminists have crippled many women with destructive ideas about womanhood and the proper place of a woman. They have targeted the basic roles women play in marriage and families. These unscrupulous females have tried to tarnish the sacred role of mother and spouse. Young women who are poorly raised are often made to feel resentment towards themselves and others who take on the roles of a homemaker and family caregiver. What these unscrupulous females are doing is wrong.

A Woman's Place....

When a person buys a new home, the home is usually equipped with a garage. The garage is designed to provide shelter for an automobile. A car or truck may be parked in the driveway or along the front curb. If someone built a ramp, an automobile may even be parked on the roof. Regardless of where one may choose to park his or her automobile, its proper place is the garage.

Many women have been led to believe that their advancement in politics, professions, and academics requires them to abandon their normal role as a homemaker, their natural place as a man's woman, or their supernatural and primary roles as a mother. This is non-sense. Although women are capable of achieving many great things outside the home, a woman's place is, was, and will always be in the home where she cares for her man and makes his babies.

The Good Ole Days....

In the old days, men and women worked by the sweat of their brow to make ends meet. When a man took interest in a woman and made his feelings known, he would demonstrate his ability to provide for his woman by buying her flower and gifts. He would invite her to his home so that she could see the type place he could provide. Men understood that a woman needed a man that could provide an adequate life for her and her children.

When a woman caught the eye of a male suitor and began courting, she would in turn demonstrate her ability to care for her man. She would put on her nicest dress to show her beauty. A woman would cook a man lunch and bring it to his work place, or invite him to her parent's home where she would demonstrate her ability to prepare a healthy full course meal for him. Women would make quilts, sow clothing, knit sweaters, and draperies to show her man how she would contribute to their lives as a homemaker and one day care for their babies.

Although men are still expected to demonstrate their ability to be a good provider, women in our society have gotten away from the role of demonstrating their ability to do anything other than pleasure a man in bed. If you ask the average female between the ages 17 and 35, what their role is during the friendship, dating, and courtship stages of a growing relationship, most of them would have hard time explaining what their responsibilities are supposed to be.

There are a number of women who think their role in a relationship is nothing short of a pet, stage prop, or tourist. They often think that being the person sitting across the dinner table at a nice restaurant or sharing an aisle seat at the theater is the grounds for a deep loving relationship. Many of them think that simply being on display, providing sexual pleasure, or bringing drama in to a relationship is the extent of their role.

When many women visit the home of a gentlemen caller, their first mind is to meet and extensively explore their world. These women investigate the lives of every potential suitor looking for anything they might find. Most women will go to great lengths to find out whether or not a man is right for them, but often dismiss the notion that men are doing the same thing with them. Many women in our society live as if men should be held to the highest standards, and women should for the most part be free from accountability.

In our society, men often engage women who know everything they want from a man in a relationship, but have given little thought to their duties to their men. With the exception of sexual pleasure, inadequate women have a difficult time putting the wants and needs of a male suitor into perspective. Many females do not seem to consider the sacrifices required of them when building a relationship. Young women should know that the greater role of a woman in a relationship begins long before marriage.

I have often asked women to take inventory of their relationships with their suitors and describe the most important details of their relationship. In most cases, women have a detailed understanding of everything their boyfriend does for them, but rarely speak of any regular good or service they offer them. Many females consider a man serving them the very basis of their intimate relationship.

In relationships where men are expected to always give of themselves no matter how unfulfilling the relationship, women should not be surprised that so few men opt marry. Those women, who misuse men and take them for granted, are often surprised when men elect to pursue other women to supplement their unfulfilling relationships.

Relationships are give and take. An intimate relationship requires men and women to give 100%. A woman should not get involved with a man until she is ready to give the way she hopes to receive. A woman should not require or accept the sacrifices of a man unless she is ready, willing, and able to make those same sacrifices for him.

I have met women who feel that not giving of themselves, in certain ways, until marriage is necessary for building a healthy relationship with a man. Although many of these women refuse to buy gifts, share intimacy, or show favor to their companions without a wedding ring, they feel it is appropriate to accept such gifts.

An intimate relationship is a privilege and not an opportunity. Setting perimeters on what one is willing to give, but not setting boundaries in what one will receive is an act of rape and exploitation. Such behavior is not appropriate for a woman.

If a woman feels a need to save herself for marriage, it is only proper that she give him the same respect. It is not appropriate for a woman to accept gifts or favor that she is not actively returning. When a woman feels a need to place limits on what she shares with a man, the limits should be fair and equal.

The women in your life should know better than to take advantage of another human being. They should learn to be sensitive to the feelings and needs of men, and learn to treat men the way they want to be treated.

A Perspective on Cheating

The word cheat is defined as a swindle or fraud. It is a dishonest or deceitful way of dealing with others. When someone consciously misuses, short changes, or takes advantage of someone else. In relationships between men and women, people often use the word cheater when describing a former companion who had other love interests. In intimate relationships, cheating is quite common for both men and women, but they do not necessarily cheat the same way. Males cheat their girlfriends the way people might cheat on their diets. Females cheat their boyfriends the way a businessman might cheat on his taxes.

Males

When males creep on their companions, it is as if they have spent months on a diet avoiding all of their favorite foods and decided to reward themselves with a taste of their favorite dessert. These males go to the grocery store and buy a New York Style Cheesecake with a carton of sweet frozen strawberries. They take their reward home, but they do not put it in the main refrigerator in the kitchen. Instead, they put their precious dessert in the rarely used refrigerator in the garage.

The cheesecake is carefully placed in the back of the refrigerator on one of its lower shelves and cleverly hidden behind a wide variety of foods and packages. They think that if the cheesecake is hidden in the spare refrigerator, no one will find out about it. The plan is to get a little nibble of their secret cheesecake everyday.

The idea is that a little nibble everyday would be good for them, but not enough to spoil their diets. These males keep their dessert out of reach so that no one can eat on it but them. Males often feel that such plans are a good way to get what they want without hurting themselves or involving anyone else.

In the social circle of most men, there are unwritten rules that men will do whatever it takes to "come up". Other unwritten rules are that no one is lower than a rat that tells another man's business, or attempts to snake the woman of a friend. In the circle of men, there are those who think men should feel free to creep on their women as long as they provide well for them.

Some men may feel being unfaithful is unacceptable, unless the circumstances are great and having another woman is genuinely a necessity. Others may stand neutral on the subject, not really caring either way. Regardless of their stand on the matter, men do not rat out other men. For this reason, there are fewer precautions taken by males who cheat on their companions. This is also why men are more likely to get caught.

Females

Females cheat as if they are business executives who have a considerable amount of money in the bank, but do not feel comfortable with the unfair tax laws and the large amounts of hard earned money the IRS takes from them every year. These intelligent, highly calculating, business minded females will study every loop hole; look in every nook and cranny, until they find every single dime they can keep for themselves.

Like an unscrupulous businessman, when a female cheats she is careful not to leave a trail. She is careful not to fall into any repeating habits, and to always maintain probable deniability. Females will not cheat everyday or even every week, choosing to only gamble when all odds are in their favor.

They will keep their options for cheating open, and have their affairs in a way that would be very difficult to track. These females will go to church with their children, leaving their husbands at home to watch a ball game, and find the best time to slip away from church and meet with their "Sugar Daddy".

While their husband is at home, and the children are in Sunday school or morning service, these women will slip away to the home of their other lover "to get their freak on". Sometimes, the best opportunity for females to creep are when the children are having piano lessons, at soccer practice, or attending some other after school function. A woman could ask one of the other mothers to watch her children while she slips away, gets her a little monkey loving, and then returns to collect her children with a few parcels of groceries and a big smile.

These are just some of the measures females will take in order, "to get their groove on" without getting caught. When businessmen cheat on their taxes, they take all precautions, and they rarely get caught. Most females recognize that members of their gender like to gossip and keep up a whole lot of drama. Such females spend most of their time either trying to hear the latest gossip about the females of their world or trying to keep their own business a secret.

In our society, females take a great deal of pride in the belief that men are quick to cheat or betray the confidence of a woman. There is so much pride in such non-sense that many females refuse to consider the dishonesty and deceit between other females and their companions. Females are not as inclined as males to cover for a cheating girlfriend.

For this reason, females take every precaution when being unfaithful. When it comes to protecting their secrets, females have to be as concerned about the women close to them, as they are everyone else.

When a female lives in a world where women out number men by a considerable margin and the number of quality men decrease as she grows older, it is only natural that females become more protective of their relationships. Under such circumstances, even if a relationship was less than satisfactory, a female may make special effort to keep her companion by her side.

Special Note:

In America and other societies greatly influenced by European cultures, people define themselves by their professional careers. There are other ways people in different cultures all over the world define and measure their success. These are the primary perspectives people may use to define themselves:

- Civil- Politics and Civil Rights
- Professional- Careers and Jobs
- Academics- Educational Credentials
- Religion/Faith- Belief Systems
- Supernatural or Spiritual- Mankind's place in the universe
- Military- Military or Paramilitary disciplines and polities
- Ecclesiastics- Faith and/or Religious philosophy
- Arts and Crafts- Artistic talent and Creative ability
- Ethnic/Cultural- Ancestry, Heritage and Tradition
- Primitive- An eclectic combination of ethnicity, faith, and family heritage. (See The Making of a Moor Woman Volume II, Book 2.)

Section 5: The Community Cure! (2)

A few years back, I had the privilege of attending a forum at the University of Texas in Austin. The sponsor of the forum was the Black Greek sorority Alpha Kappa Alpha. While I was on stage, me and the other young men invited to participate were asked many different questions. We were asked questions about the lives of Black men and women, relationships, and of course dating.

Of all the questions we were asked that night, the one that stuck out in my mind over the years was about the Black community. That question was as followed:

What is the one thing that African Americans can do to make the biggest improvement on the condition of the Black community in the United States?

When the question was asked, every man on the panel sat quietly for a minute before attempting to answer. Although I do not remember the names of the other men on stage, I do remember there answer. One of the guys said something on the lines of religion and prayer. Another guy mentioned something about getting an education and better jobs. Of the four guys that were on stage only two of us tried to answer the question with something more than a cookie cut answer.

The third young man attempted to explain the importance of Black Americans working together to build a place in the greater American family. I remember thinking that his views were insightful, but that I did not consider them at the time to be very realistic. When the question was directed towards me I remember talking about the Black institutions and our role in giving them our full support. I believed that our advancement would come from taking what was already built for us as a people and committing to adding to them.

At the time I was trying to communicate the importance of young people taking the torch that had been passed to us and traveling the well paved road of the Black Nationalists before us. I was also giving every Black American student attending the forum a playful and spirited jab for not choosing to attend a historically Black college. I gave the audience an answer that seemed to give a lasting impression, but I never felt good about it. It always bothered me that the answer really did not fix anything.

Well, to make a long story short, I never stopped thinking about that community question. It has been years since I visited the University of Texas and even longer since I have seen anyone from that forum. I do not remember who those young Alpha Kappa Alpha women were or where they wound up, but I hope you find this useful. It has taken me a long time, but I have finally found "the year book answer" to your question.

As a Black American one might say that the Black community is overwhelmed with poverty, pain, depression, and broken families. Some might say that drug abuse, crimes, and the cycles of generational dysfunction are so bad that the Black community can not be fixed. This is the common sense thinking of Black Americans who limit themselves to mainstream America and European tradition.

These Black Americans have learned to depend on mass media for direction. They see magazines, newspapers, and television as authorities on how one should live and think. In fact, many minorities in the United States look to the media to learn what society expects from them, where there place is in society, and how they are expected to function on a daily basis.

People who have spent the greater part of their lives limited to the practices and popular ideas of mainstream America have a difficult time seeing the possibilities of the Black community. Without the ability to think "outside of the box", many Black people will throw up their hands in frustration at the thought of changing the community for the better. Where the Black American will look at the community through the eyes of mainstream America and say that the Black community can not be helped and that it has too many problems, an African American would say that the Black community and its people only have one problem.

The real problem that plagues the Black community is the lack of respect for the more positive philosophies, beliefs, and practices of our African ancestry. Our lack of respect for our African heritage keeps us from learning about the common practices that helped us sustain and grow as a people for over a million years. These traditions and values common to our African brethren kept our people thriving at time when much of the world was in darkness.

One of those practices is polygamy or more particular polygyny. Polygamy is the practice of a person taking on more than one marital partner. In Africa and many other cultures throughout the world, many men and women share the responsibilities and benefits of marriage with multiple partners. Polygyny is a form of polygamy in which only men take more than one wife.

Polygyny is commonly practiced in Asia and Africa. In the Hindu culture, men can have as many wives as they desire. Among Muslims, it is believed that a man can have as many as four wives. In polygamous cultures where men have more than one wife, each wife has her own home or they live in what is known as a multiple family dwelling. A multiple family dwelling is a compound that provides for all of the wives and their children. The estate is designed to give each woman and her offspring their own private sleeping quarters, while providing an adequate living area for the whole family to share.

In 1862, the United States Congress passed a law that made polygamy illegal. In America, polygamy is still practiced by certain religious and social sects. The Mormons are native to the United States and they practiced polygamy for several years. Other American families are from foreign countries and they practice marriage according to the social mores of their home country.   Although the families that practice polygamy do not allow their business to be "put in the street", many practice this tradition faithfully.

If the average Black man had two to three wives in the African Tradition, it would solve 90% or more of the Black community's troubles. Whether it is religious, cultural, or social, everything begins with man and woman. Man, woman, and the children they produce make up the basic building blocks of society. This building block is the nuclear family and represents the center of our world.

When we speak of polygyny, we are talking about a modified marital relationship and modified building block working together to shoulder the greater responsibilities of a complex multicultural society. This modified marriage and nuclear family is a lot stronger than the traditional family. It will provide a much healthier group dynamic and greater long-term security for both the marriage and family unit. This modified unit is the key to setting the African American family and community on the right path.

Consider this....

Men   In our society, men learn that manhood is all about being a "tough guy" like John Wayne or a womanizer like the famous Elvis Presley movie roles. We get all of these backward ideas from our dealings in mainstream America. Our children are learning through the mass media to see themselves and the people in their live along the most superficial guidelines as possible.

The boys are trying to define their world by fast money and the material things it can buy, while girls see what gifts and favor they might earn through being the object of a man's sexual conquests. If we could only teach men to embrace the beauty of our African culture, we would no longer define our world through war, aggression, political corruption, and treachery. We would no longer see the world through the eyes of gangsters and warlords.

Our people would learn from the history of African ethnic groups, who before the trans-Saharan slave trade never knew war. We would learn to think along the lines of Gandhi or the Hebrew Nazarene Jesus by embracing the ethics of African societies who live at peace with all living things and define their lives by the love they share as a family. Our people would learn to govern ourselves with less politics and more virtue.

Men and women in our culture have to learn to live according to the discipline of the prophets and the light of their wisdom. They would learn that a man, who provides for his children the way the prophets provided for their followers, is a true man. They would also learn that a man, who provides for a school of women like Jesus provided for his church of disciples, is a man after His Majesty's own heart.

Women   Many African American women want to be wives and mothers while continuing their education and building their professional career. When you consider the time it takes to meet that special someone, establish the necessary trust, carefully build a responsible relationship, plan the making of your babies, pregnancy, and childbirth, becoming a new mother is very time consuming proposition. At the age of 18, a young woman is beginning the Golden Age of her sexual power (average ages 18 to 24). With this age being ideal for meeting her mate, every young woman needs the time to get out and make her claim.

During the years 18 to 24, a young woman is in the prime of her physical health and beauty. The Golden Age is a time for growth and infinite possibilities. These strong young women have a high threshold for pain, they are more open and hopeful, and they are full of youth and vigor. These years represent the height of ovarian egg production in women and they are ideal for pregnancy, childbirth, and child rearing.

At the same time, the average young woman will finish high school around 18 years of age. If she can afford to go off to college and work straight through without disruption, she will finish her four year degree by the age of 22. It will take an additional 2 to 4 years to complete a graduate or professional degree. By the time they have completed their education, the average women will already be 24 to 26 years of age.

After she invests two to three years of her life in corporate America, she will likely be almost 30 years of age.

Research has shown that fertility in women has changed for the worse by age 30, and will drop sharply after the age 35. Those women who hope to finish school and get started in their careers before starting a family will likely be well into the Bronze Age of a woman's sexual power and entering the mid-life malaise when they begin their family. When we take a close look at the emotional state and physical condition of most women during the mid-life malaise, we see that this is clearly not the best time to start a family.

Women in our culture will have to learn to efficiently build healthy intimate relationships, while also acquiring an education and building their careers. The beauty of polygamous relationships is their ability to provide each of the married women with the individual freedom needed to continue their quest for individual fulfillment.

Wife/Mother   As two or more African American women come together to care for their husband and children, practically everything in their lives will change for the better. When two or more wives work together and provide for their man, they can divide those duties and reinforce their efforts. They will share the responsibilities of cooking, cleaning, and housekeeping. They will also share the more intimate aspects of helping each other grow as individuals.

The time and energy these women spends caring for them and each other will have a profound impact on all of their lives. By building this modified family, we will cut the stress of the average women by 2/3. We will cut the stress of homemaking, raising the children, and earning a living to the bare minimum.

There are many stress related diseases and disorders that plague the lives of women. Some of the most common are PMS, postpartum depression, high blood pressure, and migraine headaches. Lowering the level of stress women have to endure on a daily bases will add years to their lives by improving their overall health. A relationship that will cut the stress and strain of being a wife and a mother is good for everyone.

Each of the wives would get the support and sisterhood they need, and husbands will get all of the love and nurturing they need. Instead of one woman trying to make breakfast, lunch and dinner, the three wives share those responsibilities. Everyone in the family would adequately provide for each other. People would rarely have to stop pushing towards their personal success in order to meet the needs of their family.

The women who come together for the good of the family will share the responsibilities of educating their babies. One woman would focus on their education or "The three R", while the second mother focuses on religion and the church. The third mother would focus on community program, extra curricular activities, and other things like the neighborhood crime watch. While the mothers care for the needs of the babies, the man of the house will keep a "watchful eye" on the corporate community and local politics.

In a traditional family, if a man and his woman have three children and either one of them suffer a severe or fatal accident, the family would be made cripple. In the case of a severe accident the surviving man or woman would find themselves overwhelmed with the challenges of caring for his or her spouse and their children. In the case of a fatal disease or accident, the man or woman would be left to raise their three children alone.

A parent having to carry such weight would not be good for them or their children. Even when parents have adequate life insurance and work hard to wisely budget their lives a bad situation may quickly overcome the family. An untimely death may leave a family stun and in need of therapy and professional counsel, and living with a deadly disease may wipe out a family savings. Families in situations like these may quickly become a burden to their extended families and communities.

In a community of traditional families, most couples would be struggling to maintain their own lives. They would not have the resources to provide adequate aid to a family in great distress. A widow or widower would have to call on the support of families, who despite their desire to help may not be able to do so. These people and their families would be at the mercy of government aid, their community, and the church.

However, if a man and his three women have three children a piece and either one of them suffered a severe or fatal accident the modified family would have a support system in place that would continue to provide for their family. In the case of a man or woman who has taken ill, the family would have the money to provide the best care for their spouse. They would also have each other to help shoulder the load of caring for the sick, as well as the other members of the family.

A mother suffering from a fatal illness would not have to worry about the lives of her husband and children. She would know that the other wives would provide adequately for her husband and help him provide for their children in her absence. She would also have the added comfort of knowing that the people taking responsibility for her children would not just finish raising her children, but would continue doing so with her dreams and ideas in mind. The husband and wives left to care for her children would be sensitive to all of her plans and expectations for her children.

It is one thing for parents to say that when they die they would like to leave their children in good hands. But it is another thing for parents to say that when they die they would want to leave their children in the best of hands. When parents can leave their children in the hands of people who understand and respect their philosophy, and beliefs, they know that their children are in a place they belong.

When a woman leaves her children in the hands of the assisting wives that will survive her, she is leaving her children with family. She would be placing her trust in two women who attended each of her pregnancies, and births. She would be trusting in women who have shared in the raising of her children. These two women would have been like sisters to her, and they would have already lived as foster mothers to her children.

If the husband and father of a modified family met with an accident or untimely death, he would have the comfort of knowing that three best friends are combining their efforts to take care of each other. These wives would continue to work together as they had since the day he took them for himself, and continue build a beautiful world for his children. He could rest with the confidence that his children would be properly cared for in his absence.

In a modern society, where many people live to a ripe old age, men and women often out live their spouse. For a person in a traditional marriage, this may be a devastating and life altering experience. Even those individuals who spent their lives in monogamous relationships raising large families are likely to find themselves old and alone.

However, members of a polygynous marriage and a modified family are least likely to grow old alone. If the three mature wives of a good man find themselves widows, they would have each other. Whenever I think of three beautiful women living together and caring for each other, I am reminded of the television program, "The Golden Girls". I believe that show give us an idea of what the lives of mature widows of a polygynous marriage could be.

Children   More than anyone, the polygynous marriage and family will best serve our children. When a man and his wives share the responsibility of caring for their children, each of their children will get more one on one attention. Working together, the modified family will give more love, and support. When the children are in need of instruction or coaching, they have more avenues within their immediate family to explore.

If children have questions about the things they are exposed to in the world, they have more people working to protect their interests. When these children want to explore arts and crafts, or participate in different sports, they will have a level of support that children of traditional families would rarely know. In matters of education, be they academic, culture, religion or militant disciplines, several parents working together will greatly reinforce their children's learning.

Structure determines function. In order to create a manageable home and family, parents have to set the perimeters that control the flow of moneys, resources, power, and information. The polygynous family will provide a better structure and offer more resources, and opportunities than the traditional family unit. A man and his wives will have a better chance of providing, protecting, and serving their family than the traditional couple.

Daughters………..

When an adolescent woman comes of age in a modified family, she has both her mother and (2) foster mothers to give her instruction in the proper way of a woman. Three different women, who are the best of friends, would be there to guide her in the ways of love, the institution of woman, the art and craft of womanhood, intimate relationships, and friendships. This would make a huge difference in a young woman's preparation for building her life.

Each of the mothers would have the kind of intimate relationship with their daughter necessary for teaching a blossoming young woman. With the love and instruction of true women, these adolescent women will be more secure with the decisions they have to make, and are less apt to folding under peer pressure or life challenges. It would be the kind of close-knit relationship that could only grow between women who have lived and grown together in the same home.

Adolescent women who grow up in modified families will learn from the examples set by their mothers' relationship with their fathers. Everything they learn will then be reinforced by the relationships their fathers have with their foster mothers. These young women will learn that the true measure of a man is not his bank roll, or some professional title, but the love and understanding he shows the women and children in his life. While many young Black adult girl lose themselves to the savagery of mainstream America and the glorification of violence, greed, and selfishness, the products of the modified family will learn the value of honor, selfless service, and integrity.

These special African American women will learn to value virtue over glamour. Virtues like patience, empathy, and the value of honest labor, will be more important than worldly riches. A man shouldering the responsibilities of loving his women and their children will set the best example from which to learn. She will learn how a man treats his woman and observe the use of skills needed to care for a modified family.

In our community, there are more young women than there are men. A young woman, who respects herself, is seeking the strongest, healthiest, and most talented man to love. Young women who live in a polygynous community are least likely to limit themselves to a male who has little or nothing to offer.

If there was 1 male for every 1 female on a college campus and 30% of the men were progressing well, 50% were progressing fairly well, and the remaining males were functioning poorly, then that population of 30% represents the acceptable candidates for certain aspects of a relationship. The 50% of males who are doing fairly well have potential, but potential good can be "hell and gone" from actually good. The greater percentage of failures, make up the troublesome "dumb-asses" that a good woman will go out of her way to avoid.

In a monogamous community, where females have not lost themselves to alternative lifestyles, each female will pair off with one male. Only the women who made connections with the top 30% will have the best chances of attaining a healthy and rewarding relationship experiences. Those females who build relationships with the 50% of men who are only doing fairly well, will likely find themselves in relationships that leave a lot to be desired. The last 20% of the college female body will likely be limited to the stress and drama of unfulfilling relationships.

However, in a polygynous community, these young women will learn to share the love and affection of a good man. Instead of putting limits on themselves and their personal future, they will learn to see the value in sharing the love of a responsible man who may fulfill their needs. Young women will quickly learn that it is better to share the love of a good man than to endure the pain and anguish of dealing with a bad one. A woman will get more out of a brief encounter with the right man than a long-term relationship with a man who is inadequate.

If the top 30% of males on campus were free to receive the attention and welcome the affection of the greater female student population, three things would happen in the male population. These males would receive the support, respect and praise they deserve. It would boost their esteem and give them a chance to better learn how to manage relationships with multiple women. It would raise the bar for the 50% of males who are only doing fairly well.

It would also send a clear message to that inadequate 20%. They would learn that no one has to entertain their failure. Once these lesser men see that young women are not willing to settle, they will see the urgency of getting their acts together. Those males who rise to the challenge of being and doing better will be rewarded by the acceptance of quality young women. Women who are as serious about giving love as they are about receiving it.

In the monogamous community, there are many weak males who have no desire to be responsible. Many of these cowardly males know that the ratio of quality women to men is off. These males know that no matter how proud, talented, educated or ambitious a woman is she will eventually settle for less than she has always wanted. They know that living flesh needs living flesh and that as a woman's biological clock unwinds, she will be pressured to compromise her principles in order to salvage some aspects of her life. Many of these young women get involved with people they otherwise would not have given a second look. These males are pimps and hustlers looking to prey on women when they are weak and unsuspecting.

Sons....
     In the modified family, a man with three wives would have three sets of in-laws. If each wife gave her man a baby, each of those children would have four sets of grand parents. This would make a huge difference in the lives of their children. Four sets of in-laws, in addition to the rest of the extended family, would give several links to the elders of past generations. Each child would have greater resources for family history and heritage. These grandparents would also provide the children with a wealth of wisdom and experiences.
     When an adolescent man begins his preparation for the life of a husband and father, he will have three mothers supporting his efforts. He will learn from his father how to properly manage a house full of women and children. These young men will have their mother and foster mothers to reinforce their father's instruction. As a man learns the way of a soldier, civil rights leader, a spiritual minister, an artist, and healer, he will acquire the wisdom and experiences of his father. He will also have the trust and support from as many as four grandfathers.
     When men of a polygynous culture meet a young woman, he will know how to treat her with chivalry and warmth. If he is called upon to interact with a young woman and her friends, he would know how to properly court the three of them. A young man would know how to read the social dynamics of the group, understand their relationships, and create a place for him within the group of young women. Everything these young men learn from their father and mothers would help them bridge any gaps that might exist between them and their potential wives.

     When people consider sending their children to school, one of the first things they want to know is the classroom size. It is understood that in a large class with thirty or more students, teachers are most likely overwhelmed with responsibilities. Studies have shown that small class sizes are better for the teacher/student relationship. In classes with fewer students, teachers can give more one-on-one attention. His or her ability to give each student the personal time they need improves their learning.
     When there is a low student to teacher ratio, children get more face time to ask questions, and they are least likely to be overlooked when there is a problem. The same way the student to teacher ratio affects our children in schools, the child to parent ratio will affect our children at home. In a family where a man has three wives with at least two children a piece, there would be four adults to six children. In a traditional family, if a man and woman have two children the ratio is two four two.
     The difference between these two types of families and their ability to provide for their children is huge. The parents of the modified family will clearly maintain better coverage over their children, than the traditional couple. The children that will receive the best preparation for life will be those who grow up in families with a smaller parent to child ratio.

Extended Family   When you consider the 50% divorce rate in America, the rate of marital separations, and the number of families struggling with abuse and infidelity, there should be little surprise at the current condition of the American family. Marriage in America and other countries greatly influenced by European cultures are all suffering the same marital fate. Marriage, as we know it in America, rarely works. Monogamy and all of the challenges that come with it, rarely not works.

Women blame men for failing marriages, and the men blame the women. The Christians say it is the devil's fault, and satanic worshipers are blaming God. Despite the fact that most everyone is at fault, no one is ready to take the blame for failed marriages. They only want to blame others.

Some believe that practically any marital relationship can be fixed, if the people involved are willing to work at it. Others may argue that in a society where people may live to be 120 years of age, and a marital relationship can last 80 or more years that all marriages are meant to be temporary agreement.

Marriage in American tradition, does not suppose to work for Black Americans. Mainstream America is rooted in the traditions of cultures foreign to the Negro man and woman. Any relationships built on romantic nonsense by a bunch of self-serving opportunists are not supposed to work.

As Africans in America, we see that our way of life in the United States leave a lot to be desired. We know that our society does not prepare us or give us the resources necessary to prepare ourselves for the challenges of building healthy relationships in America.

Polygamy is the key to most of our problems. For men who can handle the responsibility of caring for a number of women and the children they produce, it is a great opportunity to free their nurturing spirit. For the more solitary man, there is a single woman for him to love. And for those who are not fit to rule and manage a household, there is nothing wrong with the simple life of a bachelor. The bottom line is that polygyny opens doors that free our people to embrace our African heritage, and strengthen the Black family.

Men who can care for more than one woman should be encouraged to do so. Men with the wisdom needed to raise a number of families should be encouraged to teach others. When these men get together, they will be able to focus on the unique responsibilities a polygynous husband and father would face. They would be able to explore the challenges of managing and supervising more than one family. Together, these men would learn the most affective way to govern their homes.

Special Note: It should be understood that the polygynous relationship is not an alternative lifestyle. It is not an opportunity for perverts to manipulate and sexually exploit each other. It is not a bunch of fools climbing all over each other like some Greek toga party or some Roman orgy.

Polygyny is about strong, intelligent, morally responsible people working together to build a complex family unit that will provide for every member of the family. It should be understood that caring for a number of women and the children they birth would be the biggest challenge of any man's life. The greatest measure of a man is not how much money or education he has, it is his ability to properly care for his women and their children.

The extended families of monogamous marriages leave a lot to be desired. They are small and scattered. Many of these families are empty and broken, with little or no force. With the divorce rate leaving so many people without love and companionship, one would be hard pressed to find a community of healthy traditional monogamous families. Between the number of broken homes, the cost of living, and the powers exploiting our community, it is a wonder if the Black families of tomorrow will be any better.

The extended family of the modified families has a solid foundation for ensuring the healthy growth of its extended members. That is one of the benefits of the power, wealth, and prestige that the modified family brings to the community. All of the moneys, resources, and authority needed to care for the elderly, the children, and those with special needs, are in tact.

The extended modified family will bridge community gaps. The community would become smaller, and the average person would be hard pressed to find strangers in their communities. Almost everyone would be kin by blood or by marriage. This would have a big impact on how families deal with social and community issues.

In Africa, before societies were governed on caste or class systems, societies were stateless. Large areas were not ruled by government institutions separate from the private interests of people and their families. These societies were made up of large families who worked together to meet the needs of their people.

Each family was formally structured and everyone in the family worked together for the good of their family. In the old country a family was properly regarded as the primary institution. In our modern world of super power nations, the government is considered the most important institution. The nuclear family is often considered the least important and least powerful organization. The key to advancing as an African American people will be our returning the family back to its primary position in society, and returning the Negro family to its former glory.

Community   In the Black community, there are many conditions that would be greatly improve by the advancement of the modified family. There is a very high rate of sexually transmitted diseases. Black American women make up a large number of people with HIV and Aids. In a community with a large single population attitudes towards sex are casual and less responsible than the smaller married population.

When the average man has three wives, there will be a sharp drop in the single population. More men and women would enter into committed relationships, and learn to be a part of something bigger than an individual. Their attitudes and standards for sexual relationships would change for the better. They would find greater purpose and become more sexually responsible. A smaller population of single people would mean fewer casual non-committed relationships.

In our society, single people make up a large percentage of the money being spent everyday. For this reason, most businesses cater to single people. With a growing number of modified families and their unique needs, businesses will begin focusing their attention on the needs of the larger families. There will be fewer places catering to singles. Single's bars, exotic dance clubs, novelty adult shops, and other businesses that cater to the lonely would decline.

The new businesses would center on the wide variety needs common to any large family. There would be a rise in the number of private social clubs, cultural events, and religious celebrations. These new businesses would provide a number of safe and positive outlets for children of all ages, and a healthy social circle for both married men and women.

The ratio of women to men has been affected by the number of males with, special needs, physical and mental disabilities, as well as those residing in the prison system. Even though these males are part of the overall population count; they are in no position to care for a family. Another major factor is the growing number gays and lesbians. The numbers of men who practice alternative lifestyles have made it even more challenging for Black women to find a proper mate.

Many Black women are choosing to have children on their own, without an adequate support system. For this reason, many of the children in single parent homes are practically raising themselves. Children who are born to families without an adequate support system often find themselves left alone in the world. This contributes to the large number of orphaned, abandoned, and abused children in the foster care system.

For Black women who do not wish to limit themselves to males of a different race or culture, there are fewer options when seeking relationships. When Black women learn to embrace their cultural heritage and share their life's struggles, there will be fewer Black women left alone in our community. There efforts will not only provide them with the companionship they need, but give them the support system their children will greatly appreciate.

Education and Church   There are two influential institutions in the Black community, the public schools and the church. The public schools primarily teach the "three R's". Unfortunately, due to the corruption of our society, the public schools are also teaching sexual and scientific perversions. Our churches are private and teach religious beliefs, but they are no where near the status and quality they used to be or should be.

Between these the church and the public school system, there is a huge gap. There are no authorities to teach survival training, paramilitary skills, and emergency care. There is no organization that teaches ethnic and cultural training or social polities. These are the types of trainings that would bridge gaps between Black families, and improve our ability to communicate and function as a community. It would help the Negro families work and build together.

We would build private grade schools with college preparatory programs. We would also take over historically Black colleges and restructure their educational programs to better accommodate our unique community needs. Our universities would produce educated people to run our businesses, and well cultured people to govern our community. In a very short period of time, we would not only improve our education, but we would also give our community a level of wealth, prestige and power it has never known.

Business   The average highly educated man with his three educated wives may earn between $60,000 and $90,000 a year. The combined income of a husband with two wives would be $180,000 to $270,000. The combined income of a husband with three wives would be $240,000 to $ 360,000 a year.

The money these families generate would create a level of financial security, and money making opportunities that traditional Black couple would never know. On a micro level, these Black families will create solid investment groups. On the macro level, these same families are in a perfect position to connect with other modified families and build strong businesses.

As our culture of modified families become more unique, it will advance in many different ways. The nuclear families will grow large and need goods in bulk. These large families will make greater use of community resources and family oriented services. These advancements will create a demand for many goods and services. Some of which, will be unique to our African American community.

These demands will bring about new businesses, a wide variety of jobs and investment opportunities for our families. The modified families will be able to come together and build corporations that will provide a wide variety of goods and services to a fast growing community with very special needs.

Once we begin generating money for ourselves, we will no longer be limited to government aid. We will have more money to invest in social, cultural, and spiritual programs. We would no longer be limited to public schools and all of its political nonsense. As a community, we would generate enough money to build private schools that cater to our unique community needs.

Politics   As a people, we would advance in the political arena. We could collective create packs, lobbies and corporations that would hire senators and congress persons to represent our unique political interests. We would pay these state and federal officials for their consultation. Like the National Rifleman's Association or AIG, we could establish the political power needed to secure our political position in the greater American community.

Through the accumulation of wealth and a mass of political power, we could one day set our sights on the continent of Africa. We would expand our influences across the Atlantic, and make business investments that would advance the lives of our brethren while creating more business and greater wealth in America. Our families could establish second homes, start businesses, build wealth, and expand our social and cultural influences.

In the tradition of the Black Nationalists of our African American history, the members of a polygynous community will establish political organizations that would focus on the unique political and social issues that shape our lives. We would no longer be limited to the political scopes of the dominating political parties in the United States. The United States government was built on a legislative system that permits private organizations to buy into the political interests of our elected officials.

In order to strengthen the community, these newly founded political "think tanks" and political parties will work to fight for our rights and provide us with the securities we need. These organizations will represent our religious, cultural, and social agendas and give full support to the greater needs of our families. These steps forward will be among the most important advancements that a polygynous community would bring.

Crime   The crime that has plagued our community for decades is growing, but the quality of our lives do not have to continue to decline. With the money and political power our community will gain through the polygynous marriages and the families they produce, there will be a major decline in our community crime rate. As our children receive a better education and gain a better sense of self through cultural and spiritual training, we will see great improvement in our youth.

With plenty of social, academic, and cultural activity to keep them busy, there will be less time for idol minds to wander. More parents per household supervising their children will mean fewer young people living without proper tutelage. There will be less gang related activities, less vandalism, and petty thefts. There would also be fewer incidents of sexual misconduct and meaningless acts of violence.

As parents of these modified families put their resources together to blanket the community, there will be a better community monitoring system in place. There will be more money in our community budget to create the kind of security we all need for our families. Police, off-duty police, private security companies, and private detectives will be working in cooperation with the families to protect our children from rapists, child predators, drug dealers, and other negative elements in the community.

In our neighborhoods, many children see the police, fireman, health care worker, and government agents as outsiders. They learn from their parents and guardians that these individuals are the foreigners or outlanders. Many of our people grow up never genuinely understanding or appreciating the roles these individuals play in preserving our communities. The only time these individuals are recognized for the roles they play is in times of trouble.

All of the mixed feelings young people have about the police and other government authorities, would have to change in order for our community to take it proper shape. The security and safety program the polygynous community would create would go a long way towards improving our understanding and use of these government resources.

In our community, there are many children growing up in single parent homes. They are growing up with aging grandparents and distant relatives. People often think that in single parent homes young people are practically raising themselves, but many would be surprised to know that many homes with both a mother and a father have children practically raising themselves.

The challenge of building a life in our society takes its toll on even the hardest working families. Between the rising cost of living and the challenge of keeping up with a fast pace society, many mothers and fathers are working so much that they have no ideas of the troubles threatening their children. When you hear about children being kidnapped or molested, do not think that it is only the children of single parent homes. Perverts are feeding on our community. The perverts in our community target young people whose parents are rarely there to watch over them.

As families of this unique subculture come together, children will know a level of peace and harmony that can only come with growing up in a safe and healthy environment. They will grow to know less aggression and anger, and be more comfortable with themselves and the responsibilities that await them as adults. They would grow to know greater self-worth, more drive, and greater self-esteem. These changes in our youth and the world we could provide for them is perhaps the greatest argument for our people learning to embrace our African and biblical heritage.

Poverty   If the average Black person earns $35,000 to $40,000 a year, then the average couple will only generate $70,000 to $80,000 a year between them. After we make the required deductions, their combined income will be considerably less. At the same time, income of a polygamous family with a man and three wives would be more like $140,000 to $160,000 dollars a year.

There is a considerable difference in the financial power of a traditional marriage and the modified marriage. The financial "up swing" of the modified couples will ensure that they retire at an early age. Many Black Americans today would be lucky to retire at 70 years of age.

Those who are part of a healthy modified family would likely be ready to retire by the age of fifty. It would provide each one of them with adequate securities and enable them to further their education and self-development. It will also help them care for the elderly members of their extended families.

There financial position will help them provide a good education for all of their children. They will be able to live on a high socio-economic level, which will give them the resources needed to provide quality ethnic, social and religious training. The financial security these modified families will know will create opportunities that otherwise would not exist.

The traditional couple will work for years to save enough money for the down payment on a home. They will buy their start-up home with a twenty-five to thirty year mortgage. With that mortgage comes a variety of fees and costs, as well as an interest rate that may change for the worst in just a few years. Over the years, they will have to absorb a huge amount of debt in order to one day own that home. For many couples, a simple job loss or cut in salary could mean losing everything they have invested.

The non-traditional couples will accumulate enough money to buy their start-up home with cash. They would be in a position to shop for a brand new home or search the foreclosure list for a pre-owned home. When the modified couples purchase their home, it will be for cash. No beginning down payment, no "under-the-table" or earnest money, no closing balloon payments, and no changing interest rates. Working together, the modified family will achieve several times more in a much shorter period of time.

Even if the man and his wives only have high school diplomas and average twenty to twenty-five thousand dollars a year, their combined income would be $80,000 to $100,000 a year. Their combined efforts would mean quickly building a savings while only working one job a piece. They would work together to build their lives and in a short period of time create a "nest egg" of investments. They would care for each other and still have time to pursue their individual goals like earning an education, developing an artistic talent or craft.

The average Black family would find themselves elevated high above the poverty level, and that over time would transform the poorest Black community to a free flowing and financially liquid community.

Religion/Faith   When we look at religion in our society, a lot of time we take for granted just how much the world influences our beliefs, values, and perspectives on the things going on around us. Embracing our African heritage and adopting those African practices that best suit our needs will bridge gaps between us and our African brethren. It will also help bridge gaps in terms of religion and faith.

In America, much of what we learn about religion, regardless of its origin, has been altered by European Americans. When European Americans take interest in the religious philosophies of other races, cultures, or nationalities, it is common for them to alter those belief systems to fit their own. European Americans are historically pagans. Paganism is their root and the nature of their ethnicity.

Even though there are many European Americans who consider themselves Christians, many of the religious views and traditions have pagan roots. The pagan ideas that have been popular throughout Europe and America for centuries have influenced every aspect of American life. It has influenced music, books, movies, and television programs for many years. The pagan influence in Christianity can be seen in holidays like Christmas, Halloween, Mardi Gras, and Easter.

One of the most important things that we will get through bridging the gaps that separate us from our mother countries will be our reconnection with African Tradition. We will learn the true history of the Torah, the King James Bible, and the Holy Qu'ran. Our connection to Africa is our connection to the lives of Abraham, Moses, Jesus and many others. For many Black Americans, it will be the first time they ever read the original stories of the Bible.

Black Americans will finally begin studying and learning these stories the way they were originally taught. In America, most of the Hebrew teachings have been taken out of context. In a country that entertains religious freedom; many religious organizations have taken their liberties with the exploitation of the Hebrew faith. These American borne religions have given religions of all kind a European twist.

As our religion and faith make a natural connection, there will be an awakening throughout our community. We will become more defined in our ideologies and bring greater shape and form to our lives. The faith of our men, women, and children would grow in ways that we could not imagine. Bridging this gap would change the hearts and minds of our people in away that would help us in every aspect of our lives.

Ethnicity/Cultural   Another great rewards that would come with our practice of polygamy would be the bridges we would eventually build to lessen the gap between African American and the continent of Africa. We would soon have so much in common with the more successful African ethnic groups. As a people, we would quickly learn the ancient secrets that led to the advancement of our ancestors. Once we bridge the gap between us and Africa, opportunities for business, trade and investments will increase our interaction with our African brethren. It will also create new avenues to aid the greater African family with the problems that plague the old country.

As a culture, we would have to learn to govern ourselves as an ethnic group and a self-reliant social circle. We will have to learn how to address those needs common to all families and cultures, as well as those needs uniquely African American. One the most important things we will do as a people is create a liberal government to manage and supervise our community. This government will keep records of all social contract, and handle the legislative, executive, and judiciary aspects of our community.

To the greater American family, these polygamous families with the extended family connections would be regarded as small investment groups. Within the walls of our social and cultural circle, these modified families would be recognized for the formal relationships each man has with his women. They will also be formally recognized for the sacred relationship all parents share with their children and/or foster children.

Embracing our African heritage and adopting the practice of polygamy would transform the Black community practically over night. Most people would look at the condition of the Black community and say that any change for the better would take three to five generations, or as little as three to five decades. I do not believe it would take anywhere near that long. The positive impact of this change would take root relatively quick and such improvement would be apparent in as little three to five years.

Are we ready for such an extreme social change? (Great concerns for the Blended Family and Single Parenting)

Some people may be inclined to think that polygyny is a major leap for Black Americans, but it is not. The number of failing marriages, the number of broken homes, and the male to female population ratio dictates that such a change is necessary. Between the number of men and women who have lost themselves to alternative lifestyles, and the number of males and females who have lost themselves to the prison system, there are few options left.

The cost of living in the United States is constantly climbing, and for as long as I can remember the unemployment rate in the Black community has always been higher than the national average. There was a time when we could argue the importance of furthering affirmative action and our rights to reparations, but with the fall of the Berlin Wall, our voices are falling on deaf ears. Everyday there are political moves being made to push the United States of America back into the 1950's.

The family unit is the basic building block of all society, religion and culture. Our nuclear families are weak and most of them cripple. The fear and lack of trust between males and females, and the challenges of raising children in a fast paced and bankrupt culture is taking its toll on even the strongest of families. If you ask the average Black American, "What should we do to help our community?" most of them would be at their wits end. When the way that we have been taught to function no longer works, it is up to those of us who understand to make the difference.

Blended Family

When a man and woman come together and one or both of them have children from a past relationship, the merging of these two families is commonly known as a Blended Family. The blended family is made up of a man and/or woman who have on going relationships with the biological parent of their children.

In many blended families, both the man and woman have children from past relationships. In these cases, both the man and woman have to help each other build a relationship with both sets of children. Both parents have to do this without compromising their relationship with their own children. While each of their children learns to connect and function with their custodial parents, great effort has to be made to preserve their relationship with their biological parent.

The blended families with two sets of children pose very unique challenges for parents. These families require custodial parents who are organized, coordinated and have well planned strategies for governing their homes. The business of legislating, administrating, and officiating their homes must be sharply structured and prepared for just about anything.

Sometimes, only one person in the relationship has children with a former companion. In these cases, people have to try and build a healthy relationship between their children and their new companions. At the same time, these parents have to help maintain the relationships their children have with their other biological parent.

Blended families are a very special thing, and when compared to polygynous families have a lot in common. Both families deal with multiple parents sharing the responsibilities of raising children. When rules are created by custodial parents in one home, biological parents share the responsibility of respecting those rules.

Both blended and polygynous families have children from different maternal mothers building a child to parent relationship with a foster mother or father. These relationships require parent both custodial and biological to work together in the best interest of their children. Children are taught to accept their foster parent, brother and/or sister as a blood relative and an equal member of the family.

There are of course, some major differences between the blended and polygynous families. One of these major differences is the separation of the parenting groups. In the blended family, a custodial parent and their spouse may live in one home, while the biological parent of their children live in another home. That parent may have a relationship with the biological parent of their children, but in many ways the biological parent could represent an odd fixture to the family of the custodial parent.

The second major difference is the poor relationship the mothers have with each other. In the polygynous family, the women have a very good relationship and are often the best of friends. The women of a polygynous family know that they are an important part of the family unit. They know their place and willingly share in all of the duties in the home.

In the blended family, there is usually a great deal of stress and anxiety felt by the parents. Parents may feel that they are not doing right by their children or taking their foster children for granted. They may often feel that they are in competition with the other parents. Some of these parents may even feel that they are losing their children and being replaced by the foster parent.

The people who question the wisdom of polygynous marriages may think that Black Americans are not ready for such a major social change. I would strongly disagree. When we take a closer look at the blended family, we can see that the wheels of social change are already in motion. By pulling our resources and sharing our wealth, we could see the greater percentage of our community advance.

When I think about all of the challenges our people have faced over the years, it irritates me. When I think about the number of sacrifices we have made as a people to meet those challenges, it leaves me feeling kind of foolish. For a long time, we have been looking for the solution to problems that many believed could never be found. All the while, that answer was staring us right in the face.

Through hard work and confidence, the Black community would change all of our lives for the better. In a relatively short period of time, children of the community would know greater security. Women would find greater freedom through sisterhood, and men would finally receive the love and support a protector and servant needs. The African American man and woman would have all of this by doing nothing more than embracing our African heritage and being ourselves.